Close Encounters

A camera obscura *Book*

Close Encounters

Film, Feminism, and Science Fiction

Constance Penley, Elisabeth Lyon,
Lynn Spigel, and Janet Bergstrom, editors

University of Minnesota Press
Minneapolis • Oxford

A version of Henry Jenkins III, "*Star Trek* Rerun, Reread, Rewritten: Fan Writing as Textual Poaching," appeared in *Critical Studies in Mass Communications* 5, no. 2 (1988). The author and editors gratefully acknowledge permission to reprint.

Cover photograph: Yura Adams as "Yura Futura" in her 1983 performance, *Alien Streams*. Hand-colored by Sally Wetherby. Original cover design by Pat Koren of Kajun Graphics and Elisabeth Lyon. Cover design this volume by Lois Stanfield.

Published by the University of Minnesota Press
2037 University Avenue Southeast, Minneapolis, MN 55414
Printed in the United States on acid-free paper.

Library of Congress Cataloging-in-Publication Data
Close encounters: film, feminism, and science fiction / Constance
    Penley . . . [et al.], editors.
        p. cm. — (A Camera obscura book)
    Includes index.
    ISBN 0–8166–1911–5 (hc). — ISBN 0–8166–1912–3 (pb)
    1. Science fiction films—History and criticism. 2. Sex role in
motion pictures. 3. Family in motion pictures. 4. Women in motion pictures. I. Penley, Constance, 1948- . II. Series.
PN1995.9.S26C57 1991
791.43'656—dc20   90–40163
                                                              CIP

A CIP catalogue record for this book is available from the British Library.

The University of Minnesota
is an equal-opportunity
educator and employer.

Contents

Introduction *Constance Penley*   vii

Child / Alien / Father: Patriarchal Crisis and Generic Exchange
Vivian Sobchack   3

Androids and Androgyny *Janet Bergstrom*   33

Time Travel, Primal Scene, and the Critical Dystopia
Constance Penley   63

Reimagining the Gargoyle: Psychoanalytic Notes on *Alien*
Harvey R. Greenberg, M.D.   83

Ideal Hadaly *Raymond Bellour*   107

Metropolis: Mother-City—"Mittler"—Hitler *Roger Dadoun*   133

Metropolis, Scene 103 *Enno Patalas*   161

Star Trek Rerun, Reread, Rewritten: Fan Writing as Textual Poaching
Henry Jenkins III   171

From Domestic Space to Outer Space: The 1960s Fantastic Family Sit-Com *Lynn Spigel*   205

Friendship's Death (complete script) *Peter Wollen*   237

Contributors   283

Index   287

Introduction
Constance Penley

Close Encounters: Film, Feminism, and Science Fiction is an expanded
version of a special issue of *Camera Obscura* that appeared in the fall
of 1986. For that issue, entitled "Science Fiction and Sexual Difference,"
the editors had sought out essays that addressed the various ways in
which conventional notions of sexual difference are displaced or reworked by science fiction film. The impulse for doing the special issue
arose from the perception that science fiction film as a genre—along
with its evil twin, the horror film—is now more hyperbolically concerned than ever with the question of *difference*, typically posed as that
of the difference between human and nonhuman. Although science
fiction has traditionally been concerned with this question, new pressures from feminism, the politics of race and sexual orientation, and the
dramatic changes in the structure of the family and the workforce seem
to have intensified the symptomatic wish to pose and re-pose the question of difference in a fictional form that could accommodate such an
investigation. Other challenges to being able to "tell the difference" have
come not only from poststructuralist criticism, with its highly constructed and unstable subject, but also from "advances" in genetic engineer-
ing, bioengineering, and cybernetics. Such a confluence of pressures on
subjectivity and difference perhaps explains what has been for many the
rhetorical force of Donna Haraway's metaphor of the cyborg feminist,
which manages to give both a utopian and a dystopian spin to the future
of our new gendered technological bodies, and at the very least, provides a suggestive metaphor for further thinking about the breakdown
and reconstruction of what is going to count as "human" in the era that
we optimistically refer to as "late" capitalism.

The first four essays in *Close Encounters* examine how contemporary

The special issue of *Camera Obscura* (no. 15, Fall 1986) on which this book
is based was edited by Janet Bergstrom, Lea Jacobs, Elisabeth Lyon, Denise
Mann, Constance Penley, Lynn Spigel, and Janet Walker.

science fiction film consciously and unconsciously constructs new categories of masculinity and femininity, paternity and maternity, through the shifting, ambiguous, and contradictory sexual status it assigns to the robot, the alien, the monster, or even elements of the futuristic *mise en scène*.

In "Child/Alien/Father: Patriarchal Crisis and Generic Exchange," Vivian Sobchack gives a polemical account of a crisis in patriarchy and paternity as it is developed in the horror film and family melodrama, and ingeniously "resolved" in contemporary science fiction film. She exhaustively documents the tendency toward mixing genres in 1970s and 1980s American films as they attempt to redefine the place of the father—recasting him as both alien and child—given the "disintegration and transfiguration of the 'traditional' American bourgeois family."

Janet Bergstrom's "Androids and Androgyny" describes the predominance of set design over character and plot in films like *Blade Runner* and *Liquid Sky*. In part, this predominance takes its cue from new efforts in contemporary advertising to control the total perceptual field. Through an analysis of a Calvin Klein ad, she also shows how advertising commodifies an androgynous female body to which drastically different values can be assigned, from idealization to negative objectification. She then examines how this commodified body is deployed in two films, *Looker* and *Liquid Sky*.

Constance Penley's "Time Travel, Primal Scene, and the Critical Dystopia" takes *The Terminator* as the starting point for a discussion of the way in which recent science fiction film uses various structures of fantasy (the primal scene, family romance, infantile sexual investigation) to engage the spectator in scenarios of technology and apocalypse, sexuality and difference. Although the film relies on unconscious and wish-fulfilling fantasies to draw the spectator into its fictional universe, Penley argues that its extreme attention to the detail of everyday life, strewn with the debris of contemporary technoculture, throws the spectator back into the mundane world of hard choices about that technoculture and its future. Finally, in looking at *The Terminator* as the industry remake of the quintessential art film, *La Jetée*, Chris Marker's haunting tale of time travel, identity, and apocalypse, Penley challenges political film theory's privileging of the avant-garde over Hollywood and the symbolic over the imaginary.

In "Reimagining the Gargoyle: Psychoanalytic Notes on *Alien*," Harvey Greenberg argues that *Alien* is the legitimate inheritor of the motifs and conventions of the "cruel" or "hardcore" horror film, exemplified by *Psycho*, *Night of the Living Dead*, *The Hills Have Eyes*, and *The Texas Chainsaw Massacre*. Like these films, *Alien* assaults the viewer's sensibility and with a similar aim in mind: to chart the degradation of relationships within family and state. But Greenberg takes issue with those who see *Alien* as a politically engaged film, insisting that its highly touted critique of corporate capitalism is a mere tease; *Alien*, like *Psycho* and its cruel inheritors, does no more than flaunt its amoral "cool": "They dimly apprehend the primordial selfishness infecting late twentieth-century capitalism, but can only recommend convenient, escapist, individualistic solutions."

The next three essays go back into the history of science fiction film and literature to look at the origins of this genre's tendency to understand the workings of technology through fantasy, specifically the male fantasy of an idealized and yet ultimately destructive femininity.

Raymond Bellour's "Ideal Hadaly" (on Villiers's *The Future Eve*) analyzes the collusion of technology and male fantasy in the representation of the ideal—idealized—woman. In Villiers's novel, the perfect woman is an ingenious invention of Thomas Edison: an android. Bellour argues that this fantasy is a pre-cinematic representation, in nineteenth-century literature, of classical Hollywood's configuring of sexual difference. Bellour is also concerned to show how this sexing of the machine contributes to the popular idea of mass culture as feminized, insofar as the female android, like the Hollywood film, is a mass industry product that can be infinitely replicated.

Roger Dadoun's essay on Fritz Lang's *Metropolis*, "Mother-City—'Mittler'—Hitler," shows how the circumstances of the film's production—historical, political, financial, and personal—interact with the materials of unconscious fantasy that shape or enter into the composition of the filmic text. He argues that the film's various elements (characters, situations, technical procedures, and so on) "though in a sense circumscribed by history and politics, cannot be adequately organized except in terms of the unconscious processes and fantasy structures discovered by psychoanalysis." Dadoun further shows how this film about women, machines, and cities is thoroughly structured by repetition, primal scenes, and fantasies of seduction and castration. He discusses in particular the film's depiction of the "horror of the female organ," and, since the female organ is typically taken to stand for sex in general, the horror of sexuality. This depiction tells us a great deal, he says, about both the primal level of the film and the workings of the Nazi imagination.

Film archivist Enno Patalas's dramatic account of his reconstruction of "Scene 103" from *Metropolis*, missing from all existing prints, traces the logical relations between technology, femininity, and the male gaze in the construction of a robot as an idealized female image. This missing scene not only provides the motivation for the enmity between

Fredersen and the inventor, Rotwang, but shows why the robot (the false Maria) must be a woman.

In an attempt to cover some important areas of concern felt to be missing from the special issue of *Camera Obscura* on which this book is based—especially science fiction audiences and science fiction television—two new essays have been added.

Henry Jenkin's essay, "*Star Trek* Rerun, Reread, Rewritten: Fan Writing as Textual Poaching," focuses on what audiences of science fiction film and television actually *do* with the artifacts of popular culture they are typically seen to passively consume. Jenkins first looks at the zeal with which critics and academics patronize and ridicule fans, particularly *Star Trek* fans, for their "infantile" behavior and indiscriminate consumption. Far from being passive consumers, he argues, fans actively rework the givens of the *Star Trek* universe to make their own cultural meanings. Borrowing Michel de Certeau's description of popular reading as "poaching" (an impertinent "raid" on the literary "preserve" that takes away only those things that seem useful or pleasurable to the reader), Jenkins describes *Star Trek* fan activity, especially the writing in fanzines—primarily a female activity—as a "series of advances and retreats, tactics and games played with the text," a fragmenting and reassembling of found material to make sense of the fan's own social experience. Critics and academics understandably feel uncomfortable with such an outlaw notion of literary property rights, but it is one that Jenkins gleefully celebrates precisely because it questions those "rights" and the kinds of literary policing they lead to.

Lynn Spigel's "From Domestic Space to Outer Space: The 1960s Fantastic Family Sit-Com" examines the seemingly bizarre mix of suburbia and science fiction in shows like *I Dream of Jeannie*, *My Favorite Martian*, *The Jetsons*, *Mr. Ed*, and *Bewitched*. She demonstrates how the genres of science fiction fantasy and the domestic comedy merged to form a new, hybrid genre capable of presenting and containing highly contradictory ideas, values, and meanings concerning the organization of social space and everyday life in the suburban United States. By looking at these programs against the backdrop of New Frontier utopianism, particularly the space race, Spigel argues that the programs' use of space-age imagery defamiliarized the suburban middle-class dream so central to the classical family sit-coms.

The final addition to this volume is the script for Peter Wollen's 1987 film *Friendship's Death*, a film whose visual style and finely crafted writing strikingly illuminate many of the issues raised in this book. The film also exemplifies the way the themes and tropes of science fiction can be used to critically represent a fraught and topical set of circumstances, here the Palestinian struggle. A British reporter covering the terrorism and warfare in the Middle East in 1970 encounters a strange woman who claims to be an extra-terrestrial (code name: Friendship), an envoy from a distant galaxy who variously describes herself as a simulation and a computer. Friendship was programmed to land on the MIT campus, but something went wrong during entry and she has landed in Amman, Jordan, in the middle of a civil war. In the course of their many conversations, interrupted by intermittent mortar and artillery fire, and soldiers darting into their rooms to fire from their windows, Friendship and the journalist discuss her other-worldly perceptions of human political and social organization; the impulse behind his desire to know to what extent she is machine or woman, and the relation between the two; and the subjectivity of cybernetic machines and the "programming" of humans. Unable to return to her galaxy, she chooses to become a cyborg feminist and leaves to join the Palestinian forces. In a gesture toward the need for women to be techno-literate, it is the reporter's scientifically-minded daughter who, years later, cracks the code to Friendship's electronic diary, a glowing, pulsing cube given to the reporter as a gift, and whose text and images end the film.

Much that has been written previously on science fiction and sexual difference and on gender, representation, and technology has remained within the confines of sociology or traditional literary criticism. We hope that this volume will demonstrate the contribution that the reworking of semiology, psychoanalysis, and audience studies by feminist media theorists over the past decade can make to our understanding of these brave and strange new worlds.

Close Encounters

Close Encounters of the Third Kind (Steven Spielberg, 1977)

Child/Alien/Father: Patriarchal Crisis and Generic Exchange
Vivian Sobchack

Two very special babies were born to the American cinema in 1968: Rosemary's and Stanley Kubrick's. One was born in a horror film, the other in a science fiction film. One stared up from a cradle toward its earthly mother, the other down from space toward Mother Earth. Nonetheless, both the "devil's spawn" and the "starchild" condensed the *visible sight* of cultural difference, social transformation, and historical movement into the single and powerful figure of a child—one marked as an enigma by virtue of its strange eyes, and estranged, alien vision.

Both infants also signaled the replacement of previous generic displacements. Those exotic *visual sites* of horrific attraction and repulsion, and of utopian wonder and dystopian anxiety, which characterized and differentiated "traditional" horror and SF films were explicitly returned to American soil and to that domestic structure of social relations we call the nuclear family. Thus, despite their reversed visual perspectives and differing generic locations, the two newborns figured in *Rosemary's Baby* and *2001: A Space Odyssey* had a good deal in common. Born at—and as—the end or "final cause" of the narratives in which they were (re)produced, both babies not only infused a new flow of representational energy into their respective genres, but also marked the beginning of an extremely interesting and historically-situated generic convergence.

The purpose of this essay is to explore this convergence, and the cultural meanings that the figure of the child narrativizes as it is exchanged and transformed between the contemporary horror and SF film, and as it also creates an affinity between these two genres and a third—the newly revitalized family melodrama. Implicating domestic space, generational time, and family structure, the privileged figure of the child condenses and initiates a most particular and pressing cultural drama which seeks resolution in all three genres—with SF holding the most promise for its "happy end." This drama emerges from the crisis experienced by American bourgeois patriarchy since the late 1960s, and the related disintegration and transfiguration of the "traditional" American bourgeois family—an ideological as well as interpersonal structure characterized, as Robin Wood so frequently points out, by its cellular construction, its institutionalization of capitalist and patriarchal relations and values (among them, monogamy, heterosexuality, and consumerism), and its present state of disequilibrium and crisis.[1]

Although historically asymmetrical in their major periods of production and popularity, the "traditional" horror and SF film have tended toward a structurally symmetrical relationship marked by opposition. The two genres have been connected but differentiated by what seems to be a systemic and binary reversal of themes, iconographies, and strategies of narrative, dramatic, and visual representation.[2] Contemporary examples of both genres, however, tend to deny the generally neat symmetrical opposition of their traditional cinematic ancestors. In the context of the ambivalent horror and wonder provoked by the social upheavals of the last two decades, a convergence and conflation of generic difference has occurred. Indeed, many recent horror and SF films have been marked as "contemporary" not only on the basis of their release dates, but also because of their mutual spatial relocation to the American landscape and temporal relocation to the present, by their mutual figuration of the alien or Other as somehow implicated in family life, and by their common and preconscious thematic recognition that the social world can no longer be conceptualized and dramatized as an opposition between private and public concerns and spheres of action.

Figures from the past and future get into the house, make their homes in the closet, become part of the family, open the kitchen and family room up to the horrific and wondrous world outside this private and safe domain. A man's home in bourgeois patriarchal culture is no longer his castle. In the age of television, the drawbridge is always down; the world intrudes. It is no longer possible to avoid the invasive presence of Others—whether poltergeists, extra-terrestrials, or one's own alien kids.

Since the 1960s, then, the events of family life and social life have been commonly and increasingly experienced as convergent. Thus, it is not surprising that contemporary generic articulations of horror and SF have tended to *complement*, rather than oppose, each other. Their previously binary relation has been transformed into an analog(ue) one which includes the family melodrama—a genre whose representations are governed not by the conventions of the "fantastic," but by those of "realism." In the currency of today's generic economy, the once markedly different representational registers of the "fantastic" and the "realistic" are more easily able to circulate and commensurably represent similar thematic and dramatic material. Thus, even as their differentiation is seemingly still held sacred, the "fantastic" and the "real" pervade each other and insist on a closer and closer equivalence.

This triadic affinity among horror, SF, and family melodrama also entails a temporal and spatial exchange. The "past" (that temporal field usually grounding the horror film) is now commensurable with the "future" (usually associated with the SF film), and both are commensurable with the "present" (usually perceived as the temporal field of the family melodrama). Correlatively, previously distinct narrative sites have become congruent or contiguous. That is, the exotic, decadent, and alien spatio-temporal fields of the horror and SF film have geographically conflated with the familiar and familial spatio-temporal field of the family melodrama. What was once a distinctly displaced "There" has been replaced "Here"—and "Then" and "When" have been condensed as "Now." The time and place of horror and anxiety, wonder and hope, have been brought back into the American home. It is within the home and family that the institutionalization and perpetuation of the bourgeois social world is now seen to begin—and end. This is the common place, the present world, shared by horror films such as *The Exorcist, Carrie, The Fury, The Amityville Horror,* and *Poltergeist,* SF films like *Close Encounters of the Third Kind, E.T., Starman, Cocoon,* and *Back to the Future,* and family melodramas like *Ordinary People* and *Shoot the Moon.*

At a time when the mythology of our dominant culture can no longer resolve the social contradictions exposed by experience, the nuclear family has found itself in nuclear crisis. Rather than serving bourgeois patriarchy as a place of refuge from the social upheavals of the last two decades (many of which have been initiated by organized groups of young people and women), the family has become the site of them— and now serves as a sign of their representation. Not only has the bourgeois distinction between family members and alien Others, between private home and public space, between personal microcosm and sociopolitical macrocosm, been exposed as a mythological distinction, but also the family itself has been exposed as a cultural construction—as a set of signifying, as well as significant, practices. The family and its members are seen, therefore, as subject to the frightening, but potentially liberating, semiotic processes of selection and combination—and their order, meaning, and power are perceived as open to transformation, dissolution, and redefinition.

The contemporary genres of horror, SF, and family melodrama converge in their dramatization of these processes which test and represent the coherence, meaning, and limits of the "real" family as it has been constructed in patriarchal culture and suddenly exposed as horrific and alien-ated in relations and structure. Although historically asymmetrical in their peak periods of production and respectively maintaining a discrete archetypal core of generic structures and motifs, the three genres have nonetheless come together in common response to their shared cultural context and the similar social malaise which surrounds and supports the current popularity of all three. Engaging in an urgent and dynamic exchange whose goal is ultimately conservative, together the three genres attempt to contain, work out, and in some fashion resolve narratively the contemporary weakening of patriarchal authority, and the glaring contradictions which exist between the mythology of family relations and their actual social practice. In all three genres, those contradictions are most powerfully condensed and represented in the problematic figure of the child.

I began this essay by invoking two newborns: Rosemary's baby and Kubrick's starchild. My interest is in their cinematic offspring: the babies, children, and child-like changelings who have been born to the cinema in their generation and eventually transformed the cinematic shape of both patriarchy and the nuclear family. As "figures," these children coalesce, condense, embody, enact, and transform the text, cause its "trouble," and are themselves transformed through their textual work: adjusting the system of representation and the demands of the psyche and culture each to the other. In their most vital work, such figures are "more than shortcuts by way of association and substitution; they have the power to disrupt the relation of context to sign and reorient not only the discursive event but the system itself which will never be the same afterwards."[3] It is within this hermeneutic context that the production and emergence of the visible figure of the infant at—and as—the end of both *Rosemary's Baby* and *2001* can be said to have disrupted and reoriented not only the cultural meanings attached to representations of infants and children, but also the very articulation, structure, and meaning of the two "fantastic" genres in which they appeared.

The secular baby and child have held a privileged place in bourgeois and patriarchal mythology since the nineteenth century. Infancy and childhood have subsequently been popularly represented as the cultural site of such "positive" virtues as innocence, transparency, and a "pure" and wonderful curiosity not yet informed by sexuality (no matter what Freud said). Representing these virtues, the baby has been culturally produced as a figure of poignant sweetness—one helpless, vulnerable, and dependent not only because of its physical immaturity, but also because it lacks the "corrupting" knowledge so necessary to survival in the bourgeois social world. This "lack," however, also represents "hope" and "promise." Not yet having been *subjected to* the lessons of experience and history, the infant and child signify the *subject of* an experience and history still to be enacted and inscribed. In this way, the child becomes the *signifier* of the "future." But the child also simultaneously becomes the *signified* of the "past." Its familiar identity and family resemblance are produced as visible traces of the past's presence in the present, and ensure the past's presence in a future safely contained and constrained by tradition and history. At best, it will carry the father's name forward; at the least, his "seed." Thus, in its representation of the infant and child, bourgeois mythology has constructed a sign of the future which is sweetly traditional and safely adventurous, seemingly open yet firmly closed. Always informed with nostalgia, as a cultural sign of the future, the infant represents a backward longing for inexperience, and an openness to the world based on a lack of worldliness.

Both *Rosemary's Baby* and *2001* delivered infants to the screen who interrogated this mythology by their very presence, their bodies figuring a visible site of ambiguity, ambivalence, and contradiction. The two newborns were as alien as they were human. Their "baby-ness" called up familiar and familial associations, but they were not wholly the culture's own. Rosemary's emerged from the outer limits of bourgeois notions of time and Kubrick's from the outer limits of bourgeois notions of space. Given their alien parentage (Satan in one instance, a transcendental unknown in the other), the innocence and lack of knowledge of both babies were certainly questionable. Given the opacity of their eyes, their transparence and sweetness were also suspect. As well, both newborns, while appearing vulnerable and dependent in their "baby-ness," clearly possessed special power and were hardly so helpless as their bodies suggested. An irrational, unthinkable past and an unimaginable future collapsed into their visible infantile presence; they evoked no nostalgia for what was or what might be. Indeed, the children in these films threatened the mythology they represented and figured "childhood's end." In sum, the future these two children promised in their representation was not the "traditional" future, but rather a radically transformed future, an apocalyptic and/or revolutionary future— perhaps no future at all. What they delivered, however, is something quite other than radical.

Rosemary's baby has gone on to grow up in the horror film, inscribing dramas in which those negative aspects of childhood and parenthood repressed by bourgeois mythology are played out in ambivalent representations. Diachronically, this ambivalence can be bracketed between two generic declarations. "There's only one thing wrong with the Davis baby. It's alive!" pronounces the ad for *It's Alive* in 1974 (the same year which gave us the diabolic rage of the possessed but powerful Regan in *The Exorcist*). "Part of being a parent is trying to kill your kids," says the teenager in 1983's *Christine* (the same year which saw adults plotting to kill millions of American children in *Halloween III*). Over a ten-year period, the horror film has obliquely moved from the representation of children as "terrors" to children as terrorized. Unnatural "natural" infants or demonically-possessed children become sympathetic victims whose special powers are justifiably provoked or venally abused. And, where teenagers once threatened an entire populace and its social regulation with their burgeoning sexuality and presumption to authority, in recent years they have been solipsistically annihilating each other in a quarantined and culturally-negligible space.

From the early to mid 1970s and coincident with bourgeois society's negative response to the youth movements and drug culture of the late sixties and early seventies, generic emphasis was on the child not as terrorized victim, but as cannibalistic, monstrous, murderous, selfish, sexual. The child was figured as an alien force which threatened both its immediate family and all adult authority that would keep it in its place —oppressed and at home. While runaway children provided the narrative impetus, but not the focus, for such precursors of the "new" family melodrama as *Joe* (1970) and *Taking Off* (1971), the horror film focused on children not run away, but run amok. Their resentment, anger, and destructiveness, and their aberrance, their evil, were seen as unwarranted and irrational eruptions—extra-familial and pre-civilized in origin. The bodies and souls of such children as appear in *The Other* (1972), *The Exorcist*, *The Omen* (1976), and *Audrey Rose* (1977) are "possessed" by demonic, supernatural, and ahistoric forces which play out apocalypse in the middle-class home—most often graphically represented by "special effects" that rage in huge and destructive temper tantrums across the screen. Thus, while these children are verbally articulated as "possessed" and "victims," they are visually articulated as being in possession of and victimizing their households. Family resemblance notwithstanding, these kids are not their fathers' "natural" children. They are figured as uncivilized, hostile, and powerful Others who—like their extra-cinematic counterparts—refuse parental love and authority, and mock the established values of dominant institutions. They are "changelings"—the horrifically familiar embodiment of difference. Fascinating the culture which also found them abhorrent, these children collapsed the boundaries which marked off identity from difference and exercised a powerful deconstructive force utterly dangerous to patriarchal bourgeois culture. Their figural presence and work on the screen and in the home restructured and redefined the semantic field of the generation "gap"—articulating it in vertiginous imagery, as a *mise en abyme*.

In 1976, however, *Carrie* transfigures and softens the demonic and murderous child into a familiar Other whose "difference" is marked not only by her telekinetic power, but also by her relative innocence and her oppression. Adolescent Carrie is a pitiable victim of her culture and evokes sympathy. Her outrage, however horrific and excessive its expression, is a response to a comprehensible betrayal. Like Robin and Gillian who follow her in *The Fury* (1978), Carrie's fury is as "justifiable" as it is frightening. While Damien and Regan grow up in possession of relatively predetermined sequels that continue to ascribe the "cause" of children's abuse of their parents and adult authority to extrafamilial, diabolic, and ahistoric forces, the apocalyptic destruction wrought by the likes of Carrie, Robin, and Gillian seem to be as much generated by familial incoherence and paternal failure as to be the cause of it. These "furious" adolescents come from broken homes. They are oppressed and vulnerable—exposed to harm and exploitation because of the apparent weakness and instability of the bourgeois family structure deemed responsible for their protection and nurturance. Their special powers are abused, and the apocalypse that follows from their provoked and "childishly" unselective fury is seen as somehow deserved.

Correlatively, we can see the contemporary horror film's earlier representation of parents as bewildered, foolish, and blindly trusting victims of their ungrateful and aberrant children undergoing a transformation as the figures of their children change. From the terrifying Davis baby or Damien to the terrifying but terrorized Carrie, Robin, and Gillian, to the terrorized Danny (*The Shining*, 1980) or Carol Ann (*Poltergeist*, 1982), we can trace a visible shift in the ascription of responsibility for the breakdown of traditional family relations. That responsibility has been transferred from child to parent. As horror film children grow into the 1980s as smaller, younger, and less adolescent, their special powers slowly diminish also—from apocalyptic fury to a relatively helpless insight (the "shining" of Danny's prescience or Carol Ann's aura of "vital" innocence). What deserves note, however, is that this transformation of apocalyptic familial fury is generically specific. Contradictory to the most popular contemporary family melodramas and contrary to certain trends in the SF film, the horror film moves to single out Dad as the primary negative force in the middle-class family.

It is in the late seventies that the genre begins to overtly interrogate paternity and its relation to patriarchal power. In 1978, playing Robin's "natural" father in *The Fury*, iconically strong-jawed Kirk Douglas proves weak and ineffectual; he is unable to save his son from the "unnatural" father who would exploit the child in the patriarchal "name of the law." The following year shows us not only a weak, but also a "possessed" father taking to the axe and after his children. *The Amityville Horror* is not just the haunted middle-class home; it is also the haunted middle-class Dad who, weak and under economic pressure from his corrupt and demanding dream house, turns on his children. This particular corruption of paternal responsibility and perversion of paternal love follows a trajectory forward—not only to the *Amityville* sequels in 1982 and 1983, but also to the ethically lax, real-estate sales-man Dad whose willful ignorance of the ground of his business prac-tice jeopardizes his children in 1982's *Poltergeist*.[4]

The repressed in the genre is no longer the "double threat" found in the traditional horror film: an excessive will to power and knowledge, and unbridled sexual desire. Rather, the repressed is patriarchal hatred, fear, and self-loathing. As the culture changes, as patriarchy is challenged, as more and more "families" no longer conform in struc-ture, membership, and behavior to the standards set by bourgeois mythology, the horror film plays out the rage of a paternity denied the economic and political benefits of patriarchal power. The figure of the child in the genre is generated as horrific and problematic because it de-mands and generates the articulation of another figure. Father is the "repressed" who, first powerfully absenting himself, "returns" to terro-rize the family in the contemporary horror film. He is the one who, in 1968, willingly yields his paternity and patriarchal "rite" to Satan. He is the one whose absence powerfully marks the households of Regan and Carrie, who "engenders" his daughters' rage at their "lack," but is not there to constrain it culturally within the "Law of the Father."[5] Dad is also the one who—in the canny casting of John Cassavetes—carries his patriarchal pact with the devil (at Rosemary and her baby's expense) forward into his surrogate and exploitative "fatherhood" of Robin and Gillian. By 1980, the return and figuration of the repressed Father be-come fully explicit—iconically realized in the leering, jeering, mad, child-abusive hatred of Jack Torrence in *The Shining*. Looking back-ward at the frozen malevolent gaze of dead Jack, caught in a labyrinth from which he could find no escape, we can see in *Rosemary's Baby* the radical beginning of patriarchal failure: of paternity refused, denied, abandoned, hated; of patriarchy simultaneously terrified and terroriz-ing in the fact of its increasing impotence; of patriarchy maddened by a paradoxical desire for its own annihilation.

If the contemporary horror film dramatizes the terror of a patriarchy without power, and refuses or perverts paternal responsibility when it is not rewarded with the benefits of patriarchal authority, the contem-porary family melodrama plays out an uneasy acceptance of patriarchy's decline. The mode of the most popular films in the genre tends to be elegiac or comic. On the one hand, 1979 gave us *The Great Santini*, a film which found the exaggerated authoritarian power of its family patriarch excessively and pitiably inappropriate and impotent, but also celebrated its loss with a conservative nostalgia. On the other hand, the much more popular *Kramer Vs. Kramer* gave us a father without practical authority, a father lovably and lovingly bumbling to an acceptance of paternity without traditional patriarchal benefit (which includes the "surplus value" of a wife/mother). Dustin Hoffman's Ted Kramer is (if I may pun) a "little big man" hardly taller than his son: a sign of fatherhood just barely intelligible to patriarchal law and hardly able to represent it. Any real rage Kramer may feel toward runaway mom, toward his son's dependency, toward his loss of familial power and its benefits is as repressed in the text as his wife's past labor and those moments in which the adorable kid throws up or makes the bedroom look as if Regan has been there. If the horror film shows us the terror and rage of *patriarchy in decline* (savaged by its children or murderously resentful of them), then the popular family melodrama shows us a sweetly problematic *paternity in ascendance*.[6] The two genres exist in schizophrenic relation. Indeed, Greg Keeler's "*The Shining*: Ted Kramer Has a Nightmare" brilliantly elaborates this relation by viewing the mad, murderous, "bad father," Jack Torrence, as carrying out all of the negative patriarchal fury and paternal desire repressed by the nurturant "good father" in the previous year's *Kramer Vs. Kramer*.[7]

In this context, it is worth noting that both *The Shining* and the Academy Award-winning *Ordinary People* are released in 1980. The new family melodrama emerges right around the time when the horror film Father begins his active and hostile return from the repressed, and the special powers of his furious and alienated children begin to weaken in the face of his paternal hostility. In direct contradiction to the horror film Father, the "good" Dads in the family melodrama are powerless, harmless. Their patriarchal authority lessens as they paternally assume more and more of the genre's traditionally "maternal" functions. Initially, they are ambivalently figured as "soft" and "weak" in visible contrast to their "hard," "strong," and "selfish" wives. But then, as these "bad" Mothers abandon the family and the *mise en scène*, the new nurturant Dads are released from having to suffer this reversal of family power. Now playful, now "abandoned," they figure as little more than children themselves—and they transform the problematic politics of family melodrama into the playground of family comedy. With Mother gone, these Dads are given narrative license to indulge themselves in sentimental feeling and precious ineptitude. They are innocents abroad in the home—but their bumbling ignorance, while endearing, is also disempowering. Ted Kramer doesn't know how to make French toast. *Mr. Mom* (1983) is terrorized by a vacuum cleaner. In addition, their children conduct a running and critical, if finally indulgent, commentary on Dad's ineffective assumption of maternal labor and care.

The "special power" once possessed by horror film children and deconstructively directed against their parents and adult authority has been transformed and softened in the new family melodrama. In the pathetic films, that special power becomes "insight," making the child prescient and sensitive, but also fragile and vulnerable (as in *Ordinary People* and *Shoot the Moon*, 1981). In the comedic films, it becomes a cute, invincible, "precocity," (as in *Kramer Vs. Kramer* and *Author! Author!*, 1982). In both cases, however, it is the child who has the power to "authorize" the family, who evaluates Dad's abilities and performance, who denies or legitimates the particular family's existence as a viable structure. As Marina Heung points out:

> What is striking in recent films . . . is the way . . . the child not only acts as humanizer, but also as the overseer of familial roles and responsibilities. Thus, the child is a contradictory blend of precocity and vulnerability, often helpless in controlling his own situation, but instrumental in influencing the actions of adults. In fact, his control over familial relationships is so great that it is practically parental.[8]

All those "insightful" teenagers and "little adults" let Dad off the hook by themselves representing patriarchal "law" in the genre's families. And Dad, in giving up patriarchal power and authority to his children, in becoming "merely" paternal, is himself reduced—and liberated—to the status of a child.

As true of Calvin in *Ordinary People* as of more comically articulated fathers, Dad's figuration in the genre works to represent him as "positively" innocent, transparent, and cute rather than erotic. He thus becomes a poignant and sweet figure: helpless, vulnerable, and dependent upon his children not only because of his physical ineptitude in the home, but also because of his lack of the "corrupting" knowledge necessary for membership and survival in the patriarchal and bourgeois social world. If these qualities seem familiar, it is because I have used them previously to characterize the "positive" lack represented by the privileged figures of the infant and child in bourgeois mythology. In this context, an unresolvable paradox informs the contemporary family melodrama-cum-comedy. If Dad has to be figured as an innocent child to represent the "hope" and "promise" of an imaginable future for patriarchy (one which accepts paternity), he also has to give up his patriarchal power, his "authority," to his children, retaining only its illusion, its image (and that at their indulgence).

Both the horror film and the family melodrama play out scenarios which do not resolve the dilemma faced by a contemporary patriarchy under assault. The former genre dramatizes patriarchal impotence and rage, the latter patriarchal weakness and confusion—both generated by the central and problematic presence of children. If the child is figured as powerful at the "expense" of the Father, then patriarchy is threatened; if Father is figured as powerful at the "expense" of his child, then paternity is threatened. In both cases, the traditional and conceivable future is threatened—for if patriarchy is willfully destroyed by its children, no "tradition" will mark the future with the past and present, and if paternity is willfully denied by a patriarchy which destroys its children, then the future will not be "conceived." Once perceived as identical in bourgeois capitalist culture, patriarchy and paternity have been recently articulated as different and at odds—one powerful effect of white, middle-class feminist discourse. This difference emerges as a major problem when patriarchy as a political and economic power structure and paternity as a "personal" and subjective relation both locate themselves in the same place (the home) and seek to constitute the same object (the child). The horror film and the family melodrama serve to represent the horns of this dilemma—but neither is able to resolve it satisfactorily.

That resolution seems to be found in one dominant strain of the contemporary science fiction film—in a reunion of patriarchy and paternity that is as ingenious as it is also ingenuous. Rather than struggle with each other for occupation of the same place (the home), they both (temporarily) leave it; and rather than struggle to constitute the same object (the child), they both (temporarily) become it. Before "phoning home," patriarchy and paternity conflate in a single figure which is powerful, loving, and lovable: the innocent extra-terrestrial who is at once patriarchally empowered, paternal, and child-like. Indeed, it is in much recent SF that the "good" but "weak" father of the family melodrama attempts to regain his political power and patriarchal strength by moving *outside* or *beyond* the space of his "natural" family and being "born again" as an adorable child with the "special" power to again "effect" both familial and global events. Rather than the "repressed" who, first powerfully absenting himself, "returns" to the horror film to terrorize his family, Dad is the "transformed" and "transported" of the SF film. And while he, too, seems at first to abandon and deny paternity, he—unlike his horror film counterpart—returns not to savage it, but to salvage it.

The emergence of this powerful child / alien / father, who beneficently blesses the contemporary American family as both its progenitor and its progeny, is signaled but not delivered by Kubrick's ambiguously spaced-out fetus. In 1968, the "starchild" alters the semantic field of contemporary SF and provides the outer space in which to (re)produce a transformed patriarchy and a new definition of the "extended family," but it is a while before that field becomes activated as narrative space.

Although *The Man Who Fell to Earth* (1976) provides a powerful annunciation, the "starchild" gestates—ex utero—until its 1977 delivery to middle-class America in *Close Encounters of the Third Kind*. It is this film which provides the first figural contact between the powerful alien "child" and the disenfranchised human father.

The reasons for this particularly lengthy generic parturition might be attributed to a variety of factors, not the least of which is suggested by Joan Dean in "Between *2001* and *Star Wars*." She tells us:

> The science fiction films of the early seventies mirror a developing neo-isolationism (perhaps a result of a costly involvement in Southeast Asia); a diminishing fear of nuclear apocalypse (partially a result of the thaw in the Cold War); and a growing concern with domestic, terrestrial issues—most of which are related to totalitarian government control of people's lives or to overpopulation, food shortages, pollution and ecology. Consequently space travel appeared only infrequently. . . . Likewise, extra-terrestrial visitors to this planet diminished in number.
>
> The single theme . . . that dominated the science fiction imagination between 1970 and 1977 was overpopulation and its concomitant problems of food shortage and old age.[9]

The films of the period are filled with dystopian despair. Rather than figuring children (and through them "conceiving" a future), the films mark the socially necessary or externally imposed absence of children.

Having been brought back down to Earth via the domestically-directed gaze of the "starchild" in 1968, American society had nowhere to go and nothing to look forward to. The sense of failure and guilt in relation to America's constantly televised "crimes" in Vietnam (losing the war and wantonly napalming little children and child-like people) could hardly be assuaged by previous colonialist, imperialist, or militarist SF fantasies about conquering new worlds or defeating extra-terrestrial Others. (Indeed, when this narrative does return in the *Star Wars* trilogy, identification is structured so that *we* are aligned with the little, innocent, and child-like *against* the colonial, imperial, militarist and literally patriarchal Empire.) The situation at home during this period provided no better imagery. Increasing unemployment, economic recession, urban crime and decay (along with the racial and class tensions embarrassingly foregrounded by such conditions) seem the subtext of the major generic concerns Dean links with the period between 1968 and 1977.

I would also like to suggest, however, that during this period, patriarchal and capitalist America was searching for a way to transform its moral guilt and its political, economic, and social failures at home and abroad into something more supportable. Toward the end of the seventies, popular imagery began transcoding American bourgeois culture's *lack of effectivity* into *child-like innocence*, and its *failed aggressivity* into a *transcendent victimization*. It is this figural work, this transcoding and transformation, which emerges not only in the SF film and in the family melodrama, but also in the first three major films to address directly the "effects" of American involvement in Southeast Asia, and picture American men as naive and innocent "victims," of their experience: *Coming Home* and *The Deer Hunter* in 1978, and *Apocalypse Now* in 1979. Thus, it is in the late seventies that the politically, socially, and economically ineffective American male "loser" aligns himself with the "little," "innocent," and "weak" victims of patriarchal and imperialist culture: the child and the little alien Other. "Littleness," "innocence," and "weakness" become reified and celebrated in a mythically powerful and child-like figure who serves to "incorporate" concretely the bourgeois American male and the alien Other into the same small and "under-developed" body. Indeed, across those genres which attempt to resolve (rather than avenge) the social and political crisis of bourgeois patriarchy, it is of considerable importance that Richard Dreyfus as well as Dustin Hoffman and Al Pacino visibly diminish the size of the bourgeois patriarch. He first must "grow down" before he can again "grow up." And nowhere else is this process of transcoding and patriarchal transformation and regeneration made more visible than in the contemporary SF film.

It bears remembrance, however, that parallel to the birth of Rosemary's baby as the cinematic production of a horrific and demonic "hallucination," the birth of the "starchild" was the cinematic production of a "spaced-out" (drug) trip through the Star Gate. Although their delivery is delayed, the first SF babies are negative figures of the same generation as their horror film counterparts. Born in the late seventies, they are still the hostile, threatening, and alien children of the late sixties—thus, *Embryo* (1976) and *Demon Seed* (1977). Almost immediately, however, this negative sixties imagery is overtaken by a more positive dramatization which emerges from what I have suggested is bourgeois culture's attempt in the seventies to reinterpret and re-sign its ineffectiveness and failed aggressivity as child-like innocence and vulnerability.

The movement towards the conflation of American male adult, child, and alien is initially marked by the 1977 release of *Close Encounters of the Third Kind*. The film clearly valorizes the bourgeois myth of the little, innocent, vulnerable child and transcodes it as a myth of the little, innocent, and benevolent alien--who, however poignantly scrawny, is also awesomely powerful and invulnerable. Furthermore, by emphasizing its own vision as child-like and reveling in its own technology (as do the playful aliens), *Close Encounters* disavows alliance with traditional patriarchal institutions and traditional paternal behavior. The government and the military are viewed as deceitful and stupid, lacking in imagination and vision, and contemptuous of those they profess to protect. The traditional bourgeois family is seen in terms of failed paternity. (This failure is made even more painful and evident in the "special edition" of the film.)

In the Guiler family, Dad—like God—is dead. Gillian is a widow raising her son as a single parent. (She is the first of a number of unattached mothers or mothers-to-be in the genre's contemporary films, including *E.T.*, *Starman*, and *The Terminator*—and indicative of SF's generic reversal of the structure of parental presence and absence found in the serio-comic family melodrama.) In the Neary family, Dad literally abandons his paternal responsibility in an eventually successful attempt to regenerate his childhood. Misunderstood by his humorless wife and unappreciated by his conventional and unimaginative kids, Roy Neary's playfulness and curiosity are condemned by his family, who are almost as embarrassed by his childish behavior before his "close encounter" as they are after it. Literally alien-ated from traditional family structure, Gillian and Roy join together in their complementary desire to relocate the innocent and playful child they have differently lost—and, in the process, they form a "surrogate" family unit, one "elevated as the counterpart and alternative to the biological family."[10] However, the difference of their loss marks the necessarily temporary nature of their union—for Gillian's journey to Devil's Tower is an assertion of maternity, while Roy's is a negation of paternity. Gillian wants to regain her child; Roy wants to regain his childhood.

These are irreconcilable differences insofar as they concern the hierarchical structure and function of the bourgeois family and its traditional relations of power. Nonetheless, the film reconciles them in the mythology and figure of the child, in the physical relocation of personal innocence and cultural simplicity. Gillian and Roy abandon a world "cluttered" with material abundance and "noisy" with communicative complexity. In their search they encounter the empty, under-determined, and undeveloped spaces of sky and western landscape, and "noise" and "jargon" are drowned out by the universal and "simple" communication of music. (Indeed, Devil's Tower resembles Breugel the Elder's "Tower of Babel." Upthrusting from the barren Wyoming landscape, its flattened top an aborted reach to the sky, it is an iconic figure which both represents and happily reverses the biblical narrative of failed communication.) Their irreconcilable differences sublimated in their journey, Gillian and Roy's quest converges not only in their search for the innocence and wonder of childhood, but also in their flight from an incomprehensible, obstructive, over-developed, and "grown-up" world.

Thus, child-like purity and simplicity, innocence, wonder, transparency, and verbal inarticulateness are valorized by both the film and its central characters. And it is through the transcoding of the latter that the former is able to constitute equivalencies between the adult male father and the vulnerable and curious child, between the child and the powerful and curious alien, and between the vulnerable adult father and the child-like and patriarchally-benevolent alien. Child, man, and alien constitute a network of blatant displacements and homologies in *Close Encounters*. Little Barry, a smiling four-year-old with a limited vocabulary and unlimited openness to play, is displaced from his earthly home to an alien "mothership." Little Roy, the dad who's been acting a "little strange" (a "little alien"), who inarticulately babbles his wonder and excitement, who toys with his food and makes both mud pies and a mess, is dismissed and displaced as patriarchal breadwinner and authoritarian Father. Played by François Truffaut and evoking the benevolent power and innocence of his roles in *The Wild Child* and *Day for Night*, little Claude Lacombe is a geographically displaced French scientist—constantly "translated" and speaking, at best, a child's English. Representing patriarchal power as what director Spielberg calls a "man-child," he is realized as "ingenuous and wise, a father-figure with this very wide-eyed, young outlook on life."[11] And, of course, there are the little displaced aliens—unadulteratedly pure, inconceivably powerful, clearly benevolent, and completely androgynous and child-like in their physique, their playfulness, their innocence. Given this homology of innocent child, adult male, and powerful alien, it is no wonder that the end of *Close Encounters* is so affecting. Surrounded by the little and curious aliens, bathed in light, Roy Neary is a figure beatifically re-solved as powerful patriarch, loving father, and lovable child. He shines as he moves toward his imminent journey through the Star Gate, toward a culturally and politically "positive" displacement, rebirth, and eventual return to earthly power.

That journey, however, is not without potential danger. Envisioned in *Altered States* (1980), its narrative trajectory forms a cautionary nightmare dramatizing the "negative" implications of the displacement, transformation, and regeneration of patriarchy, and the apocalyptic consequences of conflating male adult, child, and alien as a means of recuperating patriarchal power. For Eddie Jessup, this conflation is hardly beatific—and culminates in a primal patriarchal scream of horror that is at once human and alien, earthly and spaced-out, and utterly displaced and decentered. Literally isolating himself in the womb of a sensory deprivation tank, alienated from both socio-political context

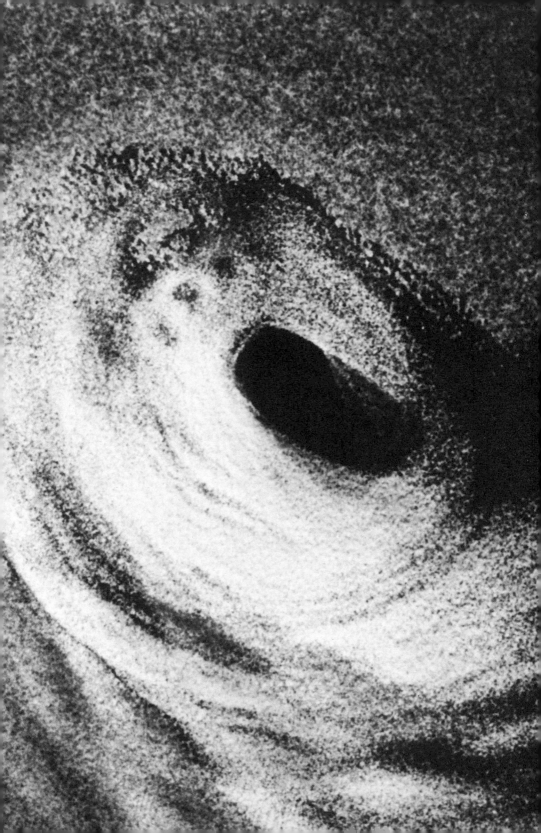

and the demands of family, Eddie's regressive escape from the modern crisis of patriarchy and paternity is conceived as a conservative, autistic journey toward self-reproduction. What he nearly achieves, however, is self-annihilation, a regeneration of patriarchy so radical it cannot be born(e).

Like Roy Neary, Eddie Jessup's psychological and evolutionary journey leads him backward from patriarchal failure to a new beginning as a child. However, unlike Roy's, Eddie's is a "bad trip." First, his hallucinatory dream-work is filled with oppressive and demanding patriarchal figures and rituals, with women who generate pleasure, but also castration anxiety and terror. Eddie regresses further and takes on the more primal and "innocent" figure of an "apeman." A powerful sign of brute masculinity and "raw" sexuality as yet "uncooked" by patriarchal Law, the "apeman" conflates male dominance, child-like innocence, and infantile need into one nostalgic figure. Yet Eddie's backward journey is not over—for the "apeman" represents no resolution of patriarchal distress in the present world, even as it represents patriarchal desire. Eddie's devolution leads him yet further backward, through the androgynous fetal stage of the "starchild" to a terrifying dispersal, a dissolution. The "pure," raw energy he seeks in his masculinist quest turns out to be a Black Hole which conflates all difference, which represents, as Eddie puts it, "hideous nothing." Proud, stubborn, selfish Eddie must ultimately choose between two states of being, both of which threaten to annihilate or emasculate bourgeois male being. Either everything that marks him as differentially sexed, gendered, and empowered is explosively and radically transformed into undifferentiated genetic energy—or, he returns to the "womb" of his family. "Delivered" from the edge of male non-being by Emily, his wife, Eddie opts for the latter and less deep space. He is finally re-signed as a chastened, "born-again" bourgeois male child; in a powerfully ambiguous Pietà, he is cradled in Emily's arms and visualized as both sacrificial Christ and "big baby." Eddie's return to Emily and his two daughters signals not only his capitulation to domesticity, but also his resigned awareness of the outer limits of patriarchy and paternity: "hideous nothing" or feminization. Horrified at becoming radically alien with the dissolution of his male difference, he must embrace Emily (woman, wife, mother, Other)—and his own literal and figurative matriarchal incorporation. Yet even as it restructures the hierarchical relations of patriarchal power as female-dominant, at least this rebirth does not annihilate the very terms of patriarchy and is, therefore, the lesser of two evils.

Altered States begins as a bold genetic fantasy, but ends with mere resignation: the adult male patriarch and paternal father is reborn as a helpless, dependent, adult male *child*. If, as Rebecca Bell-Metereau

Altered States (Ken Russell, 1980)

suggests, the "fantasy subtext" of *Altered States* "works through the male's fear and rejection of attachment to a woman in the traditional domestic situation,"[12] then it is clear that this "working through" (re)produces the adult male as a weak, powerless, and infantile figure within the structure of the traditional bourgeois family. Thus, there seems no resolution to the double-bind experienced by a patriarchy trying to conserve itself as a viable social and political structure: in order to maintain its form, it has to cede its power; in order to maintain its power, it has to change its form.

Altered States dramatizes the terror of male physical transformation, the extent to which it leads to a "hideous nothingness" which annihilates the difference upon which patriarchy is based. Nonetheless, subsequent SF films have been more sanguine about the process. Indeed, transformation of the male body is one mode of signifying a literal "physical escape" from the pressures of an untenable domestic (and terrestrial) situation. And even more common is SF's other mode of "physical escape"—the transportation of the male body to "outer" (and exotic) space. Thus, systematically, if the male body can physically escape its traditional patriarchal form, can defer and/or diffuse its sexual difference and its maturity in the androgyny and under-determined nature of an alien and/or child-like body, then patriarchal and paternal power can domestically stay at home and in the family—even if they can't quite come out of the closet. Conversely, within the same system, if the adult male body does not transform itself into a little and alien other, if it retains its signifiers of sexual difference and adulthood, then it must transport its patriarchal and paternal power to a situation and space external to traditional, domestic space. It must leave home and abandon—or, at best, spatially extend—the family. Although opposed in modality, as signifiers of a "physical escape" from patriarchal distress, the transformation and transportation of the adult male body are nonetheless completely interdependent processes.

This interdependence is, perhaps, one of the elements which makes *E.T.* (1982) so structurally satisfying and extraordinarily successful. E.T. is a transported and transformed father—and so there is a particularly deep resonance to the culturally-embraced phrase, "E.T. phone home." Physically androgynous yet paternal in function, adult, wise, and wizened, yet an innocent, childish, little "wise guy"; technologically and personally powerful, yet a vulnerable little victim of circumstance— E.T. physically escapes traditional patriarchal form *without* yielding traditional patriarchal power, and thus is able to reside in (terrestrial) domestic space and serve as Elliot's surrogate father. Linking E.T. with the childish fathers, adult children, and "surrogate families" of the new family melodrama, Marina Heung points to their conflation in the fantastic figure and narrative function of the extra-terrestrial. "Coming out of the closet" into domestic space, this alienated Dad wears the absent terrestrial father's clothing, drinks beer, reads the paper and watches TV. As Heung says, "he behaves, for all intents and purposes, like the man of the house enjoying a leisurely day at home."[13] But E.T. is also Elliot's playmate, his best friend. Thus, at the same time he fills the paternal space left empty by Elliot's "natural" father, E.T. is insistently figured as a child. He is small, toddling, curious, innocent, inarticulate. He is also particularly vulnerable and helpless—his life threatened by an alien environment and by the looming male adults who invade domestic space and the world of children to hunt him down. As well, E.T. is figured as physically androgynous and sexually unthreatening— all problematic patriarchal, paternal, and male power displaced, condensed, and conserved in the sensuously warm glow at the tip of an "innocently" elongated (and phallic) finger.

Elliot's own terrestrial father, however, is not a figure who can displace, condense, and conserve his patriarchal and paternal power. Having no recourse to a "different" and "innocent" body, Elliot's father has to escape patriarchal and paternal crisis by physically transporting himself to Mexico. Staying in traditional form, he cannot stay in his traditional place. A male adult on the run from the contradictory demands of patriarchy and paternity, Elliot's father becomes the film's real alien. Displaced in the outer-space of Mexico, he is at once narratively empowered and dispossessed. He is an E.T., a "stranger in a strange land," an alien Other (who probably doesn't speak Spanish and has problems with the water). To conserve himself as male and adult, to hold patriarchal and paternal sway over the course of the narrative, Elliot's father must stay where he is—away from its visible spaces. The most he can do is "phone home."

There is yet another fascinating off-screen narrative which, in its structuring absence, shapes E.T.'s visible drama. Mirroring the alienated and extra-terrestrialized situation of Elliot's father displaced to Mexico, this narrative is about E.T.—familial, familiar, and terrestrialized on his own home planet, in his own traditional domestic space, imagining his own physical escape from its constraints and crises, his "profession" relocating him to the outer space of Earthly suburbia. E.T. is not only Elliot's surrogate, "transformed," father. He is also the "transported" father of a little E.T. whom he, like Elliot's father, has abandoned. There is, therefore, a particular poignance in the visible narrative's insistence on E.T.'s own abandonment on a strange planet, and on his intense desire to go home. On the one hand, E.T.'s abandonment by his crewmates conflates with Elliot's—while his initial abandonment of his own family is repressed. On the other, E.T.'s longing to go home conflates the justification for his eventual abandonment of Elliot with the imagined (and narratively repressed) desire of Elliot's father to return home to his son.

Thus, the domestic absence (or extra-terrestrialism) of Elliot's father and the terrestrial presence (or domestication) of E.T. are intimately related phenomena, both predicated on the interdependent *transportation and/as transformation* of the traditional patriarchal and paternal adult male body (of whatever species) into and out of perilous, domestic, familial space. As the wish-fulfilling fantasy of separated fathers and sons who hope to bridge the distance of fragmented and spatially-extended families, *E.T.* is, as Speilberg tells us, "a love story"; "the hope [is] that they'll somehow always be together, that their friendship isn't limited by nautical miles."[14] But, despite the supposed mutuality of such love, it is finally the human male child who must absolve and resolve paternal abandonment by loving the father for leaving. Heung points out: "The lesson that E.T. teaches Elliot is that to grow up, one learns to relinquish what one loves—more specifically, one learns to accept the loss of one's father."[15]

This rationalized loss of a father is carried even further in two related SF films released in 1984: *Starman* and *The Terminator*. At first glance, the two films seem quite different. The anthropology of *Starman* is at once sentimental and comic; with a nostalgia for the simplicity of both feeling and landscape, the film borrows its non-urban but franchised geography from *Close Encounters* and *E.T.* In contrast, *The Terminator* is primarily ironic; its SF "noir" look is all urban entropy and clutter, its cinematic predecessor: *Blade Runner*. Patriarchal re-solution is also harder won in *The Terminator*—not only because Reese's death in the narrative's present confounds the logic of the future from whence he comes, but also because paternity and patriarchal power are overtly split between two opposed alien figures with whom the spectator is encouraged to identify: Reese, the loving but vulnerable rebel from the future who will father his own eventual leader, and a cyborg assassin whose nearly invincible power and determination inspire more than reluctant admiration. Less narratively problematic, *Starman* locates spectator identification in a single positive alien figure who is both vulnerable and powerful. The film's functional equivalent of the "cyborg assassin," of pure and nearly invincible patriarchal power, is the American (and male) military "machine" which inspires neither admiration nor identification, and is negatively figured in those chilling and anonymous icons of American aggression in Vietnam: "search and destroy" helicopters. (It is telling that *The Killing Fields* was released the same year as *Starman*, that the actors who played the infinitely sympathetic aliens in both films were nominated for Academy Awards, and that structures of identification with the cultural Other had been so transformed by bourgeois internalization of the defeat and guilt connected with Southeast Asia as to make the alien Other the major "human" focus of both narratives.) Its alliances quite clear, *Starman* points to an optimistic future, has a "happy"—if bittersweet—ending, its resolution of paternal and patriarchal crisis literally roseate on the screen. *The Terminator*, however, with its more temporally circular, less spatially progressive narrative, points to a ravaged and uncertain future. Its resolution is less happy; the split between paternal and patriarchal power, between caring male and male machine, is figured as a future battle to the death. *The Terminator* appropriately ends in the present of a parched desert landscape, a space which iconically accommodates both the testing ground "before" and the wasteland "after" nuclear war.

Nonetheless, whatever their differences of *mise en scène*, structures of identification, and narrative tone, the two films mirror—from opposing positions—the same narrative, the same displacements, the same newly-heroic image of an "alien-ated" maleness that is simultaneously child-like and virginal, adult and sexually potent. Both films ultimately justify the present abandonment of paternity for the future promise of a patriarchal and messianic presence who will be both child and man, both son and father. And, unlike all their recent generic predecessors (except for the "failed" *Altered States*), both films attempt to resolve patriarchal crises in the visible de-signing and re-signing of the material signifier that is the adult, human male body. A spatial and/or temporal transportation and displacement of that body narratively transforms it into the alien and different while it visibly stays human and the same. Thus, it is able to mean "something else" and remain biologically capable of domestically reproducing itself.

First, the male body is de-signed, literally stripped of conventional signifiers—not of its sex, but of its gender. Both the Terminator and Reese fall from above into the frame of a dirty modern city, their nakedness a designation of their male sexual biology and their alien-ated status. The Starman visibly incorporates himself before our eyes—transforming from an unseen alien body to fetal starchild, altering states to final figuration as a naked adult human male, who awkwardly tests, first, the marked strangeness of human embodiment and, later, of male sexual difference. Stripped to their "birthday suits," the bodies of both Reese and the Starman are de-signed, alien-ated as signifiers from their traditional patriarchal signifieds and re-signed as male adults who are "new-born."

The "new" signifieds of the "old" signifier that is the adult human male body become innocence, sweetness, inexperience, curiosity, and vulnerability—but these are semiotically linked with that body's significant patriarchal residue: biological maturity, privileged knowledge, and vast power. Thus, attributes originally mythologized on the body of the utterly lovable bourgeois child and later shared by the little and vulnerable body of the inscrutably powerful alien now become synopsized on the visible field of the full-grown (white) male body. Re-signed as inexperienced and wise, sweetly vulnerable and mysteriously powerful, childlishly innocent and biologically mature, Reese and the Starman are the patriarchs and fathers of the future. But virginal and pure, "born again" on screen, they are also present children—adult (hetero)sexual innocents, uncorrupted by and not beholden to a cultural history of masculinist sexual sniggering, and economic, political, and social exploitation. Reese and the Starman are truly alien, poignant, romantic figures whose sexual initiation at the bodies of beloved, loving, experienced, and maternal women not only reproduces them as both fathers and sons, but also nostalgically points backward towards an imaginary past. Displaced and disaffiliated from a history of patriarchal and capitalist motivations and practices which always already inform and adulterate bourgeois heterosexual relations, the alien-ated Reese and Starman enjoy a "first time" which both films figure as a sexually and spiritually "pure" and potent experience.

Here, it is appropriate to briefly consider 1984's *The Brother from Another Planet*—a film which satirically comments on SF's regressive patriarchal quest for a lost innocence it never had, and on the politically conservative motives which inform the current "mainstream" films with a seemingly "new" romanticism and humanism. *Brother* is one of a number of recent films like *Android* (1982), *Liquid Sky* and *Strange Invaders* (both 1983), *The Adventures of Buckaroo Banzai, Night of the Comet, Repo Man* (all 1984), and *Uforia* (1986) which adhere to generic SF, but also interrogate its "separatist" status. Pointing to the meaninglessness of traditional concepts like the "fantastic" and the "alien" in a totally e-stranged world marked by alienation, by temporal and spatial disorientation, by decentralization and marginalization, these films ultimately challenge the opposition between "science" and "fiction" that has traditionally structured the genre and made it unique.[16] Thus, *Brother* pokes fun at the sentimental earthly sojourn of E.T. as well as at the "alienness" of its own extraterrestrial—a black, adult male protagonist whose lack of integration into bourgeois culture and easy integration into marginal culture is hardly in the realm of the "fantastic." *Brother* draws the sexual innocence and initiation of its alien male in broad comic strokes which would find no place in the heavily romantic sexual sequences of *The Terminator* and *Starman*. But, then, the re-solution of bourgeois patriarchal crisis is not a pressing problem for a "brother" extra-terrestrialized in Harlem. While Reese and the

Starman can mark their paternal innocence and gain patriarchal power only by sexually "coming" and then going, the Brother can "come" and stay. At home in a marginal culture where paternal innocence and patriarchal power have little meaning (except as a structuring negativity), his sexual encounter is not mythologized. Nor is his brief association with a little boy and the child's pragmatic mother (and "mother-in-law"). Reese and the Starman inhabit the present only to father the future—to reproduce themselves "when" and "then" since they cannot really exist "now." The Brother, however, is unburdened by the bourgeois need, figurally and mythologically, to "overcome a contradiction (an impossible achievement if, as it happens, the contradiction is real)".[17] He can stick around here in the present, doesn't have to die or return to outer space. Indeed, he doesn't have to wait for a future resolution to social, political, and economic problems; by the film's end, the Brother has found a group of terrestrial "Others" and has settled in to start resolving things *now*. *The Brother from Another Planet* suggests that real solutions to patriarchal bourgeois crises will not be re-solutions—rather, they will be revolutions born on the margins of dominant culture (and dramatized in "marginal" films).[18]

Both figures of the "transported" and thus transformed white, bourgeois, heterosexual, and reproductive male, Starman and Reese cannot, like the Brother, realize themselves in the present—lest they betray the patriarchal sameness of their seeming paternal difference. While both are granted narrative license and patriarchal privilege to "come," physically and sexually, unable to sustain either their power or innocence, they must also go. Displaced in space, Starman (like E.T.) cannot survive on Earth and must return to his extra-terrestrial "home," while Reese, who is human but temporally alien-ated, is killed in the present to survive only—and illogically—in the future. Before their brief tenure on Earth and in the present comes to an end, however, both impregnate willing, loving, compassionate, and sexually-experienced women. In effect, the narrative teleology of both *Starman* and *The Terminator* projects a single-parent family as the necessary condition for the resolution of bourgeois patriarchal and paternal crisis. And that family has mother as the visible head of household.

Thus, like *E.T.* before them, *The Terminator* and *Starman* narrativize and justify the present loss of a husband and father. But they accomplish something further. Through their transportation and transformation of the adult male human body, through their figural work of alien-ating its traditional patriarchal meanings, they are able to *deny* the existence of the single-parent family—even as they project it. Not only are the human mothers-to-be in these films shown as strong, capable, and "understanding" in their abandonment, but it is also suggested

that they are, in fact, not abandoned at all. In some narratively satisfying (and logically impossible) time warp, the presently dead Reese will
—in the future—fall in love with Sarah's photographic image and legen-
dary "past" heroism, and will be sent back to her by an older contemporary: their rebel leader son. And, from an alien space, Starman will
keep tabs on Jenny and their future son, the latter predestined to become a "great teacher" by virtue of the concrete legacy of knowledge
and power his father leaves behind. Starman gives Jenny a small, glowing, mysterious sphere which, in effect, contains the "conscience of his
race" and is to be passed on as alien history and new human future to
his bodily male and human child. Sealed with a parting kiss, Starman's
love and paternity will transcend and synthesize the spatial (and specie-
al) fragmentation of the nuclear family. In similar ways, both defamiliarized and alien-ated, transported and transformed, Reese and the Starman are at once attached to and detached from the familiar and the
familial, and no paternal guilt or diminution of patriarchal power ad-
heres to their necessary loss.

Indeed, the literal premises of the families projected by both *The Terminator* and *Starman* transcend the traditional temporal and spatial
parameters of their presence and visibility. These families are projected
as not really singly-parented, fragmented, broken, or female-dominant.
Rather, they are re-signed as a newly temporalized and spatialized patri-
archal/paternal structure. Thus, if the necessary condition for resolving bourgeois patriarchy's social crisis is paternal abandonment of the
family, then the metaphoric and figural displacement and transformation of the adult male human body is the sufficient condition whereby
patriarchy can maintain its power over women and children. That is,
through these transformations, a "transported" patriarchy is able to
reproduce biologically and replicate itself structurally across the "nautical miles" of space and the "generation gaps" of time. The new patriarchal family is both "spaced-out" and "extended" in structures which
reverse, literalize, and transform the traditional spatial and temporal
meanings of those terms, and the final loss of these alien/earthly
fathers, while visually projected as *visible absence*, is narratively inscribed as *invisible presence*.

Both *The Terminator* and *Starman* thus construct an ingenious, if
paradoxical, narrative resolution to the atrophy of patriarchal power
and its traditional relation to paternity in the bourgeois culture of late
capitalism. But this resolution is clearly a "fantastic" one, particularly
enabled by the representational register of the genre in which it occurs.
There are no such resolutions available to either the horror film or the
family melodrama—both playing out patriarchal impotence, the one
through narratives of chaos and violence, the other through narratives

of pathos and/or comic confusion. The current science fiction film, however, plays out narratives of paternal love and benevolent patriarchal power—even as that power is deferred, is doubly displaced in space and time, once in the "transport" of the human male body and again in the awesome displays of cinematic effect wrought by an "alien" patriarchy. Seemingly the most sanguine of the three genres discussed here, it is hardly strange that the SF film has enjoyed particular privilege during the last decade.

As described and interpreted in the previous pages, the transformation of children into aliens, fathers and aliens into children, and adult males into alien fathers plays out a single patriarchal narrative, cinematically dramatized with greatest energy and force in the contemporary generic articulations of horror, family melodrama, and science fiction. In their figural and transformative work of spatially and temporally redescribing the structure and semantic field of the traditional patriarchal family, these three genres have exchanged and expended their representational energy dynamically and urgently—with the "politically unconscious" aim of seeking re-solution, or at least ab-solution, for a threatened patriarchy and its besieged structure of perpetuation: the bourgeois family.[19] In sum, their mutual project has been (and still is) aggressively regressive and conservative. Thus, while their inter-generic relations are synchronic, the various transformations explored here seem to culminate diachronically in the current dominant popularity of the SF film—that genre which most visibly figures the grandest illusions of a capitalist and patriarchal cinema, and which spatially liberates powerful born-again male "children" from social, political, and economic responsibility for the past and to the present.

And yet even SF cannot quite maintain that illusion. It keeps dissolving in the context of present structural and cultural pressure. Despite all the representational energy and urgency which have linked and revitalized the three genres in a dramatic attempt to resolve patriarchal and familial crisis in relevant but conservative narratives, there seems no viable way for patriarchy to envision a satisfying future for itself symbolically. All it can do is deny the future. There is no narrative resolution for patriarchy in the horror film—except the denial or death of the father, finally impotent and subject to the present power of his own horrific past. The family melodrama also resolves nothing; in both its serious and comic modes, its final "hopeful" articulations are a celebration of algorithmic paralysis, of a patriarchal/paternal present "on hold." And in the SF film (the most hopeful of the lot), there is no resolution of patriarchal crisis which is not patently fantastic—and no fantastic resolution which does not also annihilate any real imagination of the future in its nostalgic retreat to the "outer space" and "other time" of an impossible past. All these films symbolically enact the death of the patriarchal future.

Focusing on the problematic figure of the child and its textual transformations leads us to a "historicizing and dialectical cricitism" which reads across generic boundaries and through cultural and narrative time. What emerges from this reading is an understanding of intertextual relations of exchange which constitute "the very locus and model of ideological closure."[20] That is, the contemporary horror film, family melodrama, and science fiction film together map "the limits of a specific ideological consciousness" and mark "the conceptual points beyond which that consciousness cannot go, and between which it is condemned to oscillate."[21] Terrorized by its own past, not able to imagine and image its own presence in the future. American bourgeois patriarchy keeps getting trapped by its desire to escape the present. Nonetheless, this failure of symbolic imagination and the boredom its regressions and repetitions will eventually generate lead one to hope. Not only do we have an active and perversely popular marginal cinema which locates future outer space in the present inner city and with marginal cultures, but we also can look forward to the debilitating effects of a symbolic exhaustion so great that imaginative failure cannot be ignored. The self-revelation of an SF film blatantly called *Back to the Future* moves toward a form of ideological hysteria—the "political unconscious" of American bourgeois patriarchy teetering on the brink of babbling itself to consciousness and, perhaps, a cure.

NOTES

1. See the following articles by Robin Wood: "Return of the Repressed," *Film Comment* 14, no.4 (July-August 1978), pp.25-32; "Gods and Monsters," *Film Comment* 14, no.5 (September-October 1978), pp.19-25; "The American Family Comedy: From *Meet Me in St. Louis* to *The Texas Chainsaw Massacre*," *Wide Angle* 3, no.2 (1979), pp.5-11; "Neglected Nightmares," *Film Comment* 16, no.2 (March-April 1980), pp.24-31; and his various pieces in *American Nightmare: Essays on the Horror Film* by Andrew Britton, Richard Lippe, Tony Williams and Robin Wood (Toronto: Festival of Festivals, 1979).

2. For an elaboration of these systemic oppositions, see the first chapter in my *The Limits of Infinity: The American Science Fiction Film* (South Brunswick, NJ: A.S.Barnes, 1980). A new and enlarged edition is entitled *Screening Space: The American Science Fiction Film* (New York: Ungar, 1986).

3. Dudley Andrew, *Concepts in Film Theory* (New York: Oxford University Press, 1984), p.170.

4. On the horror film's relation to economic crisis, see Douglas Kellner, "Fear and Trembling in the Age of Reagan: Notes on *Poltergeist*," *Socialist Review* 69 (May-June 1983), pp.121-131.

5. Both *The Exorcist* and *Carrie* seem to me provocatively read in Lacanian terms; lacking both a phallus and the Phallus (or patriarchal law), the female teenagers in these films have no access to the patriarchal Symbolic. Without submission to and acquisition of patriarchal discourse, their pubescent bodies seek expression through Other means—through menstruation. Indeed, the flow uncontained by the constraints of the Father, their physical and bloody "rage" is an apocalyptic feminine explosion of the frustrated desire to "speak."

6. For a related discussion, see Dave Kehr, "The New Male Melodrama," *American Film* 8, no.6 (April 1983), pp.42-47.

7. Greg Keeler, "*The Shining*: Ted Kramer Has a Nightmare," *The Journal of Popular Film and Television* 8, no.4 (Winter 1981), pp.2-8.

8. Marina Heung, "Why E.T. Must Go Home: The New Family in American Cinema," *The Journal of Popular Film and Television* 11, no.2 (Summer 1983), p.81.

9. Joan F. Dean, "Between *2001* and *Star Wars*," *The Journal of Popular Film and Television* 7, no.1 (1978), pp.36-37.

10. Heung, p.82.

11. Tony Crawley, *The Steven Spielberg Story* (New York: Quill, 1983), p.63.

12. Rebecca Bell-Metereau, "*Altered States* and the Popular Myth of Self-Discovery," *The Journal of Popular Film and Television* 9, no.4 (Winter 1982), p.178.

13. Heung, p.84.

14. Crawley, p.114. See also p.115 where Spielberg relates the arrival of E.T. with Elliot's abandonment. Throughout the volume, both Spielberg and Crawley draw upon the bourgeois myth of the child and constitute a fascinating "rhetoric" of childhood.

15. Heung, p.84.

16. For a more detailed discussion of these films as less a category contained within SF than as an erasure of SF as genre, see "Postfuturism," the last chapter in my *Screening Space*.

17. Claude Lévi-Strauss, "The Structural Study of Myth," in *The Structuralists from Marx to Lévi-Strauss*, eds. Richard and Fernande De George (Garden City, NY: Anchor Books, 1972), p.193.

18. Much more "marginal" than the marginal films identified here is, of course, Lizzie Borden's *Born in Flames* (1982), which directly—and singularly—counters the romantic nostalgia and patriarchal "humanism" found in the contemporary mainstream SF discussed in this essay. For a theoretical and

critical discussion of this film, see Teresa De Lauretis, "Aesthetics and Feminist Theory: Rethinking Women's Cinema," *New German Critique* 34 (Winter 1985), pp.154-175.

19. Reference to the "political unconscious" is derived from Fredric Jameson, *The Political Unconscious: Narrative as a Socially Symbolic Act* (Ithaca, NY: Cornell University Press, 1981). The assertion of such a concept is based on the recognition that "nothing . . . is not social and historical— indeed, that everything is 'in the last analysis' political," and calls for the "unmasking of cultural artifacts as socially symbolic acts"(p.20).

20. Jameson, p.47.

21. Jameson, p.47.

Close Encounters of the Third Kind

Liquid Sky (Slava Tsukerman, 1982)

Androids and Androgyny
Janet Bergstrom

The overwhelming response of the young public to *Star Wars* in 1977 sparked an unforeseen renaissance in the popularity of science fiction films. *Star Wars* and the Lucas/Spielberg productions that followed were amazingly successful in capturing audience attention through high-tech special effects housed in cartoon-like stories. The appeal of this wishfulfilling narrative simplicity seemed limitless, and spilled over immediately into a lucrative series of merchandising tie-ins. Ever more fabulous effects and creatures could be accommodated by a little story modification, and indeed it appeared that stories were being written to showcase new special effects. By the time Spielberg's *E. T.* was released in 1982, the potential for massive exploitation of memorabilia was a significant factor in calculating anticipated revenues.

Thanks to this revival of the science fiction genre, a number of films were released that have a more specialized appeal, combining an unusual emphasis on visual/aural style with a less classical form of narrative. Films like *Blade Runner* (1982), *Alien* (1979), *The Road Warrior* (1981), *Liquid Sky* (1982), and *The Man Who Fell to Earth* (1976; re-released several years later in a long version) have a visual presence in keeping with perceptually aggressive and imaginative media advertising. Although their budgets and intended audiences were very different, they have all become cult movies, glittering examples of a deviation from the normal—slightly beyond what the audience for *E. T.* would find acceptable. Too much spectacle, too little story: this is exactly the kind of reaction that was so quick to dismiss *Rumblefish* (1983), *One From the Heart* (1982), *The Cotton Club* (1984), and *Streets of Fire* (1984), not to mention classics like Sternberg's *The Devil is a Woman* (1935).[1]

This deviant strain may be compared, nonetheless, to the mainstream Lucas/Spielberg productions in two significant ways. First, both types of film have an important relationship to advertising, and second, they have been accused of sacrificing story and character development to art direction. However, in the *Blade Runner/Liquid Sky* variety, the connection with advertising is more fundamental because it is conceptual rather than product-oriented. As in certain kinds of innovative media advertising, an integrated, all-over design projects ambience and doesn't necessarily focus on specific characters, objects, or actions. And rather than emphasize traditional family relationships, which is the strongest theme shared by Lucas and Spielberg, the design take-over in these films directs attention to less predictable areas of social organization and sexual identity.

A compelling visual/aural design that is perceptually insistent, but semantically uncertain or in suspension is fundamental to this type of film. These characteristics have important implications for audience identification, and are closely related to the most creative level of television advertising, including experiments in music videos. In some cases this relationship is direct. Ridley Scott had already made a name for himself with his unusual television commercials before he directed feature films. In fact, his commercials have attracted almost as much attention as *Alien* and *Blade Runner*. The ad Scott did for Apple computers, ominously called "1984," and his controversial, political advocacy commercial for W.R. Grace, where children of the future put their parents on trial for creating the national debt, exhibit the same kind of dense, perceptual involvement as *Blade Runner*, with at least as much ambiguity as to "what they say," unlike the clear messages ads are classically supposed to convey.[2]

Blade Runner could serve as a paradigm for the highly designed film. According to its critics, *Blade Runner* is an outstanding example of art direction run wild. Its style is said to be cluttered and intrusive, flaunting a disdain for character motivation and story development; in other words, instead of stylistic virtuosity, we witness a failure of narrative imagination. From another perspective, however, the visual/aural density of *Blade Runner* represents a deliberate move against the clean, spare, geometric, controlled look of such a trend-setting modern (even Modernist) science fiction film as *2001* (1968).[3] *Blade Runner* can seem confusing, a visual field that verges on incoherence. What exactly are we supposed to be looking at? Or *what is it* that we *are* looking at? The film seems to follow two different tracks at the same time: one is a story line, while the other is like a stylistic force field that resists the stabilization of the film's referential dimension at every moment.[4]

Blade Runner has the look, sound, and ambience of the totally designed perceptual experience. It is built up out of unnaturally colored beams of light and glowing neon shapes that activate parts of the screen space, filtered through haze, shadows, smoke, steam, and rain. People use degraded, hybrid languages, and costumes, to move in a disorderly, decaying urban-industrial environment. Characters emerge out of this delirium, sometimes competing with their environment for the spectator's attention. Anachronistic elements from the past are able to invade and disrupt, if not ultimately control, this "future" city. The iconography of *Blade Runner*, and also of *Alien* and *The Road Warrior*, is striking in its use of composite figures that condense the obsolete and the technologically advanced, the biomorphic and the mechanical.[5] For example, a flying machine drifts through the night skies in *Blade Runner* resembling both a heavily armored, metallic blimp and an archaic, deep-sea puff-fish, with spiked feelers protruding from its sides. Flashing lights are strung over its surface, emphasizing the "ribs" of its skeleton. An irregular patch of light is located where a fish's eye would be. This "creature" carries an electronic billboard advertising the off-world colonies, while a reassuring male voice repeats a slogan that reinforces the image verbally. This is a strange amalgamation of the ordinary and the unexpected that is not easy to adjust to. As is true of the film's style generally, it is difficult to distinguish—quickly or at all—between significant and trivial elements. The ad projected from this shuttle provides an ironic example of the kind of sound/image redundancy that the film rejects, turning instead to an indirect and "unstated" aesthetic derived from a conceptual shift in advertising strategies.[6]

The status of characters within this complex scheme is not obvious; they seem to rise and fall in importance, like an irregular pulse. Part of the rhythm of differentiating characters from decor is tied to strong generic expectations: there will be characters, but they might not be human. Androids, replicants, and aliens are not human, but more or less, depending on the film, they can approximate human physical, mental, and emotional characteristics. Genre conventions generally maintain that they cannot possess emotions: this is what differentiates them from humans. *Blade Runner* is centered on this theme and attempts to invert it. Roy Batty and Pris are meant to be replicants in love, and sexually involved with each other. They are also intended to provide a parallel with the film's main romantic couple, Rachel, an exceptionally human, exceptionally desirable replicant, and Deckard, who finds himself reacting emotionally to the replicants he is assigned to "eliminate" throughout the film, as if they were human.

Androids or replicants are differentiated from humans in these films with great difficulty, unlike the robot, R2D2, in the *Star Wars* series or the little creature, E.T. In this disturbance between categories normally kept distinct (human/non-human), another dimension is added to the standard representation of differentiation by gender in mainstream fiction film. Where the basic fact of identity as a human is suspect and subject to transformation into its opposite,[7] the representation of sexual identity carries a potentially heightened significance, because it can be used as the primary marker of difference in a world otherwise beyond our norms. The value of sexual difference in these films, however, is postclassical in that it is unpredictable. The standard use of female identity to reinforce male (dominant, institutional) identity is no longer a regular pattern of narrative development. As narrative forms have moved away from the dominance of classical story motivation and structure, so too have classical patterns of sexual (*voir* social) definition become subject to change.[8]

I am particularly interested in the representation of androids (or aliens: the non-human that is compared with the human) in these highly designed movies where they are modeled on an androgynous female type designated as ideal, or the embodiment of fashion. In a number of these films, we can see a transfiguration of what is marketed as androgyny in commercial fashion advertising. Where androgyny, as a fashionable, contemporary look, can indicate "more" sexuality, meaning *both* feminine *and* masculine appeal, virtually the same image can be used to signal the eradication of sexuality. With alarming rapidity, the narrative can lead to a withdrawal of affect and a reversal in identification; masculine and feminine connotations can cancel each other out, so that nothing is left of sexual identity in the androgynous figure. The image is the same—it has a recognizable, contemporary referent. But its value as a desirable image, a model image, has been eliminated.

This pattern of violent reversal of affect is hardly a new discovery. It provides the turning-point for E.T.A. Hoffmann's story "The Sandman" and Balzac's "Sarrazine." In both instances, the male protagonist is wrenched from an extreme pitch of idealization to abject horror by his forced realization of the non-sexual, and therefore, inhuman nature of the woman he loves. (In neither case is it really a woman: in the first, it is a mechanical doll; in the second, a castrato.) But these stories, as retold and interpreted by Freud and Barthes, respectively, are parables of castration. In other words, they are stories about male sexual identity.[9] They serve as castration parables precisely because the revelation of the "truth" of the beloved's gender does not allow the male protagonist to continue imagining his identity in terms of hers. "She"—no longer a woman—is rendered wholly alien, and this knowledge proves fatal to the hero. Here I would like to put the emphasis on female identity—the different uses and radically changing values to which a contemporary female image-type can be subjected.

Axiomatic to the "model movie" genre is the demonstration that beauty is fashion, and fashion is merchandise that must continually change its modes, or conventions, in order to perpetuate itself. In *The Rise to Power of Louis XIV* (1970), Rossellini shows how the ever-changing demands of fashion can be used to channel and intensify political power. Fashion models can be used to display social signs and meanings of many kinds. Sexual difference can be encoded; a lack of differentiation, or deliberate confusion of gender, can also be encoded. Clearly, these signs are meant to be deciphered by their intended audience, as Barthes demonstrated for magazine ads in "Rhetoric of the Image."[10] There must always be a reference to the world of real bodies, or there would be no fashion industry. But the reference is made through desire and fantasy. Frederick Wiseman shows this by way of negative example in his documentary *Model* (1980). The fact that the fashion industry is revealed by Wiseman to be ugly, degrading, and deeply unglamorous only heightens the miracle of this transformation away from reality (or this version of it) and the imaginary investment in the fantasy status of the fashion image by the public.

In the following sections, I would like to describe three cases where the androgynous fashion image is assigned a different value. In the first, a celebrated magazine ad for Calvin Klein underwear (1985), the androgynous image is used to connote "more" sexuality, both masculine and feminine aspects of seductiveness. In the second, a science fiction/detective film, *Looker* (1981), the positive or "surplus" sexual connotations of a highly idealized androgynous female image are reversed when the image reappears as an electronically simulated, depersonalized double. The third example, *Liquid Sky* (1982), uses androgynous models to project a negative presence, where masculine and feminine sexual connotations cancel each other out. This extreme use of the androgynous image brings the discussion back directly to the design-dominated film, for in *Liquid Sky*, androgynous characters are subsumed within a spectacular frame that overshadows them.

Fashion and the Androgynous Model

Androgyny is fashionable today, and it has been for some time. It is not only fashionable, it can be commodified and packaged; it is marketable and profitable. David Bowie's brilliantly theatrical image of androgynous perfection may have been ahead of mass consumption in the early seventies, but it made history and has seen numerous and ever more popular transformations in the meanwhile. "Nightflight," a cable television program that presents thematic selections of music videos, highlights androgyny at regular intervals. The last few years of Calvin Klein ads for nearly identical underwear worn by androgynous male and female models probably best exemplifies the appeal of fashionable androgyny. In an article in *Newsweek*, Klein said that he was trading on narrative ambiguity. In one ad, a woman lies on a bed between two men, all three androgynous types, wearing a minimum of designer underwear. They are posed lying very close to each other, not quite touching, as if they are asleep. The photograph has a gauzy, soft-focus look, rendered in delicate pastels. The *Newsweek* reporter suggests possible scenarios: an innocent nap, or perhaps they had just had sex? (If so, who? All three? How?) The point, underlined by Klein, is to leave the story to the viewer.[11]

This is an example of the use of androgynous images to connote *more* sexuality. The ad is clearly designed to be sexually suggestive. It can be imagined in many ways, but one of this image's most potent aspects is its soft ambience of indefinite sexuality. As for gender, it is clearly marked. But practically nothing else about sexual identity is indicated—not object choice, not preference for any variety of sexuality. Perhaps the strongest theme of the Calvin Klein ad campaign is narcissism. But that can easily be overlaid with any number of other fantasies. The powerful thing about this ad is that the consumer is under no obligation to choose. Ambient sexuality is completely non-restrictive. It is not even restricted to the bodies photographed. It is a function of the total image: its colors, its textures, its design. This is obviously the lesson that advertising has brought home to the modern, image-conscious filmmaker.

In film there is historical precedent for playing up connotations of ambiguity or non-resolution of sexual identity. Louise Brooks as Lulu in *Pandora's Box* (1928) was seductive and desirable to everyone around her, causing her admirers to transgress traditional boundaries of class, age, gender, and family. It was never possible to define her sexual identity in a predictive or restrictive way. Likewise, one might argue that the seductiveness of Pabst's visual style, as in many other Weimar films, was used deliberately to entrance the spectator in a general sense, not necessarily related to anything erotic in the narrative. By contrast, films like *Victor, Victoria* (1982), *Tootsie* (1982), and *Yentl* (1983) that supposedly open the public's eyes to the ambiguities of sexual object choice work by limiting their plots to comedies of mistaken sexual identity. The audience knows all along what the mistake is, and that a normal, heterosexual choice will be made in the end. This is reinforced in *Victor, Victoria* by including a "real" homosexual couple among the characters, carefully bracketed off as such. These films congratulate themselves on not passing a negative judgement on homosexual relationships, but there is no ambiguity here, and no real experimentation with identification either. Heterosexuals fall in love with heterosexuals, homosexuals with homosexuals. They are absolutely separate categories.

In contrast, Pasolini's *Teorema* (1968) introduces a young stranger (Terence Stamp) who seduces, in turn, every member of a traditional, wealthy Italian family: son, maid, mother/wife, daughter, and father/husband/patriarch. Their lives are each uniquely and irrevocably changed by the illicit desire his presence forces each one of them to recognize in themselves. The Calvin Klein ad campaign is geared toward a similar ambiguity of attraction and seduction. But by leaving its "story" so undeveloped, it can attract an audience who would find identification with seduction in *Teorema* too dangerous, or incomprehensible. The ad isn't threatening because it allows the viewer to hold on to traditional sex role expectations while denying them at the same time. For those who would like to see it that way, sex role expectations in the ad are quite conventional, except for the "modern" semi-nudity, which might be appropriate on a European beach. For others, various imaginative possibilities—some conventional, some not—are evoked the moment the ad is seen. The primary impact might not even be connected with sexual expectations, but with an abstract design of shapes, textures, and colors. The body as landscape has an important place in the art history of photography (Edward Weston, Imogene Cunningham, and countless others). The potential for different kinds of identifications is calculated to let the ad appeal to the broadest spectrum of the fashion conscious public.

Looker: Reversing the Value of Perfection

In these designer films, there is something that speaks directly to the world of advertising and simulated response. Although *Looker*, ironically, is a very ordinary-looking film, including its deceptively routine TV ads, it is about the phenomenon that is actually realized in the *Blade Runner/Liquid Sky* type of film, where the artfully controlled ambience (the total look) controls perception without even seeming to provide it with a focus.[12]

Looker is about beautiful fashion models, and about the potential for television advertising to exercise total control over the public's desires. The ultimate goal is political power, to be gained by means of hypnotic suggestions repeated during campaign ads. A strikingly lovely woman tells a Beverly Hills plastic surgeon that her modelling agency has requested several changes to perfect her face. She presents him with a computerized analysis that lists a series of minute "defects" to the millimeter. Dr. Roberts has already performed plastic surgery on three models from the same agency, who had brought in similar lists. As it turns out, after these models have corrective surgery, they are duplicated by an electronic scanning device and murdered. Their image has been reconstituted by a computer for television commercials; the simulated model cannot be distinguished on the screen from the original.

The ad research unit connected with this modelling agency has almost reached the point of controlling the viewer's eye at every moment of their commercials. Absolute control of the perceptual field is necessary in order for the hypnotic effect to be achieved. Only the human movement in the ads still poses a problem, because no matter how perfect the models can look, they can't match the exact body placements of their computer analogues. Computer simulations are *more* perfect: they are more perfectly controlled.

Cindy Fairmont is an androgynous model whose life is endangered by this scheme. (Eventually she is saved by Dr. Roberts and her own resourcefulness.) Cindy is highly desirable, and a kind of ideal, female androgynous type that the modern consumer of fashion products would see everywhere in fashion magazines. But the positive sexual connotations associated with her boyish good looks will be reversed in a sequence of shots heavily emphasized in the film. Cindy is taken to a lab, where, left alone, she is given instructions by a disembodied voice to undress and stand still on a small, revolving platform. Her body is covered by a moiré pattern while computers copy her image electronically. Scanning beams encircle her, much like the scene of Maria's transformation into a robot in Lang's *Metropolis* (1926). But here the image of fascination is about to be negated, not created. We see schematic representations of a woman's head, hand, and body on a bank of video monitors to her side. These images evolve rapidly until they look just as life-like as the real model.

Meanwhile, upstairs, Dr. Roberts is given a demonstration of the ad

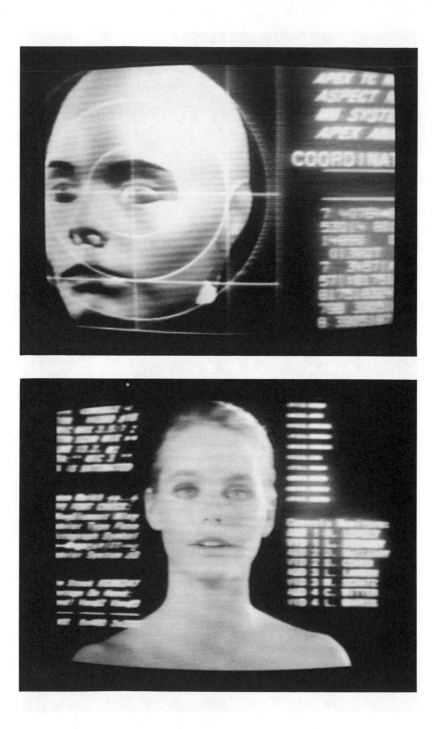

agency's voice synthesizer. He is taken by surprise when he sees Cindy's reconstituted face on a video screen, framed by two columns of statistical information. At first her voice is obviously artificial. It is easy to believe she is a robot as she repeats mechanically: "Hi. I'm Cindy. I'm the perfect female type, 18 to 25. I'm here to sell for you." But by the fifth repetition (the sound appears to speed up a bit each time), her voice has become as natural as her image. Before his eyes, she has become "real." What this means, of course, is that she didn't look real to begin with, or, more accurately, that she didn't *seem* real. Watching her face as she speaks, knowing, in other words, that "Cindy" is computer-generated, her image is voided of identity: "she" is no longer human. The image is the same, but its desirability has been reversed. This is paradoxical since her image is intended by the agency to connote desirability in television ads, where no one would know that the image was only a copy of a copy, not a copy of a woman.

This demonstration impresses Dr. Roberts with the gravity of the situation. He takes steps to save the real Cindy, who is still really desirable, from being replaced by her electronic double. But doesn't this negative use of the ideal type reflect on the model who is saved and her own looks, which have, after all, been perfected?[13] This is a question the film doesn't dwell on, because we're not really ever supposed to doubt the attractiveness of Cindy's image. Even at its most robotic, it serves to emphasize the fact that her "real," sensual self is present somewhere, and is a more powerful image.

In *Looker*, the female androgynous type is entirely taken for granted as modern and popular. (In the Looker Labs, Cindy is told: "You're perfect in your category.") However, it *is* this type that we see being subjected to a reversal in value in its transformation from a woman into an electronic robot. Near the end of the film, we watch Cindy, amazed and aghast ("That's *me*!"), as she *sees herself* on a video monitor transformed into an ordinary, young (electronic) housewife in a commercial for "New Formula Blast." Her image is not only deglamorized, but depersonalized as she wipes off her kitchen table and addresses the audience: "I admit I have troubles with bugs and roaches, even in my perfect and spotless kitchen. What with everybody coming and going, the rush and bustle of a large family, what is a mother to do?" *Looker* demonstrates how the female androgynous image is *used*, how it is exploited. Its value isn't inherent, but relative and variable: it can be given or taken away. The bearer of this image isn't the one who controls its value.

Liquid Sky: Hostile Fashion

> Conventional ideas of prettiness were jettisoned
> along with the traditional lore of cosmetics.
> Contrary to the advice of every woman's maga-
> zine, make-up for both boys and girls was
> worn to be seen. Faces became abstract por-
> traits: sharply observed and meticulously ex-
> ecuted studies in alienation.
> Dick Hebdige, *Subculture: The Meaning of
> Style*[14]

Revulsion and cynicism go hand in hand with modelling in *Liquid Sky*. Unlike model movies of old, the film is not designed to show off either clothes or faces. Dick Hebdige, in characterizing a moment of punk aesthetics, also describes the New Wave fashion poseurs in *Liquid Sky*. By way of contrast, remember how ugly duckling Audrey Hepburn is discovered by fashion photographer Fred Astaire in *Funny Face* (1957). He falls in love with her quite visibly, in her absence, watching her eyes and the lines of her face materialize on his high-contrast photographic paper. Soon Audrey Hepburn is transformed into an elegant fashion model, embodying the *Vogue* look in the heyday of Richard Avedon's influence.[15] Stark compositions highlight her face and wardrobe as angular, graphic designs, countered in their severity only by the emphasis on Hepburn's expressive eyes. The androgynous models in *Liquid Sky* are worlds apart from the charm and warmth of Audrey Hepburn's character. They project hostility and aggressiveness toward each other, the camera, and the audience. *Liquid Sky* shows an extreme use of the androgynous fashion image, where masculine and feminine qualities violently and nihilistically cancel each other out. Sexual desire, and sexual identity, have been almost willfully eradicated. The characters are represented as alienated, clearly; but they are also represented as aliens.

In *Liquid Sky* a sketchy and far-fetched science fiction plot intersects a fantasized version of eighties punk subculture in New York City.[16] The subcultural group is characterized by a sense of its own outsider status, to the point of extreme, narcissistic self-destructiveness; lack of emotion, other than derisiveness or hostility; attention to surface, as seen in the fashion obsession, the importance of being in costume, the Club; and forms of dependency, especially drug dependency and the passivity associated with it. (Liquid sky is a euphemism for heroin.) Sexuality in the film is hostile and aggressive. Disinterest in sex and violent sex are both associated with drugs. The loss of sexual identity, whether in deliberate gender confusion or in a withdrawal from sex,

is paralleled by a loss or abandonment of social identity. This is particularly evident in the case of the main character, Margaret, and her gay male counterpart, Jimmy, both of them androgynous New Wave fashion models. (They are played by the same person, Anne Carlisle.)

A number of standard science fiction elements are present in *Liquid Sky*: a flying saucer; a German scientist who arrives in New York to track down the aliens; a theory about what they want, namely a chemical substance produced in the human brain during orgasm, or similarly induced by heroin; electronic imagery, like fluid, colored X-rays, seeming to represent the point of view of the aliens observing the orgasmic substance as it accumulates in the brain. But I would suggest that the science fiction elements and the "normal" elements of the film are transposed: it is the fashion poseurs who are on display as the real aliens. This identification is suggested in the dialogue, but comes across largely through the over-all design of the film, its look and its sound.

The science fiction elements are visually unimpressive: the flying saucer is tiny, and the aliens' electronic point-of-view shots are rather crude and predictable. The aliens are never seen, and the scientist is awkward. Scenes in which he interacts with New Yorkers, such as Margaret's former acting professor or Jimmy's mother, are filmed in a banal manner, offset by comedic touches relating to the use of familiar stereotypes. The fashion/performance scene, on the other hand, is filmed entirely differently, providing more visual interest than could possibly be absorbed. An unending variety of objects enters into the frame and prevents stability of vision. Colored neon lights interact with wildly inventive makeup painted across faces, bodies, and hair, and a kaleidoscope of shapes and styles of costumes. Editing is rhythmic and jagged; the electronic score emphasizes the separation of this group from the normal. These performers, who parade for each other with the greatest affectation of disinterest, are seen mainly in the Club or in Margaret's apartment. Both locales are scenes of aggressiveness, confrontation, and visual splendor. In effect, the science fiction elements of *Liquid Sky* have been taken over by its design elements.

The fashion photo session in Margaret's apartment provides a violent, stylish centerpiece for the film. A montage sequence presents a quick series of "stills" of the "twin" boy-girl models, Jimmy and Margaret, photographed against the night sky of Manhattan. Costume changes are perceived as flashes of brilliant color and angular, unnatural body positions. The emphasis is on fashion as ambience—as attitude and as posturing, rather than on costumes, which extend, like disguises, into the elaborately painted faces and hairstyles of the models and their mannered cynicism. The brittle mood of hostility essential to

the negative magnetism of the photos increases in direct proportion to the depersonalization of the models. In the last "photos," Margaret wears a black band of paint across her eyes, like a mask. Her expression is a function of design, color, movement, and light, not interiority. The film is Expressionist in that it exteriorizes and objectifies the alienation of its characters.

The masculine and feminine aspects of the androgynous fashion image are split into two antagonistic characters who are used to cancel each other out. The derisive looks and comments of the photography entourage contribute to this end in a calculated, sadistic way. Sex has been used against Margaret (she has been raped); now sex becomes Margaret's passive-aggressive weapon. However, it is a weapon she has no more control over than she has over her victimization. As the audience knows, anyone who experiences orgasm within view of the aliens will die. (Margaret, notably, doesn't.) Jimmy is brutally abusive to Margaret during the photo session, and finally she retaliates by playing on his biggest weakness—love of his own image. Looking into a mirror held up by the photo crew, Jimmy gives in to their sarcastic compliments, and is brought to sexual climax by Margaret (off-screen). We see the abstract, alien representation of events (their "point of view" shot), and Jimmy vanishes. Adrian, Margaret's lesbian roommate, is contemptuous in the face of these events. She has two women hold Margaret down on the bed. Despite Margaret's distraught pleading, Adrian won't stop. Suddenly she disappears, exactly as Jimmy had.

Visual style as controlled ambience is emphasized further as Margaret circles the room, pulling the cords out of the colored neon signs that line the walls—each time changing the configuration of light and color—and finally knocking down the photographer's lamp, leaving a harsh light from below. In breaking up the space of her apartment and the photography crew, she translates psychological disruption into physical disruption. She sits down in front of the mirror where her fashion image had been elaborately constructed and wipes blue fluorescent paint over her face. Paradoxically, as she destroys the image of her fashion identity (her elaborate makeup and expression), Margaret tells everyone who she is (her identity as a history) by describing a series of images she had learned and rejected: suburban life in Connecticut as a lawyer's wife, with beautiful children and barbecues; an alternative life in New York—independence, success.

> I was taught that to be an actress one should be fashionable. And to be fashionable is to be androgynous. And I am androgynous not less than David Bowie himself.

At this point, her disillusionment, her alienation, are externalized and visible: even the contours of her face have disappeared in the glowing blue color so that she is no longer recognizable. (She is now lit only by blacklight.) Her appearance is completely dehumanized; it looks like the mask that figures prominently on the wall. In Margaret, androgyny was perfected as an image, and a posture. But androgyny didn't bring with it anything very different about sexual, or social, relationships. Women can exploit women as well as men can. Not only is sexual identity eliminated in this scene, but a larger sense of community or social identity is rendered ludicrous. Margaret is no longer within a community at all.

Style as Resistance

Dick Hebdige, in *Subculture: The Meaning of Style*, describes the function of style as resistance for youth subcultures in post-war England through the late 1970s.[17] Like the function of myth, and the kinds of popular icons and rituals analyzed by Roland Barthes in *Mythologies*, style is what subcultural groups use to mediate between irreconcilable realities.[18] The adoption of anti-social styles by youth subcultures doesn't resolve political problems directly, but Hebdige argues that it provides a form of expression for ideological conflict. Style functions as indirect communication; it is like a language spoken among initiates, signalling the resistance of subcultures to the norms established by the dominant culture. In the case of the British punk subculture, Hebdige finds a particularly aggressive, expressive example.

> Like Duchamp's "ready mades"—manufactured objects which qualified as art because he chose to call them such, the most unremarkable and inappropriate items—a pin, a plastic clothes peg, a television component, a razor blade, a tampon—could be brought within the province of punk (un)fashion. Anything within or without reason could be turned into part of what Vivien Westwood called "confrontation dressing" so long as the rupture between "natural" and constructed context was clearly visible . . . .[19]

Hebdige would like to show the subversive side of this movement "against nature," in contrast to the dismissal of youth subcultures as ephemeral, trivial, offensive, and incoherent.[20] Jean Genet is the emblematic figure for this study. Hebdige sees in both Genet's life and his art recurring themes that also provide a focus for youth subcultures: "the status and meaning of revolt, the idea of style as a form of Refusal, the elevation of crime into art (even though, in our case, the 'crimes' are only broken codes)."[21]

The appearance of androgyny is an important component of this movement against nature, because predetermined, restrictive sex roles

all too often were assumed to be natural, including dress. Girls were supposed to look like girls, boys like boys. Rock music played a key role in changing these kinds of image expectations. David Bowie's influence was particularly strongly felt.

> . . . Bowie was responsible for opening up questions of sexual identity which had previously been repressed, ignored or merely hinted at in rock and youth culture. In glam rock, at least amongst those artists placed, like Bowie and Roxy Music, at the more sophisticated end of the glitter spectrum, the subversive emphasis was shifted away from class and youth onto sexuality and gender typing.[22]

In *Liquid Sky* style is clearly intended as provocation—this is stated repeatedly by various characters. However, style-as-revolt is trapped in its own narcissistic and romantic image of negation. The communication model of style doesn't seem to apply here, or at least not communication among the characters in the film. They seem quite determined, in fact, *not* to communicate with each other, despite a certain shared anti-aesthetic. This seems to be the point of several scenes where Margaret tries to express her sense of loneliness and isolation to Adrian; but Adrian has no emotional bond with the past, and she is dismissive of Margaret's crisis of identification.

According to Dick Hebdige's description of British punk subculture, "faces became abstract portraits: sharply observed and meticulously executed studies in alienation"; *Liquid Sky* presents a fictionalized image of punk ten years later, in New York, when punk has been appropriated by the media. These characters—New Wave fashion poseurs— are not masquerading for each other to make an anti-social visual statement; the film shows how they are dressing up for the fashion industry and its media (a live fashion show in the Club, the photography session for a pictorial spread, the interview for *Midnight Magazine*; Margaret and Jimmy identify themselves as models, and are pressured to perform in order to advance their careers). Style no longer represents revolt. But because it once *said something* within a community, this style can act as a facade, allowing its participants to believe they are outsiders while attempting to win the rewards of mainstream approval. *Liquid Sky* is able to crystallize the powerlessness of this subcultural group by focussing almost exclusively on its spectacular appearance, as it falls prey to commodification.

In this film, style as communication functions in a way that largely transcends characters. Style needs to be understood as communication between the film and its audience. The unusual style of the characters is part of the overall design of the film, with design understood broadly as the integration of acting, makeup, costumes, sets, lighting, camera style, editing, and sound.[23] The failure of communication among characters, or among representatives of groups, doesn't preclude communication on another level, where Hebdige's concept of the social and aesthetic function of "spectacular" subcultures as indirect communication could translate with greater success into a similarly spectacular film style.

Androgyny as a Masquerade

> When you meet a human being, the first distinction you make is "male or female?" and you are accustomed to make the distinction with unhesitating certainty.

Freud uses this observation as the point of departure for his last major article on feminine psychology in 1932.[24] He wants to show that gender differences in humans cannot serve as an a priori explanation for psychological differences, and that, therefore, a description of feminine psychology has to be developed apart from social roles women have been accustomed to playing and prevailing attitudes about women based on convention. He is primarily concerned to modify, or clarify, his earlier explanations of "activity" and "passivity" when used in psychological description and explanation, particularly in the light of biological evidence which doesn't allow one to equate the male gender with activity and the female with passivity. Freud repeats his frequent warning against prejudging the causes of psychological characteristics: "But we must beware in this [study of feminine psychology] of underestimating the influence of social customs, which similarly force women into passive situations."[25] Freud's own analysis, however, is not free of such limiting stereotypes. Later in the same article he, too, is influenced by the conventions of his own society:

> The fact that women must be regarded as having little sense of justice is no doubt related to the predominance of envy in their mental life; for the demand for justice is a modification of envy and lays down the condition subject to which one can put envy aside. We also regard women as weaker in their social interests and as having less capacity for sublimating their instincts than men.[26]

My purpose is not to examine Freud's cultural bias regarding women, in spite of his goal to eliminate this kind of prejudice (among others) in the name of science. This subject has already received a great deal of attention.[27] But I am interested in the fact that Freud and his developing school were deeply, and necessarily, embedded in a classical period of conceptualizing sexual difference. This can be seen in the many references to commonly-held sex role expectations, whether the purpose is to argue against their "naturalness" or even sometimes to accept them without a great deal of reflection. This powerful stability of sex role expectations, whether contested or accepted, is fully operative in the classical Hollywood cinema.

A case study published by Joan Riviere a few years before Freud's article on "Femininity" reveals the same preoccupation with sex role stereotypes, and it has proven to be highly suggestive for the analysis of classical cinema. "Womanliness as a Masquerade" was written as a contribution to the debate on feminine psychology within the International Psychoanalytic Society.[28] Riviere's aim is to show that "women who wish for masculinity may put on a mask of womanliness to avert anxiety and the retribution feared from men."[29] Even though Riviere was conscious of cultural bias as a problem to be avoided in her research on feminine psychology, her description of masculine and feminine characteristics reads as normative from a contemporary vantage point. Consider the following statement:

> In University life, in scientific professions and in business, one constantly meets women who seem to fulfil every criterion of complete feminine development. They are excellent wives and mothers, capable housewives; they maintain social life and assist culture; they have no lack of feminine interests, e.g. in their personal appearance, and when called upon they can still find time to play the part of devoted and disinterested mother-substitutes among a wide circle of relatives and friends. At the same time they fulfil the duties of their profession at least as well as the average man. It is really a puzzle to know how to classify this type psychologically.[30]

Few people today would claim that "complete feminine development" entails being a capable housewife. Indeed it is doubtful whether one would want to endorse *any* of the characteristics she lists as necessary to "feminine development." Nonetheless, this description seems to me most interesting for the way in which socially conventional roles or opportunities for women are confused with "psychological types," because it is an indication of how strongly these characteristics must have been accepted as common knowledge. The article would make no sense during a time when sex roles were not clearly defined.

Riviere's more general thesis, that "normal" femininity can also function as a mask, has inspired a number of important articles on "femininity as a masquerade" in film.[31] It is appropriate that their subject is the image of women in the classical Hollywood cinema, because these films depend on sex role expectations as an obvious fact. This is all the more true for unconventional heroines such as the pirate queen in *Anne of the Indies* or Amy Jolly in *Morocco*.

Masquerade is a major preoccupation in *Liquid Sky*, but the difference in the kind of masquerade—androgyny as masquerade—is an indication that a radical change in sex role definitions has occurred in our society, and has been adapted in various ways in this particular film. This is one of the strongest, clearest signs of the film's movement away from the classical paradigm. The subcultural group, with Margaret as a prime example, rejects gender stereotyping altogether. This is explicitly discussed in the course of the film with respect to sexual preference as well as visual appearance. The rejection of sex roles and sexual definitions is one of the most coherent aspects of this subcultural group; gender is disguised by elaborate costumes, and sexuality is rechannelled in various non-standard ways, including the substitution of drugs for sexual activity.

The family is virtually non-existent in the film, but there are still vestiges of more or less traditional family relationships that have an important function. The subcultural group doesn't exist in a vacuum. It is a small part of a larger social context where traditional sex roles haven't disappeared, but have become unpredictable, a question of more or less, now and then. Figures like Jimmy's mother, who is a television producer, the heroin addict's professional girlfriend, Margaret's former acting professor, and the family Margaret remembers nostalgically indicate a larger social sphere that is still determining, although the meaning of sex roles and definitions has become destabilized. The subcultural group attempts not to acknowledge this world around them, but ends up defining itself in opposition to its standards and norms, even if it does so in an irregular manner. In *Liquid Sky*, the importance of costume, of masquerade, and of androgyny both as a look and as a move away from expected sexual norms is directly related to Hebdige's analysis of spectacular subcultures.

> They *display* their own codes (e.g., the punk's ripped Tshirt) or at least demonstrate that codes are there to be used and abused (e.g., they have been thought about rather than thrown together). In this they go against the grain of a mainstream culture whose principal defining characteristic, according to Barthes, is a tendency to masquerade as nature . . . .[32]

Margaret is an important character not only because she embodies spectacle, but because she represents contradictions within her society, as the film interprets them, and she is unique in this respect. In Margaret, we can see the conflict between a traditional past, seen in the conventionally pretty and obliging photographs she has saved of her childhood and early college days, and the attempt to replace her privileged background with an alternative, anti-social fashion identity in New York City. This conflict cannot be resolved, as it is presented in the film. Instead of resolution, there is regression.

Margaret's alternate identities have all been marked by dependency. At the end of the film she is alone (the people she has depended on are dead, and the fashion group has disappeared), and she has negated her identity as an image of androgynous fashion. In response, she turns back to the images of her past in a regressive, self-destructive sense. Margaret puts on a traditional white wedding dress left behind in the wake of the photography session. She wipes off all her makeup, and runs to her balcony to beg her unknown helper to take her. In an improbable turn of events, the German scientist rushes in and conveys all the basic facts about the aliens before Margaret stabs him to death as an intruder. She sees the spacecraft rising in the air, and, in desperation, injects heroin so that the alien will take her. In a strobe sequence, she dances spasmodically in her bridal gown, presumably inducing orgasm at last. She disappears. This is a nihilistic and almost unbearably Romantic conclusion, a dance of death and apotheosis.

Margaret, as a character, is controlled by a larger system of surveillance of which she is largely unaware. An alien eye is trained on her apartment during the entire sequence of events, and the German scientist watches her apartment from a telescope. Surveillance is a way of exercising power through looking that operates in one direction only; there is no exchange or implicit agreement as in the dynamics of voyeurism and exhibitionism. It doesn't allow for reciprocity, and in this sense, it is like rape—it takes. Rape, which occurs with alarming frequency in *Liquid Sky*, functions almost as a rhetorical figure to illustrate the depersonalized assertion of power. It is not photographed or edited to appear erotic: it represents the kind of uninvited, mechanical appropriation that characterizes surveillance. While sex, often violent sex, takes place within view of the surveillance systems, it is the abstract result of sex that is the object of both the aliens and the scientist. (The aliens want the chemical by-product; the scientist wants the aliens.)

The photographer's camera also operates as an instrument of surveillance during the fashion shoot, but it affects the main characters more directly. The camera is represented as a predator; it feeds on the accelerated mood of hostility and destructive narcissism between the androgynous models, rather than anything explicitly sexual. This depersonalized attitude is clear from the cut-away shots to the technical crew and fashion entourage. The models are both willing participants and passive victims of the cooptation, or commercialization, of their negativity.

Our own look is distanced from the characters; it seems to share the impersonal and de-eroticized power, the objective interest, so to speak, of the surveillance system. Yet it is outside the surveillance system, observing its mode of operation. Identification is transferred to the "spectacular" look of the film, to its showy surface, which is so well organized that it occupies our attention almost aimlessly, superceding the improbabilities of the plot, and masking the unremitting negativity and entrapment of the subcultural group. At the end of the film, the androgynous image is not only depersonalized but eliminated. And although the Romanticism Hebdige associates with Genet is present,[33] the subversive edge to the idea of style as revolt seems entirely absent. At least style doesn't function as communication among characters. The conflicts presented by Margaret's uneasy choice between images from her past and her present are not able to be resolved. However, the contradictions present in Margaret's character are absorbed by, and reflected in, the total design of the film, which negotiates a form of indirect communication with its audience. Not that this dense surface is reducible to a meaning that could give us a sense of power over it: the design elements of *Liquid Sky*, and *Blade Runner*, and films of this type, are powerful because they destabilize classical narrative expectations at the same time as they demonstrate how classical sex role expectations in our society have become unreliable. *Liquid Sky* represents changing social conventions embedded within a more conservative framework that is *itself* unstable. Integration occurs on the level of design, and, paradoxically, in an absorbing distraction of visual/aural style that demonstrates different levels of conflict indirectly to its audience.

I would like to thank Yuri Neyman, cinematographer for *Liquid Sky*, for generously providing photographs. Earlier versions of this paper were presented at the conference on "Italian and American Directions: Women's Film Theory and Practice," at New York University (December 1984), and at the Symposium on Film Theory, Yale University (March 1985). I would like to thank many participants for their comments; I have attempted to clarify a number of points in response to them.

NOTES

1. Sternberg's sardonic account of his design extravaganzas and Dietrich's ambiguous role within them can be found in his autobiography. For example, on *The Devil is a Woman*: "With the dice loaded so that I could not win, I paid a final tribute to the lady I had seen lean against the wings of a Berlin stage, at the same time planning an affectionate salute to Spain and its traditions. As if I were a computing machine, I built scene after

scene to form an exact pattern, allowing nothing but the future audience to escape my attention, and adding to my normal duties the task of handling the camera mechanism." *Fun in a Chinese Laundry* (New York: Collier Books, 1973), pp.166-167.

2. The "1984" ad was planned to be shown only once, during the Superbowl on January 22, 1984. Not only was the commercial advertised in advance in *The New York Times*, but Chiat/Day, the agency that produced it, took out a full-page ad in *The Wall Street Journal* on May 1 to proclaim its success.

> ABC, CBS, NBC and CNN featured the commercial in network news segments. Dan Rather covered it at night. Bryant Gumbel covered it at dawn. The BBC ran it in England. Associated Press put it on the wire. 27 TV stations in major US markets ran it on local news programs. Steven Spielberg called. As did *The New York Times, The Wall Street Journal, The Washington Post,* [etc.] Not to mention *Time, Newsweek, Fortune, Forbes, Business Week* and, of course, *Advertising Age*.

> Apple is now producing one Macintosh every 27 seconds. And selling one every 20 seconds. Not bad for one 60-second spot on the Super Bowl.   —Chiat/Day

Controversy over the W.R.Grace & Co. commercial, "The Deficit Trials: 2017 A.D.," can be seen in *Broadcasting* (August 11, 1986), p.60; the *Los Angeles Times* (August 21,1986), p.16; and The *Hollywood Reporter* (August 21, 1986), p.1. The networks originally refused to air it because it contained a reference to a bill then before Congress to limit federal spending.

3. Annette Michelson's important article on *2001* takes this film to be a paradigm of cinematic modernism. "Viewing becomes, as always but as never before, the discovery, through the acknowledgement of disorientation, of what it is to see, to learn, to know, and of what it is to be, seeing . . . .As a film which takes for its very subject, theme and dynamics—both narrative and formal—movement itself, it has a radical, triple interest and urgency, a privileged status in the art that is ours, modern." "Bodies in Space: Film as 'Carnal Knowledge'," *Artforum*, 7 (February 1969), p.58.

4. On first viewing: during subsequent screenings, a classically strong referential logic relating space, time, and characters emerges with greater clarity and subtlety. This no doubt contributes to the "repeater" phenomenon for *Blade Runner*.

5. This is perhaps even more obvious in *Alien*, where the monster, in all its transformations, advances through a series of biomorphic shapes in the midst of the mechanical, metallic ship, likewise cluttered (as in *Blade Runner*) with obstacles to vision and movement. See Harvey Greenberg's article in this issue on the "Alien's" transformations. The Swiss artist, H.R. Giger, designed the monster in *Alien*; his drawings were an important in-

fluence on the visual style of the film. (He received an Oscar for "Best Achievement for Visual Effects" for *Alien*.) See *H.R. Giger's Necronomicon 2* (Zurich: Edition C, 1985), which includes four sketches for *Alien*. Drawings and photographs from other series in this collection have similar composite designs that blend mechanical and human parts, often resembling internal or sexual organs in both erotic and dehumanizing ways. I would like to thank Michael Friend for showing me Giger's work.

6. For a description of this conceptual shift, where the product is not center-stage and clearly labelled, see "U.S. Creative Upsurge?" in *Ads* (December 1984), which discusses the Calvin Klein ad campaigns and "1984," among others; and "The Advertising Game Tilts Toward the West" in *Newsweek* (March 4, 1985), which describes metallic, "sexy" robots selling canned goods, "Levi-Strauss's MTV-style '501 Blues' spots," and the billboards for Nike running shoes "that often feature gigantic blowups of star amateur athletes, the company's logo and nothing more."

7. Examples of changing into the opposite: Ash in *Alien*; Rachel's ambiguous status in *Blade Runner*, and the many references to Deckard's identification with the replicants; the David Bowie character in *The Man Who Fell to Earth*, convincingly human *and* alien; in *Mad Max* and *The Road Warrior*, Max devolves into near-machine status (a survival for revenge machine).

8. An example of a designer film without any interest in redefining or destabilizing sexual norms is *Brazil* (1986).

9. Sigmund Freud, "The 'Uncanny'" in *On Creativity and the Unconscious* (New York: Harper and Row, 1958); Roland Barthes, S/Z, trans. Richard Howard (New York: Hill and Wang, 1974).

10. In *Image, Music, Text*, trans. Stephen Heath (New York: Hill and Wang, 1977).

11. "A Kinky New Calvinism," *Newsweek* (March 11, 1985), p.65. "An underwear ad appearing this month in *Vogue* and other fashion magazines pictures two men and a woman (wearing only Klein's briefest briefs) sleeping together on a towel-laden bed. There is no caption, no explanation. The reader is left wondering: is this an innocent nap or a sexually spent *ménage à trois*?

    "It doesn't matter," explains Klein. "I'm not out to offend anyone, but the ads are meant to be ambiguous—to make people stop and think. I don't want women flipping through 600 pages of *Vogue* and not even noticing my ads."

12. *Looker* was directed by Michael Crichton, and stars Albert Finney and Susan Dey. It had a brief release period, and is interesting here for its illustrative value; cult status isn't being claimed for the film.

13. Dr. Roberts, after all, has surgically corrected the models with the aid of computer analysis; the electronic simulations seem like logical extensions of his craft. The music we hear while Cindy's body is being copied in the

lab is the same Vivaldi theme he had used earlier when he was performing cosmetic surgery. This puts him in an ambivalent position with respect to "saving" Cindy, her autonomy, and the film's conventionally romantic happy ending. See Elizabeth Cowie's commentary on similar themes in an earlier film directed by Michael Crichton, a doctor himself, in "The Popular Film as a Progressive Text—A Discussion of *Coma*," published in two parts in *m/f* (London), no.3 (1979) and no.4 (1980).

14. In *Subculture: The Meaning of Style* (New York: Methuen, 1979), p.107.

15. Richard Avedon was a photography consultant on the film.

16. *Liquid Sky* was an independent production made in New York, largely by a group of Russian émigrés: Slava Tsukerman produced and directed; Nina Kerova, his wife, was associate producer; Yuri Neyman was director of photography; Marina Levikova, his wife, was production and costume designer; the screenplay was written by Slava Tsukerman, Anne Carlisle (the American actress who plays the dual role of Margaret and Jimmy), and Nina Kerova.

17. Hebdige, pp.17-18.

18. *Mythologies*, trans. Annette Lavers (New York: Hill and Wang, 1972); see Hebdige, pp.8-19.

19. Hebdige, pp.106-107.

20. Hebdige, following a Gramscian model of hegemony, sees the coherence and interaction among subcultural groups as a form of communication that challenges the uniformity of dominant social structures. See pp.15-19.

21. Hebdige, p.2.

22. Hebdige, pp.61-62.

23. For a description of the way the visual style was planned to integrate all design elements in the film, including characters, see "Photography for *Liquid Sky*" by Linda Trefz, *American Cinematographer* (February 1984). The article is largely drawn from an interview with the cinematographer, Yuri Neyman.

24. Sigmund Freud, "Femininity" in *New Introductory Lectures on Psychoanalysis*, edited and translated by James Strachey (Norton, 1965 [1933]), p.113.

25. *New Introductory Lectures*, p.116.

26. *New Introductory Lectures*, p.134.

27. For example, see the last chapter of Juliet Mitchell's *Psychoanalysis and Feminism* (New York: Pantheon, 1974).

28. Joan Riviere, "Womanliness as a Masquerade," *The International Journal of Psycho-Analysis* 10 (1929), pp.303-313. Riviere refers specifically to an earlier article by Ernest Jones, as well as Karen Horney, Freud, and others.

29. Riviere, p.303.

30. Riviere, pp.303-304.

31. The first important use of Riviere's concept of the masquerade for film analysis was in "*Morocco*: A Collective Text" by the editors of the *Cahiers du Cinéma* in no. 225 (Nov.-Dec. 1970). An English translation appeared in *Sternberg*, edited by Peter Baxter (London: British Film Institute, 1980). Claire Johnston introduced Riviere's concept to an English-language audience with her influential essay "Femininity and the Masquerade: *Anne of the Indies*," in *Jacques Tourneur* (Edinburgh Film Festival, 1975). Mary Ann Doane extended the idea of the masquerade to include the imaginary activity of the female spectator in "Film and the Masquerade: Theorising the Female Spectator," *Screen* (Sept.-Oct. 1982).

32. Hebdige, pp.101-102.

33. At the end of his study, Hebdige refers again to Genet's importance as an emblematic figure. He then observes: "The emphasis has thus been placed on deformity, transformation and Refusal. As a result, this book no doubt succumbs to a kind of romanticism"(p.138).

The Terminator (James Cameron, 1984)

Time Travel, Primal Scene, and the Critical Dystopia
Constance Penley

If the sure sign of postmodern success is the ability to inspire spin-offs, *The Terminator* was a prodigy. The film was quickly replicated by *Exterminator*, *Re-animator*, *Eliminators*, *The Annihilators*, and the hardcore *The Sperminator*, all sound-alikes if not look-alikes. It then went on to garner one of popular culture's highest accolades when a West Coast band named itself *Terminators of Endearment*. And just to show that postmodernity knows no boundaries, national or otherwise, an oppressively large (2 ft. × 3 ft.) and trendy new Canadian journal has appeared, calling itself *The Manipulator*.

For some science fiction critics, Fredric Jameson among them, *The Terminator*'s popular appeal would represent no more than American science fiction's continuing affinity for the dystopian rather than the utopian, with fantasies of cyclical regression or totalitarian empires of the future. Our love affair with apocalypse and Armageddon, according to Jameson, results from the atrophy of utopian imagination, in other words, our cultural incapacity to imagine the future.[1] Or, as Stanislaw Lem puts it, in describing the banality and constriction of most American science fiction, "The task of the SF author today is as easy as that of the pornographer, and in the same way."[2] But surely there are dystopias and dystopias, and not all such films (from *Rollerball* to *The Terminator*) deserve to be dismissed as trashy infatuations with an equally trashy future. While it is true that most recent dystopian films are content to revel in the sheer awfulness of The Day After (the Mad Max trilogy and *A Boy and His Dog* come readily to mind), there are others which try to point to present tendencies that seem likely to result in corporate totalitarianism, apocalypse, or both. Although *The Terminator* gives us one of the most horrifying postapocalyptic visions of any recent film, it falls into the latter group because it locates the origins of future catastrophe in decisions about technology, warfare and social behavior that are being made today. For example, the new, powerful defense computer that in *The Terminator* is hooked into everything—missiles, the defense industry, weapons design—and trusted to make all the decisions, is clearly a fictionalized version of the burgeoning Star Wars industry. This computer of the near future, forty years hence, gets smart—a new order of intelligence. It "began to see all people as a threat," Reese tells Sarah as he tries to fill her in on the future, "not just the ones on the other side. It decided our fate in a microsecond. Extermination."

A film like *The Terminator* could be called a "critical dystopia" inasmuch as it tends to suggest causes rather than merely reveal symptoms. But before saying more about how this film works as a critical dystopia, two qualifications need to be made. First, like most recent science fiction from *V* to *Star Wars*, *The Terminator* limits itself to solutions that are either individualist or bound to a romanticized notion of guerilla-like small-group resistance. The true atrophy of the utopian imagination is this: we *can* imagine the future but we *cannot* conceive the kind of collective political strategies necessary to change or ensure that future. Second, the film's politics, so to speak, cannot be simply equated with those of the "author," James Cameron, the director of *The Terminator*, whose next job, after all, was writing *Rambo* (his disclaimers about Stallone's interference aside, he agreed to the project in the first place). Instead *The Terminator* can best be seen in relation to a set of cultural and psychical conflicts, anxieties and fantasies that are all at work in this film in a particularly insistent way.

Tech Noir

What are the elements, then, of *The Terminator*'s critical dystopian vision? Although the film is thought of as an exceptionally forward-thrusting action picture, it shares with other recent science fiction films, like *Blade Runner*, an emphasis on atmosphere or "milieu," but not, however, at the price of any flattening of narrative space. (In this respect it is closest to *Alien*.) *The Terminator* is studded with everyday-life detail, all organized by an idea of "tech noir." Machines provide the texture and substance of this film: cars, trucks, motorcycles, radios, TVs, time clocks, phones, answering machines, beepers, hair dryers, Sony Walkmen, automated factory equipment. The defense network computer of the future which decided our fate in a microsecond had its humble origins here, in the rather more innocuous technology of the film's present. Today's machines are not, however, shown to be agents of destruction because they are themselves evil, but because they can break down, or because they can be used (often innocently) in ways they were not intended to be used. Stalked by a killer, Sarah Conner cannot get through to the police because the nearest phone is out of order. When she finally reaches the LAPD emergency line, on a phone in the Tech Noir nightclub, it is predictably to hear, "All our lines are busy . . . please hold . . . ." Neither can she get through to her roommate, Ginger, to warn her because Ginger and her boyfriend have put on the answering machine while they make love. But Ginger wouldn't have been able to hear the phone, in any case, because she'd worn her Walkman to bed. Tech turns noir again when the Terminator, not Ginger, takes the answering machine message that gives away Sarah's location. Later Sarah will again reveal her whereabouts when the Terminator perfectly mimics her mother's voice over the phone. And in one of the film's most pointed gestures toward the unintentionally harmful effects of technology, the police psychiatrist fails to see the Terminator entering the station when his beeper goes off and distracts him just as their paths cross. Lacking any warning, scores of policemen are killed and the station destroyed. The film seems to suggest that if technology can go wrong or be abused, it will be. To illustrate this maxim further, Kyle Reese is shown having a nightmare of his future world where laser-armed, hunter-killer machines track down the few remaining humans; he wakes to hear a radio ad promoting laser-disk stereos. It comes as no surprise, finally, to see that his futuristic concentration camp number is the ubiquitous bar code stamped on today's consumer items.

That tech turns noir because of human decision-making and not something inherent in technology itself is presented even more forcefully in the "novelization" of *The Terminator* by Randall Frakes and Bill Wisher.[3] The novelization adds a twist, perhaps one that originally appeared in the script but was discarded because it would have generated a complicated and digressive subplot. Or perhaps the authors of the book made it up on their own, unable to resist pointing out, once again, that it is humans, not machines, that will bring on the apocalypse. Near the end of the book, after the Terminator has been destroyed, a man named Jack, a Steve Wozniak-like computer prodigy, discovers a microchip in the debris. His entrepreneur friend, Greg, decides that they will go into business for themselves, once they figure out how to exploit what they take to be a new kind of microprocessing unit. Sixteen months later, they incorporate under the name Cyberdyne Systems . . . the company that goes on to make the same defense network computer that will try to destroy humanity in Reese's day. Here the case is being made not so much against the tunnel vision of corporate greed, but against the supposedly more benign coupling of golly-gosh tech-nerd enthusiasm with all-American entrepreneurship.

The film, moreover, does not advance an "us against them" argument, man versus machine, a Romantic opposition between the organic and the mechanical, for there is much that is hybrid about its constructed elements. The Terminator, after all, is part machine, part human—a cyborg. (Its chrome skeleton with its hydraulic muscles and tendons of flexible cable looks like the Nautilus machines Schwarzenegger uses to build his body.) And Kyle's skills as a guerilla fighter are dependent upon his tech abilities—hot-wiring cars, renovating weapons, making bombs. If Kyle has himself become a fighting machine in order to attack the oppressor machines, Sarah too becomes increasingly machine-like as she acquires the skills she needs to survive both the Terminator and the apocalypse to come. The concluding irony is that Kyle and Sarah use machines to distract and then destroy the Terminator when he corners them in a robot-automated factory. At the end of one of the most harrowing, and gruelingly paced, chase scenes on film, Sarah terminates the Terminator between two plates of a hydraulic press. This interpenetration of human and machine is seen most vividly, however, when Sarah is wounded in the thigh by a piece of exploding Terminator shrapnel. Leaving aside the rich history of sexual connotations of wounding in the thigh,[4] part of a machine is here literally incorporated into Sarah's body ("a kind of cold rape," the novelization calls it). While the film addresses an ultimate battle between humans and machines, it nonetheless accepts the impossibility of clearly distinguishing between them. It focusses on the partial and ambiguous merging of the two, a more complex response, and one typical of the critical dystopia, than the Romantic triumph of the organic over the mechanical, or the nihilistic recognition that we have all become automata (even if those automata are better than we are, more human than human, as in *Blade Runner*).[5]

Time Travel

The Terminator, however, is as much about time as it is about machines. Because cinema itself has the properties of a time machine, it lends itself easily to time travel stories, one of the staples of science fiction literature. Surprisingly, however, there have been relatively few attempts in film to create stories around the idea of time travel. Hollywood, to be sure, has always been more drawn to conquering space and fighting off alien invaders than thinking through the heady paradoxes of voyaging through time. The exceptions have been very successful, however, and so it is curious that the industry has not made more effort to produce such stories. George Pal's *The Time Machine* (1960) was so exquisite (it brought the MGM look to science fiction film) that one even forgave the film's suppression of H.G. Wells's kooky class analysis of the Eloi and the Morlocks, which was, after all, the conceptual center of the original tale. And the runaway success of the banal and clumsily made *Back to the Future* should have convinced Hollywood that there is something commercially attractive about the idea of time travel. Indeed, *The Terminator*'s appeal is due in large part to the way it is able to put to work this classical science fiction theme.

Compared to the complexity of many literary science fiction time travel plots, *The Terminator*'s story is simple: in 2010 a killer cyborg is sent back to the present day with the mission of exterminating Sarah Conner, a part-time waitress and student, the future mother of John Conner, the man who will lead the last remnants of humanity to victory over the machines which are trying to rid the world of humans. John Conner chooses Kyle Reese, a young and hardened fighter, to travel back in time to save Sarah from the Terminator. If the Terminator succeeds in his mission, John Conner, of course, will never be born, and the humans will never be able to fight back successfully against the machines. Kyle has fallen in love with Sarah through her photograph, given to him by John Conner. He says he always wondered what she was thinking about when the photo was taken for she has a faraway look on her face and a sad smile. "I came across time for you," he professes. "I love you. I always have." They make love, he is killed soon after, Sarah destroys the Terminator and leaves for the mountains to give birth to her son and wait out the holocaust to come. The film ends South of the Border with a Mexican boy taking a Polaroid of Sarah as she is thinking of Kyle. It is the photograph that John Conner will give to Kyle, forty years later, knowing that he is sending his own father to his death.

This sort of story is called a time-loop paradox because cause and effect are not only reversed but put into a circle: the later events are caused by the earlier events, and the earlier by the later.[6] If John Conner had not sent Kyle Reese back in time to be his father, he would never have been born. But he was born, so Kyle Reese must *already* have traveled back to the past to impregnate Sarah Conner. As another instance of paradox, John Conner's fighting skills were taught him by his mother. Sarah Conner, however, learned those skills from Kyle Reese, who had himself learned them while fighting at John Conner's side. (The novelization adds another time-loop paradox in locating the origin of the defense network computer in the microchip found in the Terminator debris.) Small wonder then that Sarah looks slightly bewildered when Kyle says he has "always loved" her. How could this be true when, from the perspective of her point in time, he hasn't been born yet?

What is the appeal of time loop paradox stories? They are so fascinating that many people who used to read science fiction but have long since given it up will usually remember one story in particular, Ray Bradbury's "A Sound of Thunder," even if they can no longer recall the author or the title (others have also noted this phenomenon). In this famous story, big-game hunters from the future travel back to the age of the dinosaurs. They don't have to fear that their shooting and bagging will affect the future, however, because dinosaurs will soon be extinct anyway. They are strictly warned, though, not to step off the walkway that has been prepared for them over the primeval jungle. One hunter disobeys and in doing so crushes a tiny butterfly under his boot. When the hunting party returns to the future, everything is ever so slightly different, the result of killing one small insect millions of years earlier.

Primal Scene

The essential elements of time travel and its consequences are witnessed in a very succinct way in "A Sound of Thunder." That is why the story is remembered. But when plots of this kind become more complex, one theme tends to predominate: what would it be like to go back in time and give birth to oneself? Or, what would it be like to be one's own mother and father? Robert Heinlein has given us the seminal treatment of this paradoxical situation in "All You Zombies." A time traveler who has undergone a sex-change operation not only encounters both earlier and later versions of himself but turns out to be his own mother and father. Similarly, in David Gerrold's *The Man Who Folded Himself*, each time the protagonist travels in time, he reduplicates himself. Eventually this results in a large group of identical men who find each other to be ideal lovers. One of them goes very far back in time and meets a lesbian version of himself. They fall in love, have children, and then break up, to return to their copy-lovers. (As the narrator says in "All You Zombies," "It's a shock to have it proved to you that you can't resist seducing yourself.") The appeal of *Back to the Future* should now be apparent—it is only a more vulgar version of the desire manifested in these stories. There is of course a name for this desire; it is called a primal scene fantasy, the name Freud gave to the fantasy of overhearing or observing parental intercourse, of being on the scene, so to speak, of one's own conception. The desire represented in the time travel story, of both witnessing one's own conception and being one's own mother and father, is similar to the primal scene fantasy, in which one can be both observer or one of the participants. (The possibility of getting pregnant and giving birth to oneself is echoed in *Back to the Future*'s TV ad: "The first kid to get into trouble before he was ever born.") The reconstruction of a patient's primal scene assumes, in fact, a great deal of time travel. (Freud said the most extreme primal scene fantasy was that of observing parental intercourse while one is still an unborn baby in the womb.)[7] The Wolf-Man, supine on the analytic couch, is sent further and further back in time to "remember" the moment when, as a child, he saw his parents having sex. Although Freud's interpretation depends upon the Wolf-Man witnessing such a scene, he decides, finally, that it was not necessary for the event to have *actually occurred* for it to have had profound effects on the patient's psychical life. A patient can consciously fabricate such a scene only because it has been operative in his or her unconscious, and this construction has nothing to do with its actual occurrence or nonoccurrence. The idea of returning to the past to generate an event that has already made an impact on one's identity, lies at the core of the time-loop paradox story.

What is *The Terminator*'s primal scene? The last words that Kyle Reese throws at the Terminator, along with a pipe bomb, are "Come on, motherfucker!" But in the narrative logic of this film it is Kyle who is the mother fucker. And within the structure of fantasy that shapes the film, John Conner is the child who orchestrates his own primal scene, one inflected by a family romance, moreover, because he is able to choose his own father, singling out Kyle from the other soldiers. That such a fantasy is an attempted end-run around Oedipus is also obvious: John Conner can identify with his father, can even *be* his father in the scene of parental intercourse, and also conveniently dispose of him in order to go off with (in) his mother.

Recent film theory has taken up Freud's description of fantasy to give a more complete account of how identification works in film.[8] An important emphasis has been placed on the subject's ability to assume, successively, all the available positions in the fantasmatic scenario. Extending this idea to film has shown that spectatorial identification is more complex than has hitherto been understood because it shifts constantly in the course of the film's narrative, while crossing the lines of biological sex; in other words, unconscious identification with the characters or the scenario is not necessarily dependent upon gender. Another element of Freud's description of fantasy that also deserves attention, particularly in discussing fantasy in relation to popular film, is the self-serving or wish-fulfilling aspect of fantasy. In "The Paths to the Formation of Symptoms," Freud constructs two analogies between the creation of fantasy and instances drawn from "real life." He begins by saying that a child uses fantasies to disguise the history of his childhood, "just as every nation disguises its forgotten prehistory by constructing legends" (p.368). A fantasy is thus not "just a fantasy" but a story *for* the subject. The fantasy of seduction, for example, serves to deny the subject's acts of auto-eroticism by projecting them onto another person. (Such fantasy constructions, Freud says, should be seen separately from those real acts of adult seduction of children that occur more frequently than is acknowledged.) Similarly, in the "family romance" the subject creates another parent, an ideal one, to make up for the perceived shortcomings of the real mother or father. Thus a film like *The Terminator* that is so clearly working in relation to a primal fantasy, is also working in the service of pleasure (already a requirement for a mass audience film), a pleasure that depends upon suppressing conflicts or contradictions. (Because such suppression does not always work, and because desire does not always aim for pleasure— the death drive—much recent film analysis is devoted to examining those aspects of film that go distinctly "beyond the pleasure principle."[9])

Take, for example, the seemingly contradictory figure of Kyle Reese. The film "cheats" with his image in the same way that *The Searchers* "cheats" with Martin Pauley's image, which is, variously, wholly Indian, "half-breed," "quarter-blood" Cherokee, one-eighth Cherokee, or wholly white, depending upon the unconscious and ideological demands of the narrative at any given moment.[10] In *The Terminator* Kyle is the virile, hardened fighter barking orders to the terrified Sarah, but alternately he is presented as boyish, vulnerable, and considerably younger in appearance than her. His childishness is underscored by Sarah's increasingly maternal affection for him (bandaging his wounds, touching his scars), and in the love scene, he is the young man being initiated by the more experienced, older woman. Kyle is thus both the father of John Conner and, in his youth and inexperience, Sarah's son, John Conner. The work of fantasy allows the fact of incest to be both stated and dissimulated. It is only in fantasy, finally, that we can have our cake and eat it too. Or as the French equivalent puts it, even more aptly, that we can be and have been—*peut être et avoir été.*

Freud also compared the mental realm of fantasy to a "reservation" or "nature reserve," a place set aside where "the requirements of agriculture, communication and industry threaten to bring about changes in the original face of the earth which will quickly make it unrecognizable" (almost a description of a post-apocalyptic landscape). "Everything, including what is useless and even what is noxious, can grow and proliferate there as it pleases. The mental realm of fantasy is just such a reservation withdrawn from the reality principle" (p.372). Can a film like *The Terminator* be similarly dismissed as merely escapist, appealing as it does to a realm of fantasy "withdrawn from the reality principle," where even our incestuous desires can be realized? For one possible answer we can turn to the end of Freud's essay on symptom formation, where he tells us that there is "a path that leads back from fantasy to reality—the path, that is, of art." An artist, he says, has the ability to shape a faithful image of his fantasy, and then to depersonalize and generalize it so that it is made accessible to other people. Even if we do not have as much faith in "art" or the "artist" as Freud has, we can still draw some useful conclusions from what he says.

One could argue that *The Terminator* treads the path from fantasy back to reality precisely because it is able to generalize its vision, to offer something more than this fully, though paradoxically, resolved primal fantasy. This *generalizing* of the fantasy is carried out through *The Terminator*'s use of the topical and everyday: as we have seen, the film's texture is woven from the technological litter of modern life. But this use of the topical is not, for example, like *E. T.*'s more superficial referencing of daily life through brand name kid-speak, that is, topicality for topicality's sake. Rather, it is a dialogue with Americana that bespeaks the inevitable consequences of our current technological addictions. To give another example, the shopping mall in George Romero's *Dawn of the Dead* is more than a kitsch ambience, it is a way of concretely demonstrating the zombification of consumer culture. By exposing every corner of the mall—stores, escalators, public walkways, basement, roof—the location becomes saturated with meaning, in a way that goes far beyond *E. T.*'s token gesturing toward the commodification of modern life. If *The Terminator*'s primal scene fantasy draws the spectator into the film's paradoxical circle of cause and effect and its equally paradoxical realization of incestuous desire, its militant everydayness throws the spectator back out again, back to the technological future.

Science Fiction and Sexual Difference

In the realm of the unconscious and fantasy, the question of the subject's origin, "Where do I come from?" is followed by the question of sexual difference, "Who am I (What sex am I)?" It is by now well-known that the narrative logic of classical film is powered by the desire to establish, by the end of the film, the nature of masculinity, the nature of femininity, and the way in which those two can be complementary rather than antagonistic.[11] But in film and television, as elsewhere, it is becoming increasingly difficult to *tell the difference*. As men and women are less and less differentiated by a division of labor, what, in fact, makes them different? And how can classical film still construct the difference so crucial to its formula for narrative closure? Ironically, it is science fiction film—our hoariest and seemingly most sexless genre—that alone remains capable of supplying the configurations of sexual difference required by the classical cinema. If there is increasingly less practical difference between men and women, there is more than enough difference between a human and an alien (*The Man Who Fell to Earth*, *Starman*), a human and a cyborg/replicant (*Android*, *Blade Runner*), or a human from the present and one from the future (*The Terminator*). In these films the question of sexual difference—a question whose answer is no longer "self-evident"—is displaced onto the more remarkable difference between the human and the other. That this questioning of the difference between human and other is sexual in nature, can also be seen in the way these films reactivate infantile sexual investigation. One of the big questions for the viewer of *Blade Runner*, for example, is "How do replicants *do it*?" Or, of *The Man Who Fell to Earth*, "What is the sex of this alien who possesses nothing that resembles human genitals (its sex organs are in its hands)?"

But if recent science fiction film provides the heightened sense of difference necessary to the classical narrative, it also offers the reassurance of difference *itself*. In describing one important aspect of the shift in the psychical economy from the nineteenth century to the twentieth century, Raymond Bellour maintains that in the nineteenth century men looked at women and feared they were different, but in the twentieth century men look at women and fear they are the same.[12] The majority of science fiction films work to dissipate that fear of the same, to ensure that there is a difference. A very instructive example is the NBC miniseries *V*, broadcast during the 1983-84 season. A rare instance of science fiction on television (*Star Trek* to the contrary, the television industry insists that science fiction does not work on television), *V* tried to be as topical and up-to-date as possible, particularly in the roles it gave to women. The Commander of the alien force that takes over Earth's major cities, the Supreme commander of the aliens, the leader of the Earthling guerrillas, and the leader of the alien fifth column aiding the Earthlings, are all played by women. They are seen performing the same activities as the men (planning, fighting, counterattacking, infiltrating, etc.), thus removing the most important visible signs of difference. The only difference remaining in *V* is that between the aliens (scaly, green reptiles in human disguise) and the humans. That difference, however, comes to represent sexual difference, as if the alien/human difference were a projection of what can no longer be depicted otherwise.[13] The leader of the guerrillas is captured and brainwashed by the alien commander. Although she is eventually rescued by her comrades, it is feared that the brainwashing has turned her into an alien. She even begins using her left hand rather than her right one, a reptile-alien characteristic. Thus when she and her boyfriend, the second in command of the guerillas, are shown making love, we realize, as they do, that this could be interspecies sex—the blond, all-American Julie may be a lizard underneath it all, whether in fact or in mind. It gives the otherwise banal proceedings a powerful source of dramatic tension, while it reassures TV-viewing audiences everywhere that there is a difference. (Such a radical disposition of difference always risks, of course, tipping over into the horror of *too much* difference.)

Similarly, it is instructive to see how *Aliens*, directed by James Cameron following his success with *The Terminator*, cracks under the strain of trying to keep to the very original *lack* of sexual differentiation in its precursor, Ridley Scott's *Alien* (not counting, of course, the penultimate scene of Ripley in her bikini underwear). Dan O'Bannon's treatment for the first film was unique in writing each role to be played by either a man or a woman.[14] Ridley Scott's direction followed through on this idea, producing a film that is (for the most part) stunningly egalitarian. In attempting to repeat the equal-opportunity camaraderie of the first film, Cameron's sequel includes a mixed squad of marines, in which the women are shown to be as tough as the men, maybe tougher. And Ripley is, again, the bravest and smartest member of the team. But this time there is a difference, one that is both improbable and symptomatic. Ripley "develops" a maternal instinct, risking her life to save the little girl who is the only survivor of a group of space colonists decimated by the aliens. Tenaciously protective, she takes on the mother alien, whose sublime capacity for destruction is shown nonetheless to result from the same kind of maternal love that Ripley exhibits. Ripley is thus marked by a difference that is automatically taken to be a sign of femininity. (We do not see Hicks, for example—played by Michael Biehn, who was Kyle Reese in *The Terminator*—acting irrationally in order to rescue a child who is probably already dead.) *Aliens* reintroduces the issue of sexual difference, but not in order to offer a newer, more modern configuration of that difference. Rather, by focussing on Ripley alone (Hicks is awkwardly "disappeared" from the film in the closing moments), the question of the couple is supplanted by the problem of the woman as mother. What we get finally is a conservative moral lesson about maternity, futuristic or otherwise: mothers will be mothers, and they will *always* be women. We can conclude that even when there is not much sex in science fiction, there is nonetheless a great deal about sexuality, here reduced to phallic motherhood: Ripley in the robot-expediter is simply the Terminator turned inside out.

Just as it is ironic that science fiction film can give us the sharper notion of sexual difference lost from contemporary classical film, so too it is ironic that when this genre does depict sexual activity, it offers some of the most effective instances of eroticism in recent film. The dearth of eroticism in current filmmaking is pointed up by Woody Allen's success in providing the paradigm of the only kind of sexual difference we have left: the incompatibility of the man's neuroses with the woman's neuroses. Understandably, this is not very erotic. But science fiction film, in giving us an extreme version of sexual difference, coincides with the requirements of the erotic formula, one which describes a fantasy of absolute difference and absolute complementarity (the quality of being complementary, of course, depending upon the establishment of difference). Unlike in classical cinema, the science fiction couple is often not the product of a long process of narrative differentiation; rather, the man and the woman are different *from the very beginning*. The narrative can then focus on *them together* and the *exterior* obstacles they must overcome to remain a couple. The erotic formula has, in fact, two parts: first, the two members of the couple must be marked as clearly different. (In non-science fiction film, for example, she is a nun, he is a priest; she is white, he is black, she is a middle-class widow, he is a young working-class man; she is French, he is German/Japanese, etc.) Second, one of the two must die or at least be threatened by death. If the man and the woman, in their absolute difference, are absolutely complementary, then there is nothing left to be desired. Something has to be taken away to regenerate desire and the narrative. Thus, although the lovemaking scene in *The Terminator* is not a very distinguished one in terms of the relatively perfunctory way that it was filmed, it nonetheless packs a strong erotic charge, *in its narrative context* because it is a kiss across time, a kiss between a man from the future and a woman from the present, an act of love pervaded by death. For Kyle has to die in order to justify the coda, in which Sarah ensures the continuity of the story, now a legend, of their love for each other.

Time Travel as Primal Scene: *La Jetée*

If time travel stories are fantasies of origins, they are also fantasies of endings. Mark Rose has pointed out that many of the narratives that deal with time travel tend to be fictions of apocalypse.[15] (As in *The Terminator*, however, these visions of endings may also be visions of new beginnings—in the Genesis version, after God destroys the world by flood, it is Sarah who is anointed "mother of all nations.") Rose cites Frank Kermode's *The Sense of an Ending* to show that we create fictions of endings to give meaning to time, to transform *chronos*—

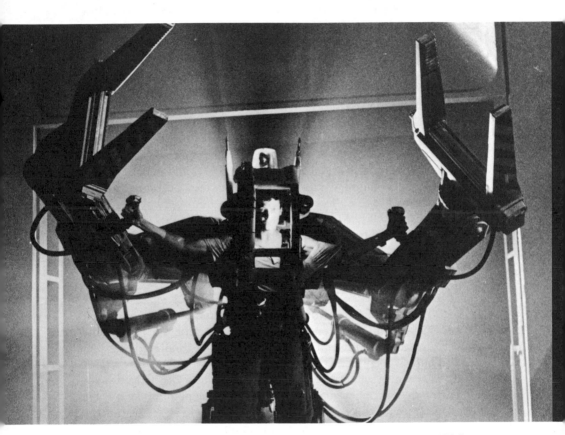

Aliens (James Cameron, 1986)

mere passing time—into *kairos*, time invested with the meaning derived from its goal. History is given shape, is made understandable by spatializing time, by seeing it as a line along which one can travel. Such spatialization of time, however, introduces the paradox of time travel. "Much of the fascination of the time loop is related to the fact that it represents the point at which the spatialization of time breaks down" (Rose, p.108). If I could travel back into the past, I could (theoretically) murder my own grandmother. But I would cease to exist. How then could I have murdered her?

If this example illustrates the collapse of time as we know it, it also shows that it is impossible to separate ourselves from time. (The time traveler who murders her grandmother ceases to exist.) Thus time travel paradox narratives typically explore either the question of the end of time or the reciprocal relation between ourselves and time (Rose, p.108). Although *The Terminator* is concerned with both apocalypse and the question of time in relation to personal identity, another film which preceded it by more than 20 years, Chris Marker's *La Jetée*, weaves the two together in a way that still haunts the spectator of this stunning film. *The Terminator*, in fact, bears such an uncanny resemblance to *La Jetée* that Cameron's film could almost be its mass-culture remake. Marker's film too is about a post-apocalyptic man who is chosen to be a time traveller because of his fixation on an image of the past. It too involves a love affair between a woman from the present and a man from the future, and an attempt to keep humanity from being wiped out.

A crucial difference between *The Terminator* and *La Jetée*, however, is that Marker's film explicitly addresses the paradox of time travel. After being sent on numerous journeys through time, *La Jetée*'s time traveller attempts to return to the scene from his childhood that had marked him so deeply. On that day, a Sunday afternoon before a third World War which will drive the few remaining survivors underground, his parents had brought him to Orly to watch the planes take off. He remembers seeing the sun fixed in the sky, a scene at the end of the jetty, and a woman's face. Then, a sudden noise, the woman's gesture, a crumbling body, the cries of the crowd. Later, the voice-over tells us, he knew that he had seen a man die. When he tries to return to that Sunday at Orly, he is killed by one of the scientists from the underground camp who had sent him voyaging through time; they no longer have any use for him. The moment, then, that he had been privileged to see as a child and which had never stopped haunting him, was the moment of his own death. In the logic of this film he has to die, because such a logic acknowledges the temporal impossibility of being in the same place as both adult and child. In *La Jetée* one cannot be and have been.

The film goes even further when it insists on the similar paradox at work in the primal scene fantasy by depicting the psychical consequence of attempting to return to a scene from one's childhood: such a compulsion to repeat, and the regression that it implies, leads to the annihilation of the subject.[16] But the subject is also extinguished in another way, this time through a symbolic castration depicted as a very real death. The woman he is searching for is at the end of the jetty, but so is the man whose job it is to prevent him from possessing her, the man and the woman on the jetty mirroring the parental (Oedipal) couple that brought the little boy to the airport. (This film's version of the Terminator succeeds in its mission.) While *The Terminator* gives us a time travel story that depends upon a primal scene fantasy for its unconscious appeal, its fantasmatic force, *La Jetée* shows that the two are one and the same: the fantasy of time travel is no more nor less than the compulsion to repeat that manifests itself in the primal scene fantasy. Moreover, since *La Jetée*'s circular narrative is wholly organized as a "beginning toward which [one] is constantly moving,"[17] it suggests that all film viewing is infantile sexual investigation.

The *Terminator*, in many respects, merely abstracts and reifies *La Jetée*'s major elements. Marker's film, for example, is composed almost entirely of still images, photographs that dissolve in and out of one another in a way that constantly edges toward the illusion of "real" filmic movement. As Thierry Kuntzel has pointed out,[18] such a technique allows *La Jetée* to be a film about movement in film, and our desire for movement. Using still images to make a film is also a perfect way to tell a time travel story because it offers the possibility of mixing two different temporalities: the "pastness" of the photographic image and the "here-nowness" of the illusionistic (filmic) movement.[19]

Although I suggested that *The Terminator* could be seen as the industry remake of *La Jetée*, it should now be clear that Marker's film could not be remade because in its very structure it is *unrepeatable*. Inasmuch as it acknowledges the paradox of the time loop and rejects the rosy nostalgia of a wish-fulfilling version of the primal scene fantasy, it is not likely remake material with respect to popular film's demand for pleasure without (obvious) paradox. Similarly, one could not imagine a *sequel* to *La Jetée* because of the way the film collapses time in its rigorous observance of the fatalistic logic of time travel. But one can be sure that *Terminators* is already more than a gleam in a producer's eye. After all, what is to stop John Conner, in another possible future, from sending Kyle Reese back in time again, but at a later date, perhaps so that he could rendezvous with Sarah in her South of the Border hide-out?

Would it not be too easy, however, to conclude by pitting *La Jetée* against *The Terminator*? To end by falling back on less-than-useful dichotomies like the avant-garde versus Hollywood or even the Symbolic versus the Imaginary? It is true that *La Jetée* is governed by "the laws of recollection and symbolic recognition" (in Lacan's terms) while *The Terminator* is ruled by "the laws of imaginary reminiscence."[20] But it is precisely the way *The Terminator* harnesses the power of "imaginary reminiscence" (the primal scene fantasy of time travel) that allows it to present one of the most forceful of recent science fiction tales about the origins of techno-apocalypse. The film is able to do so, as I have argued, by generalizing its core of fantasy through the systematic use of the topical and everyday, reminding us that the future is now. As a critical dystopia, *The Terminator* thus goes beyond the flashy nihilism of apocalypse-for-the-sake-of-apocalypse to expose a more *mundane* logic of technological modernity, even if it is one that is, finally, no less catastrophic.

NOTES

1. Fredric Jameson, "Progress Versus Utopia; or Can We Imagine the Future?" *Science Fiction Studies* 9 (1982).

2. Stanislaw Lem, "Cosmology and Science Fiction," trans. Franz Rottenstein, *Science Fiction Studies* 4 (1977), p.109.

3. Randall Frakes and Bill Wisher, *The Terminator* (a novel based on the screenplay by James Cameron with Gale Anne Hurd) (New York: Bantam Books, 1984).

4. See Jessie L. Weston, *From Ritual to Romance: An Account of the Holy Grail from Ancient Ritual to Christian Symbol* (Cambridge: Cambridge University Press, 1920), pp.42-48.

5. For a full and very interesting discussion of the political dimensions of the cyborg, see Donna Haraway, "A Manifesto for Cyborgs: Science, Technology, and Socialist Feminism in the 1980s," *Socialist Review*, no. 80 (March-April, 1985).

6. Useful essays on time travel and its paradoxes include Stanislaw Lem, "The Time-Travel Story and Related Matters of SF Structuring," *Science Fiction Studies* 1, 1974; Monte Cook, "Tips for Time Travel," *Philosophers Look at Science Fiction* (Chicago: Nelson-Hall, 1982); and David Lewis, "The Paradoxes of Time Travel," *Thought Probes*, eds. Fred D. Miller, Jr. and Nicholas D. Smith (New Jersey: Prentice Hall, 1981).

7. Sigmund Freud, "The Paths to the Formation of Symptoms," *The Standard Edition of the Complete Psychological Works of Sigmund Freud*, ed. and trans. James Strachey (London: Hogarth Press, 1958), vol. 16, p.370.

8. See, among others, Elisabeth Lyon, "The Cinema of Lol V. Stein," *Camera Obscura* no. 6 (1980); Elizabeth Cowie, "Fantasia," *m/f* no. 9 (1984); and Steve Neale, "Sexual Difference in Cinema," *Sexual Difference*, special issue of *The Oxford Literary Review* 8, nos. 1-2 (1986).

9. For the best formulation of this idea, see Joan Copjec, "*India Song/Son nom de Venise dans Calcutta désert*: The Compulsion to Repeat," *October* 17 (Summer 1981).

10. Brian Henderson, "The Searchers: An American Dilemma," *Film Quarterly* 34, no. 2 (Winter 1980-1981); reprinted in *Movies and Methods* Vol. II, ed. Bill Nichols (Berkeley: University of California Press, 1985).

11. There are, of course, important exceptions to this standard narrative logic, as Jacqueline Rose has shown, for example, in her analysis of *The Birds*, in which Mitch's "successful" attainment of a masculine and paternal identity comes at the price of regression and catatonia for Melanie. "Paranoia and the Film System," *Screen* 17, no. 4 (Winter 1976-1977).

12. Raymond Bellour, "Un jour, la castration," *L'Arc*, special issue on Alexandre Dumas, no. 71 (1978).

13. This wholly unremarkable series seems surprisingly capable of taking on a great deal of cultural resonance in its radical presentation of "difference." Andrew Kopkind (*The Nation* 243, no. 17, Nov. 22, 1986) reports that *V* is currently one of the most popular shows in South Africa. He speculates that the show's success lies in the unconsciously ironic, allegorical reading that it allows. Kopkind cites the newspaper description of the week's episode (broadcast on the state-controlled television channel):
    TV 4: 9:03. "Visitor's Choice." The Resistance Stages a daring attack at a convention of Visitor Commanders where Diana intends to show off the ultimate device in processing humans for food.
Robit Hairman in *The Voice* (Jan. 13, 1987) also reports on the cult that has grown up around *V* in South Africa because of the allegorical readings that escaped the government censors. Before the series was over, anti-government forces were spraying slogans from the series on walls in Johannesburg and Soweto, and T-shirts with a large V painted on front and back became a feature on the streets: "*V* joined the mythology of the resistance."
    There are also at least two fanzines devoted to *V*, the newest of which, *The Resistance Chronicles*, describes its first issue in terms that evoke infantile sexual investigation:
    This volume will contain the answers to the following burning questions—Why is that blue Chevy with the fogged-up windows rocking back and forth??? How does Chris Farber feel about virtue . . . and boobs? What color underwear does Ham Tyler wear? What do Ham

and Chris keep in their medicine cabinet? Plus a musical *V* parody, 'We're off to See the Lizard . . . '."
Description taken from *Datazine*, no. 44 (Oct.-Nov. 1986).

14. Danny Peary reports this in his interview with Sigourney Weaver, "Playing Ripley in *Alien*," *OMNI's Screen Flights/Screen Fantasies: The Future According to Science Fiction Cinema*, ed. Danny Peary (Garden City, N.Y.: Doubleday, 1984), p.162.

15. Mark Rose, *Alien Encounters: Anatomy of Science Fiction* (Cambridge, Mass.: Harvard University Press, 1981), p.99.

16. My discussion of primal scene fantasy in *La Jetée* is indebted to Thierry Kuntzel's lectures on that topic in his 1975-1976 seminar at the American University Center for Film Studies in Paris.

17. Ned Lukacher's formulation of the primal scene fantasy in *Primal Scenes: Literature, Philosophy, Psychoanalysis* (Ithaca: Cornell University Press, 1986), p.42. This book contains the best recent discussion of the structure of the primal scene fantasy.

18. In his lectures on *La Jetée* at the American University Center for Film Studies.

19. The distinction is made by Roland Barthes in "Rhetoric of the Image," trans. Stephen Heath (New York: Hill and Wang, 1977), p.45.

20. Jacques Lacan, *Ecrits: A Selection* (New York: Norton, 1977), p.141. A distinction cited by Lukacher, p.43.

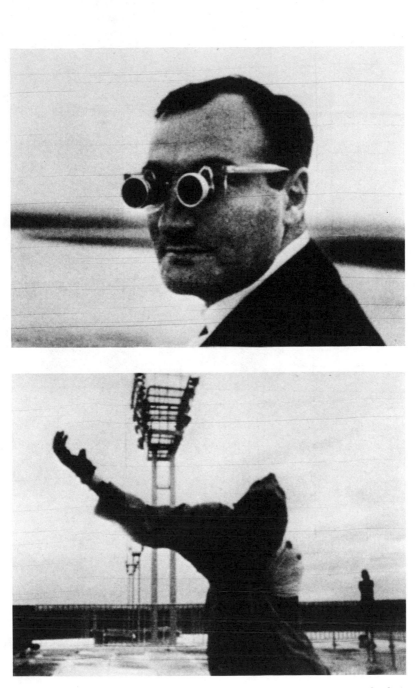

La Jetée

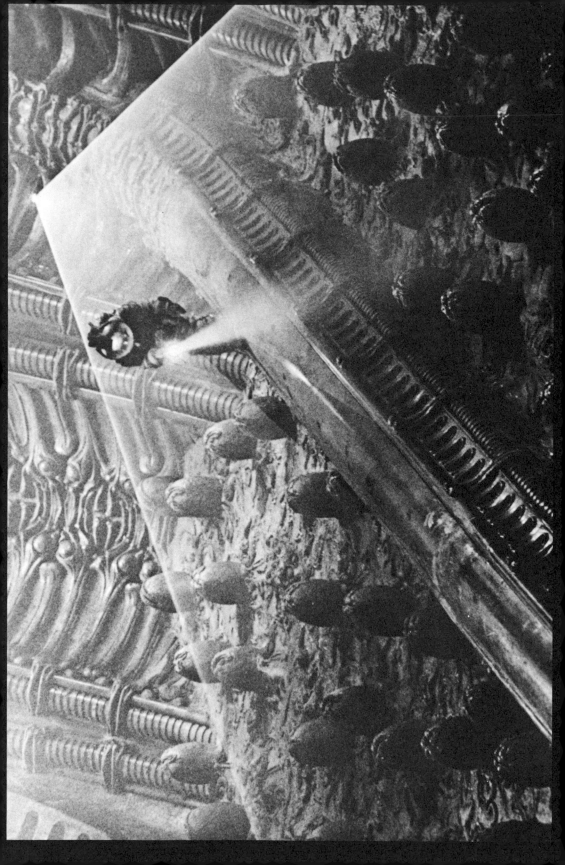

Reimagining the Gargoyle: Psychoanalytic Notes on *Alien*
Harvey R. Greenberg, M.D.

> *I admire its purity. . . . a survivor, unclouded by*
> *conscience, remorse or delusions of morality. . . .*
> Ash, Science Officer, the Nostromo

If *Hair* proclaimed the Age of Aquarius, *Close Encounters of the Third Kind* surely celebrated its last gasp. According to Steven Spielberg's vision, our troubles would be resolved by Aquarian consciousness-raising sessions conducted by relentlessly benevolent extraterrestrials. But then a *stretto* of disasters put paid to the aspirations of Woodstock Nation. Three Mile Island, the plunging dollar, the spectacle of the American imperium held hostage by shabby ideologues—these and sundry other narcissistic injuries refurbished our pessimism, setting us to brood upon apocalypse.

With the situation so grim below, how could we remain sanguine about the good intentions of celestial messengers? Through that obscure feedback process by which the cinematic dream factory translates inchoate collective angst into extravagant scenarios, we have been served up an outerspace ghoulie to match the proper paranoia of the day—*Alien!*

Despite its contemporary iconography, *Alien* hearkens back to the malignant conception of unearthly life found in fifties science fiction, during another watershed of national self-doubt and paranoia. In the setting of spreading global communism, fading postwar prosperity, and the renewed threat of nuclear holocaust, Hollywood disgorged an army of implacable invaders feasting upon flesh and blood, like the brainy carrotman of *The Thing*; or cannibalizing consciousness, like the emotionally sanforized Pod People of *Invasion of the Body Snatchers*.

Alien contains numerous citations from these fifties classics, allusions to *Forbidden Planet* and similar arcana that excite cultists, but hardly make for big box office. Nor does *Alien*'s populist political stance and debatable feminism explain its staggering popularity. "In space, no one can hear you scream," the promo poster tantalizes. It shows a cracked egg, backlit harshly. Dared to discover the source of this soundless

Alien (Ridley Scott, 1979)

scream, we go to the theater, gag on bloody recognitions, then—according to demographics—return again for more. The "repeater" phenomenon of past "weird" films has become even more significant with recent horror hits like *The Exorcist* and *Alien*. How to explain it?

In an earlier essay I suggested that part of the weird genre's vast appeal resides in its flamboyant catharsis of our *timor mortis*.

> By participating in the macabre pageant of weird cinema . . . we tilt at the myriad deaths conjured up from childhood conflict and injury. We shriek and grin and mock at alien yet familiar deaths, delighting for a few moments in a dubious victory over our infantile distortions and the grim truth of mortality . . . .[1]

This bizarre cure grows worse than the disease it addresses when

> horror beyond psychological tolerance cancels enjoyment, nullifies catharsis. The film becomes a nightmare from which it is impossible to awaken after leaving the safety of the theater, an unmastered trauma that continues to plague the mind . . . .[2]

With few exceptions, the creators of vintage fantasy refused to violate our child-like faith that the weird movie might scare us but never really harm us, saving the rare catastrophic reaction of the exceptionally vulnerable viewer. This fragile trust was irrevocably abrogated by Alfred Hitchcock's 1960 benchmark masterpiece, *Psycho*. The English Hammer Studio productions flooded the screen with stylized gore in the fifties, but *Psycho* truly legitimized the showing of violence to large general audiences. With extraordinary craft, Hitchcock welded the excesses of the Grand Guignol to a panoply of disturbing, perverse psychological motifs—rape, voyeurism, necrophilia—which had previously been explored more distantly and tactfully. Never had viewers been so cunningly seduced by a mere "thriller" into attending scenes of eroticized butchery.

Paradoxically, this species of trauma encouraged repeated exposure; not out of masochism, but the very human wish for *mastery*, to prove to the vulnerable self that one can face mortal danger and survive. Many viewers rushed to *Psycho* on a dare, as they would later rush to *Alien*, and got far more than they bargained for. They told their friends, everyone came back in droves. Concentration camp survivors, in a desperate attempt to master the unmasterable, often dream themselves back into torment. Analogously, *Psycho*, more than any previous horror film, compelled us against our better judgement to seek out hell at the Bijou . . . .

"Cruel" Horror Cinema

Psycho's financial and artistic success spurred the escalation of violence throughout cinema, especially within the weird genre. It became the prototype for a sub-genre I will categorize as "cruel" or "hardcore" horror, comprising pictures that skirt the edge of the impermissable visually and psychologically, or plunge over the edge.

Shot on low budgets, employing unknown actors and waning Hollywood luminaries, many cruel films piled up fortunes on the drive-in exploitation circuit. The best—or most notorious—of these frightful cheapies are *The Texas Chainsaw Massacre, Night of the Living Dead, The Hills Have Eyes, Last House on the Left*; more recently *Halloween, Friday the 13th, Nightmare on Elm Street* (and sequels). Huge profits from exploitation screenings eventually restored cruel cinema to the legitimacy *Psycho* had acquired. Expensive, high production value shockers like *The Exorcist, The Omen,* and *Carrie* generated megabucks through massive distribution to family audiences. Although the number of cruel films produced has declined today, the sub-genre still does well at the box office, and exceptionally well in home video rentals.

It is a monument to *Psycho*'s enduring power that its elegant or execrable spinoffs continue to reflect its cynical appraisal of the human condition and its cooly harmful attitude towards the audience. In cruel cinema, any possibility for a healing catharsis is deliberately sacrificed in favor of overwhelming the viewer's capacity to endure psychic pain. The attack may be crafted with exquisite visual manipulations, and little if any actual on-screen violence—viz., John Carpenter's work in *The Fog*. It may be unremittingly raw, as in the nonstop carnage of George Romero's films. Or it may modulate between a raw and cool approach, as in the cinema of DePalma.

The *Weltanschauung* which informs *Psycho* and its cruel successors is paranoid/Hobbesian. Hitchcock predicates exploitation as the central experience of relatedness. He elaborates an articulating chain of victims and victimizers which culminates in a monstrous exploitation within the family. Norman Bates, murderous motel manager and avian taxidermist, is a psychological zombie. The marrow of his ego has been sucked dry by his mother during her life; after her death, her malignant internalized image continues to rule him. *Mutatis mutandis,* Norman has slaughtered, gutted, and stuffed his mother after she threatened to abandon him for a new husband. To affirm their tainted symbiosis, he carries her mummy about the house as if she were an invalid, maintaining a creepy illusion of *her* need for him.

Since *Psycho*, the cruel movie has busily engendered similar monstrosities, born out of disturbed family relations (*Carrie, Rosemary's*

Baby, The Exorcist). Alternately, the entire family is presented as a deviant monster (*The Texas Chainsaw Massacre, The Hills Have Eyes*). For a lengthier discussion of this trend and its ramifications the reader is referred to Robin Wood's admirable essay, "The Return of the Repressed."[3]

Cruel cinema has also powerfully discoursed on the exploitative viciousness Hitchcock saw lurking within family life. Sometimes a family member will transform suddenly into a monster, turning savagely upon spouse, parent, siblings (*Night of the Living Dead, The Children*). Or, monstrous from birth, the child beast feeds upon strangers (*It's Alive!*). The monstrous family preys upon its own, or maintains its perverse solidarity by attacking outsiders (*The Hills Have Eyes*). Murder and rapine flourish, but the signatory crime of cruel cinema is cannibalism.

The taint of cannibalism is subliminal in *Psycho*. Hitchcock dwells predominantly on the devouring of psychic identity—a theme privileged in the weird genre. Norman and his mummified Mum dine upon each other's egos. Mrs. Bates's withered husk is emblematic of that foul feast; the ghastly image of her shrunken skull, her leathery lips pulled back into a charnel house grin, evoked a ravening orality. Vastly potent, it provoked less fastidious talents after Hitchcock to "embody" the devouring of the self's substance, in the loathsome consumptions of the cannibalistic family monster.

The celebration of cannibalism reaches its zenith with the most traumatizing movies ever made—George Romero's "Dead" trilogy, *Night of the Living Dead, The Texas Chainsaw Massacre*, and *The Hills Have Eyes*. In the Romero cycle, the newly dead rise again through some inexplicable agency to become ghouls. Amidst the wholesale slaughter, the cannibalistic corruption of family relationships is particularly harrowing. Mortally wounded loved ones succumb, then resurrect to tear their bereaved into pieces. *The Texas Chainsaw Massacre* and *The Hills Have Eyes* respectively present psychotic and mutant families which sustain themselves by eating intruders. Their bloodthirsty orgies leave nothing to the imagination. Norma Bates's mummified skull is repeatedly reincarnated: in the half-eaten skull which first reveals ghoulish attack in *Night of the Living Dead*; in the skull-cum-lamp of *The Texas Chainsaw Massacre*; in the severed head of the tourist father which the mutant patriarch of *The Hills Have Eyes* impales upon a stake.

Besides deriding the family "togetherness" valorized by the American heartland, these films also satirize the competitiveness central to the American dream. In *Dawn of the Dead*, Romero's zombies are drawn to a huge shopping mall. They totter about the aisles in a grotesque parody of conspicuous consumerism until living prey attracts them. In

The Texas Chainsaw Massacre and *The Hills Have Eyes*, the cannibalistic behavior of the deviant families is wittily counterpoised against the competitive striving of the "normals" who have wandered into their turf. Capitalism is pictured as a less egregious form of the deviant's cannibalism, a normative rapacity sanctioned by culture and family. Wood mordantly observes that the family of *The Texas Chainsaw Massacre* only carries to its logical conclusion "the basic (though unstated) tenet of capitalism that people have the right to live off other people . . . capitalism represents the ultimate in possessiveness, hence the logical end of human relations under capitalism . . . ."[4]

I will now undertake a reading of *Alien* as legitimate inheritor of *Psycho* and its cruel lineage regarding its stylistic conventions, its frontal attack upon viewer sensibility, and its re-invention of the above motifs in outer space—particularly its Hobbesian perception of degraded relationships within family and state. My interpretations are based upon what the film shows and says, plus information furnished by Ridley Scott, *Alien*'s director and guiding intelligence.[5]

Alien's *Mise en Scène*

The film opens with the letters A — L — I — E — N slowly etching themselves in a futuristic/runic script. Behind them the camera tracks across the galactic void. Cut to a long shot of a space vehicle, hovering over subtitles:

    COMMERCIAL TOWING VEHICLE: "THE NOSTROMO"
    CREW: SEVEN
    CARGO: REFINERY PROCESSING TWENTY MILLION TONS OF MINERAL
        ORE
    COURSE: RETURNING TO EARTH

After these slim facts about the Nostromo and its mission, the viewer is set squarely down *in medias res*. One then pieces out an exceptionally vivid impression of *Alien*'s time, unencumbered by those self-conscious explanations about "how we came to be here" that so often have marred the science fiction film.

The Nostromo's formidable technology constitutes a dull given for its people. The ship is a high-tech rustbucket, an old warhorse of the interstellar "Company's" merchant fleet, returning not from Ulyssean adventures, but prosaic commercial enterprise. Its crew is also unextraordinary. Like their well-worn surroundings, they are utterly and rather wonderfully *there*, a collection of competent loners one would find aboard a similar vessel in ancient Phoenicia or the East India Trade.

Most viewers come to *Alien* old cinema spacehands, too—not as inclined to gasp at outerspace vistas after a glut of *Star Wars* special effects. *Alien*'s creators have subsumed the audience's tacit acceptance of the previously marvelous, in order to manipulate the gleaming mechanics of "straight" science fiction towards darker ends.

The Nostromo complex consists of several refineries—half-spheroids topped by towers and spires—linked to a central tug module. In the first long-shot the entire structure looks like a warren of abandoned gothic cathedrals, suspended in midair. One's impression is distinctly *not* of the future, but of some indeterminate fantasy realm—Oz, or more pointedly, the terrible dark houses of vintage horror cinema: Dr. Frankenstein's mountain laboratory, Dracula's eyrie, even the Bates's Victorian mansion.

The next shot is a tight close-up of the Nostromo's massive ventral plane rumbling across frame. This detailed immensity has been a commonplace of genre iconography since *2001*, rendering tomorrow's apparatus awesome and tangible. But here, instead of being lit starkly (another commonplace), the ship's surface is sunken in shadow, vaguely threatening. The Nostromo's "terrible house" equivalencies, combined with the darkness of the ship's surface in the subsequent passing shot, at once kindle a feeling of disquieting ambiguity that pervades the flat "suchness" of space-age technology throughout the film. More than any previous work (including *Metropolis*), *Alien* evokes simultaneous resonances within the horror and science fiction canons in representing a future milieu.

This feat is accomplished by exceptional design which imbues futuristic hardware with haunting "horrific" connotations quite apart from function; viz., the hieratic helmets—they resemble *Aztec skulls*!—resting upon the dead computer terminals in the deserted control room at the film's beginning. Ridley Scott's vision of Nostromo's hardware also shifts facilely between the locutions of science fiction and the horror/suspense film. For example, the decks are first presented as a maze of unexceptional storerooms, conduits, grills, and greasy machinery. As tension mounts, Scott transforms them into a tenebrous labyrinth, filled with false leads and murderous cul-de-sacs, through which the crew members stalk or are stalked by the elusive monster.

I cite only one of the numerous paraphrases of classic horror cinema during these sequences: Brett, seeking Jones the cat, approaches the Nostromo's cavernous undercarriage storeroom. Through subjective camera work, the gates seem to advance *towards him*, charged with an ineluctable menace—just as the front doors of the Bates house in *Psycho* seem to move eerily towards Vera Miles as she goes to penetrate the mystery behind them.

The unsettling quality of the "ordinary" future environment foregrounds the unabashed weirdness of the wrecked derelict. Much of the

uncanniness in the derelict's exploration derives not from the outland-
ishness of the vessel, but from the nagging similarity of its structures
to human organs, particularly the organs of reproduction (reflecting
Alien's preoccupation with monstrous gestations).

The entire craft resembles a stupendous uterine-fallopian system. The
crew members enter the ship through one of three unmistakably vagi-
nal hatches. The main deck is shaped like an enormous spine/rib cage.
Kane, lowered into the bowels of the derelict, discovers the Alien hatch
laid out in the pelvis of a mighty vertebral column. The fossilized "space
jockey's" giant skeleton rests upon a control chair, from which juts a
huge penile shaft. The chair itself resembles an operating table; here,
eons ago, some unfortunate pilot from another race died of the same
catastrophic Caesarean which later terminates Kane.

Science fiction frequently offers an "acceptable" rationale for frightening psychotic or archaic mental phenomena. Clinical corollaries of
the derelict's megalithic anatomy are found in the changes in body image
experienced during a hallucinatory drug trip or an acute schizophrenic
episode. One recalls Victor Tausk's intriguing hypothesis that the paranoid schizophrenic projects the skewed sense of his own body into the
crazy design of the "influencing machine."

These distortions are thought to be extravagant elaborations of early
percepts of self and "other." The uncanny feelings aroused in the viewer
by the derelict's great innards may likewise be rooted in infantile oceanic
impressions of one's body and of the immense, ineffably mysterious
physicality of nurturing adults. In this regard, the investigation of the
derelict has been interpreted as a symbolic return to the maternal womb
and beyond, an oneiric quest for truth about the origins of being.[6]

The Anatomy of a Monster

No matter how evocative the milieu, the monster film ultimately stands
or falls on the believability of its inhuman protagonist. Many promising films have foundered when the monster stood ludicrously revealed.
Neither talent nor cash was spared by *Alien*'s production team in manu-
facturing a credible being.[7] Superbly executed and artfully deployed,
the Alien is one of the most frightening monsters ever brought to the
screen. The qualities owned separately by the best of the breed have
been gathered together under one hide: the creature is *mysteriously un-
graspable, viciously implacable, improbably beautiful,* and *lewd.*

A. Ungraspability

Weird literary masterpieces like the stories of M.R. James triumph
through discretion, and an elegant paucity of illustration. In the hor-

ror film the naked face of Thanatos is best sparingly revealed as well, lest the indescribable be described or the unnamable named. Like the dim memory of repressed trauma, what frightens us most is likely to be half-glimpsed, seized, and rehearsed in each viewer's intuition of the terrible. In this regard, Ridley Scott made an astute decision, over the objections of others in his production team. He shows his exquisitely designed monster briefly and ambiguously.

The explosion of a seething tongue of flesh out of the Alien egg lasts the blur of an instant. The only version of the creature that registers in detail is the "face hugger"; besides the egg form, it's the most quiescent of the Alien's stages, befitting its relatively passive function as Kane's nurturer. The "chest burster" form is still for a few seconds before it careens out of the mess.

The adult Alien is photographed so obliquely that a coherent gestalt can never be constructed. When it drops upon Brett it seems like a huge phallic tube; during Lambert's slaughter, one only sees a sinuous tail curling around her leg. Fully ninety percent of the Alien footage consists of close-ups of its head and jaws, from which one bears away a hobgoblin vision of metalloid skullbrow, cruelly curling lips, needle-teeth dripping luminescent saliva—*Alien*'s reprise of Norma Bates's skull. The entire creature appears for the first and last time in the shuttlecraft, but the viewer's sight is obscured by flashing strobes within the ship, and by the dazzling engine exhaust outside. Scott thus compels the viewer to piece together an impression of the monster based on tantalizing fragments, fleshed out by the potent nuances of subjective fantasy, surely the scariest beast of all (shades of Orwell's Room 101 in *1984*!).

The Alien's enigmatic appearance is further compounded by its *mutability*. King Kong's genes dictate no other form but hairy apehood, nor is Frankenstein's monster likely to burst his stitches and assume other shapes. But like the Old Man of the Sea, awful transformations are native to the Alien's life cycle, central to its survival. The awareness of its quick-change potential keeps the viewer in a state of even greater unease, anticipating what chimerical composition the creature will choose in its next reincarnation.

In keeping with this ambiguity of shape, Ridley Scott deliberately provides the sketchiest information about the Alien's developmental phases. It is a Linnean nightmare, defying every natural law of evolution; by turns bivalve, crustacean, reptilian, and humanoid. It seems capable of lying dormant within its egg indefinitely. It sheds its skin like a snake, its carapace like an arthropod. It deposits its young within other species like a wasp.

Intermediate or alternate stages are hinted at, but never clarified. Scott deleted a sequence in which Ripley discovers Brett and Dallas in co-coons. Dallas is still alive, in agony and recognizably human. Brett is dead; the shrunken husk of his body contains the larval Alien and has further progressed in dreadful metamorphosis towards the egg form. From this scene, one could easily discover that the eggs in the derelict's hatch were the implanted, mutated bodies of *its* crew, awaiting yet another unwary host. But Scott obviously thought the satisfaction of closure would be better sacrificed in order to keep the Alien an awesome enigma.

One further intuits that the Alien's mutability is not solely dictated by a fixed if remarkably various life cycle, but by formidable mechanisms that allow it to mutate literally second by second, in conformation with the changing stresses of its milieu. It responds according to Lamarckian *and* Darwinian principles. When it attacks Ripley, it looks much smaller and more humanoid than before. Several observers, Ridley Scott included, have rather horribly suggested that its next manifestation would be fully human—at least on the outside!

B.   Implacability

Movie monsters frequently provoke fear and pity because they embody the persecuted outsider, excluded from quotidian joys and sorrows. In Karloff's poignant portrayal, Frankenstein's creation became a misunderstood, battered child who identified with its oppressors. It only gave back in kind the ill-treatment afforded by its laboratory "parents" and society at large. Even Dracula drew a measure of compassion from Lugosi's performance because of the eternal torment of his immortality.

The Alien stems from a different line of monsters, creations that provoke terror untempered by sympathy by virtue of the inhumanity of their form, their divorce from human concerns, or the catastrophic nature of their onslaughts. Examples of "unsympathetic" monsters with inhuman shapes include the giant insects, birds, and crustaceans of the post-atomic era (*Them, The Giant Claw, Attack of the Crab Monsters*); assorted globs of undifferentiated protoplasmic goo like *The Blob* or *Caltiki, the Immortal Monster*; vile extraterrestrial phantasmagoria like the demonic Martian grasshoppers of *Five Million Years to Earth.*

The unsympathetic creature's lack of empathy may originate in its lack of wit wedded to an enormous appetite. On the other hand, its brainpower may be so vastly superior (viz., the invaders of *War of the Worlds*), that humankind appears to it as mere fodder, or so much underbrush to be cleared away. Its attack is devastating, merciless. The victim is expunged, erased, body disintegrated, dismembered, or consumed; or else the marrow of psychic identity is sucked dry, leaving an envelope of dumb flesh for colonization.

The Alien being is patently inhuman in its earlier versions, and the adult form is never sufficiently humanoid to promote easy identification. Its IQ is problematic; it cannot be easily dismissed as a digestive machine propelled by a peabrain—*Jaws* in space. It demonstrates exceptional cunning while hunting the crew in its instant grasp of the Nostromo's layout, and its decision to secrete itself aboard the shuttlecraft. It is not inconceivable that it can read the crew's thoughts (the possibility that they might communicate with it is never entertained).

The ruthlessness of the Alien's attack is typically unrelenting; its victims are sundered or totally annihilated. Kane is eviscerated by the nativity of the beast; Brett is hauled off by the adult Alien, leaving only a scream behind. Dallas vanishes in the airshaft as if into thin air, a dot on Lambert's tracking screen, there one moment, gone the next.

Cornered by the Alien, Parker is garrotted—by what is not made clear. Next, there is a quick shot of an uncertain gourd of flesh (head? belly?) pierced by a toothy ramrod. Then the Alien's tail snakes around Lambert's leg, and the camera cuts briefly to a close-up of her terrified face. When Ripley arrives, all the viewer is allowed to see is Parker, hunched against a bulkhead, intact but obviously dead, as Lambert's naked and bloody foot dangles out of focus in foreframe. By careful editing, Ridley Scott leaves the exact manner of the victims' passage nearly blank, once again compelling the viewer to conjure from fantasy the direst account of their deaths.

C. Beauty

Much of the Alien's fascination resides in its unexpected loveliness. The "face-hugger" and "chest-burster" stages are frankly repellant. But the adult Alien owns a sumptuous elegance. The robotic simulacrum of the heroine in *Metropolis*, and the Gillman of *Creature from the Black Lagoon* nearly approach this nacreous beauty. The creature's architecture is skeletal, fleshed out with a kind of flayed musculature reminiscent of Vesalius's anatomical engravings. The bony elements are supplemented by strange, streamlined mechanical structures, cartilaginous rods and pistons. The creature's skin is glistening black; a long, lustrous grey porpoise head is fitted behind a skull's facies; the outsize jaws are studded with rows of stainless steel teeth. Here is the charnel house aesthetic of the medieval Dance of Death; the hellish apparitions of Bosch; the figurations of Tibetan demonology.

D. Sensuality

A few inhabitants of Monster Alley are not without lubricious intentions —viz., Kong's moony courtship of Anne Darrow, or the Frankenstein monster's confused erotic designs upon its creator's fiancee. However, sensuality is not usually within the purview of the unsympathetic movie monster. With rare exceptions—the mutant amphibians of *Humanoids from the Deep*—the unsympathetic creature's depredations are too obliterating, its appearance or disposition insufficiently humanoid to project a believable sexuality.

The Alien manifests no erotic intention until its lust erupts during the final showdown with Ripley. Until then the crew members have shown little sexual interest either, compared with the clumsy yearnings weird cinema frequently depicts between heterosexual shipmates cloistered in deep space, mad scientists and their intended brides, intrepid military types and their scientific girlfriends. When Ripley steps out of her fatigues, she becomes intensely desirable and achingly vulnerable. The sight of her nearly nude body is highly arousing, in the context of the film's previous sexual neutrality, as well as the relaxation that follows the Nostromo's destruction and the creature's supposed death. Precisely at this moment, the Alien unfolds out of its hiding place.

Unlike the blinding speed of its earlier assaults, it moves slowly, languorously. It stretches its phallic head out, as if preening. Ripley, her horrified gaze fixed hypnotically upon it, retreats stealthily into the equipment locker. It extends a ramrod tongue, tipped with hinged teeth from which drips luminescent slime (KY jelly!), and hisses voluptuously. The very air is charged with the palpable threat of rape—and worse. There is no square-jawed hero to rescue this damsel in distress. Unlike Fay Wray and a legion of impotent screaming Mimis, Ripley saves herself. Her combat with her exhibitionistic assailant bears the patents of sexual engagement.

She slips into a spacesuit, crooning a *love ditty* to curb her panic: "You . . . are . . . my . . . lucky . . . star. . . ." Repeating "Lucky . . . lucky . . . lucky . . . ," she creeps out of the locker, and straps herself into the pilot's chair. Her breathing, amplified within her helmet, is heard in accelerating gasps and moans (a libidinous variation on the famous sequence in *2001*, where Dave Bowman's breathing is heard echoing in his own ears, as he goes to disconnect the murderous HAL).

The Alien rushes upon her, maddened by poisonous gases she has triggered. Her face is sweaty, her expression dazed, very nearly ecstatic. With an orgastic wail, she slams her hand down upon the control panel and blows away the hatch. The monster hurtles out, then grips the

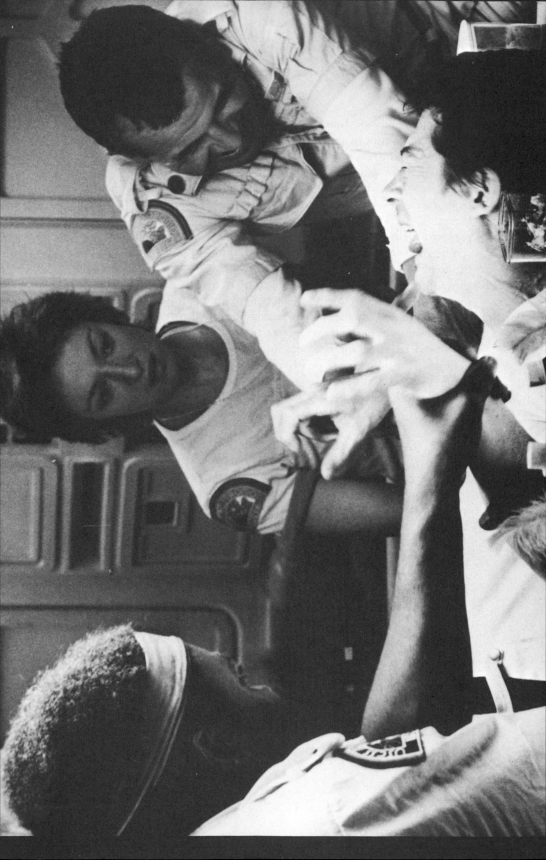

entryway. She discharges an ejaculatory bolt from the grapnel gun, which strikes the creature full in its chest, flinging it into space. Simultaneously suffering with her, and voyeur to her victimization, the viewer (especially the male viewer) experiences a powerful commingling of raw sexual excitement and mortal terror; an effect often sought but rarely achieved so well in suspense cinema.

Innards and Other Outrages

Like Hitchcock and DePalma, Ridley Scott incites terror in *Alien* through a clever blend of suggestion, indirection, and confrontation. The film contains almost as little actual on-screen mayhem as *Psycho*; horror is elicited rather by sophisticated manipulations of the medium.

Alien's considerable cruel reputation is based on two extraordinary gobbets of overt violence flung in the viewer's face: the birth of the Alien through Kane's shattered chest, and the Science Officer Ash's dismantling by Parker. The "chest-burster" sequence merits particular attention since it is probably the main reason many people have been dared into seeing the movie, or have returned to see it again.

Scott sets up the scene by lulling the viewer into a state of false calm. The anxiety which has been adroitly built abates with the creature's supposed death and Kane's reawakening. The viewer identifies with the crew's relief, is disarmed by their highjinks during the celebratory meal; then is plunged into even deeper disorganizing terror by Kane's awful fate. This "ratchet" effect—sharply lowering tension with a leaven of humor, then sharply escalating it so that it impacts more profoundly —is a staple of the genre, and never employed to better effect.

When Kane sickens, Parker and Ash wrestle him onto the mess table. His chest heaves, swells, a stain of blood spreads over his tunic, then the head of the infant Alien thrusts out viciously, spattering the appalled onlookers with gouts of gore and visceral shreds (Ridley Scott had his actors unexpectedly showered with entrails purchased from a nearby butcher shop to achieve their howls of shocked surprise!). The Alien looks like a dehisced organ or loop of gut, until it fully emerges as a murderous embryo. One is marginally aware of Kane's hands in the frame's periphery, clawed in agony. Parker lunges forward, a knife in his hand. Ash stops him. The creature emits a sizzling hiss and rockets away, a long reptilian tail whipping out behind it.

The most traumatizing aspect of the sequence is Kane's unexpected *disembowelment*. The overwhelming loathing and fear related to evisceration has rarely been addressed in the psychoanalytic literature. While the smooth exterior is readily conceptualized, a completely realistic or pleasing picture of the "insides" is not likely to be found in the average citizen's body image. A nauseous vision is usually summoned up of a smelly claustrum, stuffed with slippery ropes and lumps of flesh. One knows the vitals are vital to life, that food is processed, energy generated, the seeds of life itself planted within one's proper entrails, but it still seems necessary to the psychic economy to keep the guts safely contained, relegated to darkness.

Disembowelment abrogates this touchy sequestration irrevocably. The self's fragile envelope is definitively breached; once the abdomen is ripped open, how can Humpty Dumpty ever be put right again? After his tiny invader leaves him a gutted husk on the mess table, Kane's deadness is absolutely unassailable, a crushing narcissistic wound (like Janet Leigh's death in *Psycho*) to viewers who had imagined themselves omnipotently secure outside the screen.

The discovery that Ash is a robot doesn't make the spilling of his entrails less unpalatable. His evisceration, coupled with his bizarre resurrection, is even more traumatic. Ridley Scott gives the viewer a closer look at Ash's guts—unwholesome gizmos which spout greenish hydraulic goo. After Parker decapitates him with a fire extinguisher, Ash's head is rewired at a distance from his unpacked torso. His voice a dispassionate gurgle, a tiny smile plays across his lips as he expresses genteel sympathy for his shipmates' fate: "I can't lie to you about your chances, but you have my sympathy. . . ." The utter morbidity of the moment beggars description.

Kane serves as prime focus of *Alien*'s complex birth imagery. His intrusion into the hatch, his penetration of the blue force field, the touch of his hand that discharges the Alien out of its egg, are symbolic fertilizations. Kane is thereby uncannily implicated as subject *and* object in a horrific account of the primal scene. As if in talion retribution, the scene recoils upon *him*; his punishment for viewing and participating in the forbidden act of conception is a spectacular (*sic*) death precipitated by the Alien's birth.[8] I submit that each viewer's catastrophic response to Kane's disembowelment may well be determined by reactivation of personal archaic fantasies about the primal scene and the birth process, in addition to the dynamics elucidated above.

Finally, the "chest-burster" sequence epitomizes the leitmotif of *Alien*: within a dark claustrum filled with real, simulated, or symbolic vitals, a supremely potent menace lurks, waking to tear apart and devour its unsuspecting victims. For Kane, the menace literally lives within his guts. For the remaining crew, their ship becomes one great *cloaca* through which the beast prowls, Grendel-like, to pick them off at its pleasure. Their plight acquires an added claustrophobic piquancy by the immensity of galactic space surrounding them into which they can neither "shit out" the Alien, nor expel themselves! The menace concealed within Ash's bionic entrails is the proof he functions as the Company's creature. And the Company is the direst menace of all, a treacherous Leviathan that gnaws away at the vitals of *Alien*'s society.

Of Corporate Depredations and the Family Monster

The Nostromo's crew may be analyzed as a symbolic family. In this context, Dallas, the Father/Captain; appears initially passive, increasingly withdrawn, until he is completely eliminated mid-film. The real source of power within this family system is "Mother," the computer. "She" and the Company she prefigures are futuristic versions of the classic "bad" witch-mother of myth and fairytale.

The crew is symbiotically dependent upon "Mother," but her nurturing is at best ineffective, exemplified in the meager sustenance provided by her life support systems in hypersleep. When the crew awaken, her ministrations turn definitively noxious. With full knowledge beforehand, she reroutes them to certain doom on the asteroid. After Ripley exposes her complicity, the female Warrant Officer emerges as the nearest thing to a "good" mother on board. But Ripley can only rescue herself and Jones, the ship's cat, narrowly escaping "Mother's" last revenge, the Nostromo's detonation.

One is told almost nothing about *Alien*'s culture, but one may draw powerful inferences about it from studying the crew. For the most part, they are skilled technicians from a conforming middle or upper-middle class. They observe the outward tenets of contemporary American democracy. No one is a focus of obvious discrimination because of sex, class, or color (Parker is black). Everyone seems well-fed, well-educated, and reasonably well-off.

Differences exist in station, but an air of unauthoritarian informality is maintained, possibly consistent with the Nostromo's status as a merchant rather than a military vessel. Each individual's competence is tacitly respected. Ripley, one notes, perceives Ash's failure to provide more information about the Alien as a function of his untrustworthiness rather than ineffectiveness. The importance of teamwork is implicitly emphasized.

Yet, on closer scrutiny, the Nostromo's democracy smacks of the ant-hill. The crew address each other by last names only, work efficiently like anonymous cogs. Women are on an exactly equal footing with men to the point of androgyny; they wear no makeup, use the same serviceable clothing as their male counterparts—floppy surgical whites or fatigue uniforms. Although not unattractive, both sexes evince little if any sexual interest.

Except for a few convivial moments, the crew's interactions are impersonal, tense, and slightly abrasive. Hardly a trace of empathy exists, with the notable exception of the "chum" bond between Parker and his taciturn fellow mechanic Brett (their origins seem working-class). Some affection is also elicited by Jones the cat, indicating the capacity for engagement has not withered entirely, if only with the nonhuman environment.

As the Alien's threat escalates, relations aboard grow more alienated. Dallas betrays a nasty paranoid streak. When Ripley tries to discuss her suspicions about Ash, he snaps: "I don't trust *anybody*!" The crew seem bound to each other only by shared fear and vulnerability. They betray little real mourning for their dead except for Parker's grief when Brett is killed. Even Ripley, who evolves into the most humanized character, never overtly shows more than momentary anguish over her lost comrades.

Kane's maimed funeral rites offer a paradigm of the pervasive dehumanization afflicting the crew. Dallas reads no formal service over him, an intriguing departure from the convention of fifties classics like *Forbidden Planet*, wherein departed shipmates were assured of a Christian burial in deep space. Instead, the Captain coldly inquires, "Does anyone want to say anything?" and when no answer comes, flushes the corpse out of the airlock as dispassionately as emptying a toilet.

It is strongly implied that the source of the Nostromo's impoverished relationships lies in an overweaning lust for gain, a life-denying greediness that has extended from the highest levels of *Alien*'s world to become rooted within the individual psyche. The theme of insatiable orality is subliminally sounded in the beginning of the film: the camera tracks through the empty mess to a close-up of two perpetually feeding plastic Goony-birds, bobbing up and down over a cup of water.

After the crew awakens, their first conversation involves Parker's noisy demands for a larger share of the profits. He claims that those who do the dirty work below decks are exploited by the technocrats above (shades of *Metropolis*). When Dallas orders the landing, Parker protests that since Nostromo is a commercial ship he will only undertake a rescue operation for extra pay. He complies after Ash dryly points out that a clause in his contract makes the investigation mandatory "under penalty of total forfeiture of shares. No MONEY!!!"

Parker strikes a keynote of sour appropriativeness that echoes throughout the film. His type is recognizable today, the "I'm all right, Jack" union stalwart, jealous of petty prerogative, spoiling for a strike, his true ideology to the right of Bismarck. But one should not be misled by the coarseness of his rhetoric: those who walk the upper decks share his greediness. Their motives are merely more suavely disguised. Dallas, for instance, does not seem any more touched by mercy in conducting the rescue operation. The Captain is simply a better servant of his employers.

Ingrained personal selfishness may be taken as a pallid reflection of the maniacal greed of the corporate masters ruling *Alien*'s society. They would appear to govern a corrupted galactic democracy that maintains the pretense of libertarian ideals while shamelessly plundering outsiders and covertly abusing its own citizens. The resources of the Nostromo are deployed to exploit a distant planet's natural resources. In past centuries, the lucre from similar missions legitimized subjugation and slaughter of colonial populations; even the death of those enlisted by the exploiters in pursuit of their golden dreams could be justified by appropriate compensation of their survivors. The Nostromo's real mission, and the heartless manner in which it has been contrived, illustrate the depth of the inhuman exploitiveness which has developed out of the earlier terrestrial excesses of capitalism.

It may be extrapolated that the Company actually deciphered the derelict's transmissions some time *before* the Nostromo's departure. After gleaning that a highly dangerous presence had been encountered by whatever agency responsible for planting the warning beacon, the Company felt that this entity might be useful for its "weapons section." Perhaps it is one of many battling for galactic hegemony like our Krupps or DuPonts; perhaps it competes with other conglomerates, hawking ordinance across the universe.

Since it constantly seeks a competitive edge, the Company opts to keep its profile low while retrieving the Alien. Sacrificing safety for stealth, it elects *not* to send a large, well-equipped expedition. Instead, an ordinary merchant vessel is chosen, whose course has already been scheduled to take it near the planetoid on which the acoustic beacon is located.

Hopefully, the beacon site can then be reconnoitered, and the Alien recovered under the guise of a rescue operation, without unduly alerting the suspicions of the crew *or* potential competitors. After all, investigation of unknown transmissions *is* required under prevailing maritime law. A rescue operation *is* what the crew members will probably think they are undertaking to earn their pay, and will perhaps keep thinking if survivors are actually found together with whatever danger lurks on the planetoid.

Profit, always the Company's primary concern, may also dictate its stratagems concretely. Besides preserving security, the use of a merchant vessel saves the major cost of outfitting an expedition. The Company therefore can possibly kill two birds with one stone, acquiring both the Nostromo's cargo and a new weapon. The complete success of the gamble is, of course, contingent on a docile, or at least manageable

Alien—never a reliable possibility in the genre since Kong broke out of his chrome-steel chains at the Rialto.

But the mission's complete success is by no means mandatory. The Company has neither issued the crew disintegrator weapons to vaporize the creature, nor the means of creating a force field to contain it—devices well within the capabilities of a faster-than-light technology. One theorizes that the highly limited low-tech defenses alloted to the crew—the best they can jury-rig are primitive prods and flame-throwers—indicate the Company's miserliness, as well as a bias in favor of eliminating the human crew to preserve the Alien (and the cargo).

To cover every contingency, the Company substitutes for the Nostromo's regular Science Officer an android totally obedient to its will, programming Ash and "Mother" to implement its intentions on the mission. One surmises the Company prefers to bring back the Alien without incident, without disclosing the evil uses to which it will be put, if Ash can fog the issue by insisting the creature needs to be studied for its intrinsic research value, or possible humanitarian benefits. But Ash is also empowered if necessary to sacrifice crew, survivors, the Cargo, himself, to return the Alien to the "weapons section." His tactics are passive-aggressive and obfuscatory until Ripley discovers the conspiracy. Then he explodes into an impersonal fury that quite matches the Alien's.

Conceive, then, that the "family" of the Nostromo is victimized by three monstrosities, within and without. The clearest danger to its integrity is the Alien, but it is monstrous *only* from its victims' viewpoint. Objectively, there is nothing evil in its nature, for its ceaseless feeding and breeding merely fulfills the imperative of its genetic code—to survive in shifting, inimical environments.

Ash is the second monster, inserted from outside to dwell deceitfully within the family's bosom, preserving group integrity if it will further his aims, but equally capable of destroying the group to protect the Alien. But Ash is no more culpable or intrinsically evil than the creature, for he is not his own man. His morality is pre-programmed, a cog-and-wheels Darwinism engineered by others to make him a tool fit for their dirty tricks. For him, the Alien's purity constitutes a robotic ego-ideal, and he is more than halfway towards achieving it . . . .

The authentic moral monstrosity of the piece is the Company, and its fellow corporate predators. The Company's materialism has infected the heart, corroded relationships almost beyond redress, struck hurtfully at the center of individual, group, and family identity. Like the family of *The Texas Chainsaw Massacre*, the Company's feeding upon others to survive and prevail is completely ego-syntonic; it perceives nothing in the least reprehensible about its machinations.

Cruel Cinema as Sullied Polemic

Many critics have theorized that art reflects the psychic tensions generated by a culture's historic, economic, and technological circumstances. Inimical conditions are believed to provoke dark, disintegrative resonances in the psyches of a culture's members; more "affirmative" percepts may evolve whenever favorable environments promote higher levels of cultural integration. Employing formal devices consistent with his or her medium and prevailing stylistics, the artist is said to "capture" the culture's "negative" or "positive" collective psychological valence, a process which occurs largely outside conscious intent.[9]

The motion picture has been widely heralded as an exquisitely sensitive litmus for collective psychic tensions. Weird cinema offers a particularly sensitive index of disintegrative cultural thrusts, elaborated into a highly idiosyncratic vocabulary of apocalyptic imagery. Both trashy and artful productions of the weird canon therefore deserve serious attention in a politically committed critical practice. Robin Wood observes that, paradoxically, the very *lack* of seriousness with which horror movies are conceived and received encourages *loosening* of censorship for maker and viewer. Superficially innocuous, or downright disreputable, weird films may consequently be far more "radical and fundamentally undermining than works of social criticism, which must always concern themselves with the possibility of reforming aspects of a social system whose basic rightness must not be challenged. . . ."[10]

In opposition to the liberalism of "establishment" reformists like Capra or Kramer, cruel cinema has been waxing exuberantly nihilistic about sacrosanct American values. *Alien* is the culmination of this trend: it recapitulates in one concentrated scenario the cruel film's fragmented, or disguised preoccupations with the deterioration of the quality of life —notably of family life, and the degradation of the social contract under capitalism.

The omnipotent monster who preys on puny humans is a common figure in art of earlier phases of cultural disintegration. As the despair of the Dark Ages gave way to the hope of the Gothic Middle Ages, the indomitable Grendel dwindled into the gargoyle, a peripherally removed figure of fun, waiting in the wings to flourish again in darker times.[11] *Alien* moves the gargoyle back to center stage. Late twentieth-century corporate capitalism, with its unslakable thirst to propagate its vast institutions, is nominated as the sinister force which has reincarnated the omnipotent beast.

The condemnation of a callous, consumerist ethos, obliquely set forth in *The Texas Chainsaw Massacre* and the Romero *Dead* opera, now emerges undisguised. The Company, playing out its intergalactic scenario of contemporary corporate smash-and-grab, is emphatically labelled villainous; the Alien recognized as avatar of its unholy scavenging.

The script implies that the Alien is also a warning to the Company cast in its own image. For had the creature been brought to Earth, a dreadful retribution would surely have followed as it fed upon the flesh of its rescuers and bred its own kind with Malthusian vigor. Ripley's courage narrowly averts the extinction of her culture. It is left moot whether she will unmask the Company's perfidy after her return, which might precipitate a galactic Watergate or even send interplanatary revolutionaries to the barricades.

Several critics have suggested that *Alien* is agitprop in genre masquerade. Lyn Davis and Tom Genelli believe the film functions "as a kind of wakeup call to present day society. . .to shock us out of our psychic 'hypersleep'."[12] Our "technological society" breeds environmental and economic ills as numerous as the Alien's mutations because "our left brain 'mothers,' the computers and the technocrats who run them, are unable to *generate* what is needed to solve these problems. . . ."

Davis and Genelli categorize the Alien as the *dernier cri* of the "masculine principle, total aggression without emotion or regard to life . . . ." The answer to the phallic expansionism it symbolizes is the affirmation of "the conservation instinct which we need to reacknowledge, to reincorporate within our collective human body."[13]

This "feminine principle" is epitomized by *Alien*'s heroine. Ripley, as avatar of Kali, the Mother Goddess, perceives the danger of letting Kane and the other explorers back aboard; she is ready to sacrifice a few lives that millions may live. She searches out the Company's scheming, and exposes Ash's empty "fathering" of the Alien. She jeopardizes her own escape to rescue Jones the cat, demonstrating her empathy with the nonhuman manifestations of the life force.

I found the Davis-Genelli arguments doubtful in 1980; they seem even less helpful in reassessing *Alien* and the problematics of cruel cinema in 1986. Several decades of work in psychoanalysis and feminist studies enjoin wariness about erecting gendered "principles" as eternal spiritual/biological verities. Beyond their essentialism, Davis and Genelli have fundamentally erred—perhaps falling prey to wishful thinking—in ascribing to *Alien*'s creators a degree of mindfulness that simply doesn't sort with its deliberately traumatizing aspects. *Alien* remains a marvelous masterpiece of the genre. But it also replicates the uncompromising hurtfulness, the amoral "cool" of *Psycho* and its cruel inheritors, while teasing the audience with a politically "engaged" facade.

Robin Wood remarks that contemporary horror cinema brings "to a focus a spirit of negativity, an undifferentiated lust for destruction, that seems to be not far below the surface of the modern collective consciousness. . . ."[14] Not content with mocking the values of its characters as it tears their flesh, I submit that cruel cinema assails its audience with that same spirit of negativity, destructiveness, and exploitation Davis and Genelli would have us believe *Alien* decries. And what vast profit is garnered in the process—shades of the Company!

The past few decades have witnessed the spread of violence throughout American culture, perpetrated within the family, on our streets, sanctioned at the highest levels of government, whether in the napalming of children or in subsidizing foreign torturers. The show of overt violence in media has become a commonplace never conceived of in the worst excesses of yellow journalism. Television news passes equably from the commercial break to the unsparing depiction of the atrocities of war and urban crime. We have gradually become inured, desensitized to violence; its victims grow increasingly "thing-like," exciting only the briefest twitch of pity or horror before the bloody scene dissolves to the hawking of toothpaste and designer jeans.

It seems to me that cruel cinema merely takes up where the TV screen leaves off, with a greater *cachet* to treat characters and audience as dumb objects to be exploited towards enormous gain. In the course of transforming the collective angst bred out of a corrupt and corrupting capitalism, the creators of cruel movies, wittingly or otherwise, have allowed their medium to become tainted by the sordid practices of their *bête noire*. The creators of *Alien* have perhaps beheld the greedy beast lurking in its lair more accurately; but then, to paraphrase Blake, they have become what they beheld.

In sum, films like *Alien* cannot legitimately be recommended as polemics against capitalism. They should instead be properly recognized as collective artistic derivatives of its depredations. With rare exceptions, their means of production and, inevitably their ideology are dictated by corporate parameters. At best, these texts constitute sullied jeremiads. They dimly apprehend the primordial selfishness infecting late twentieth-century capitalism, but can only recommend convenient escapist, individualistic solutions.[15] At worst, they are signatory of its callous manipulations of our fellow creatures and our environment, which have brought us to the brink of universal ambiguity, destructiveness, and despair.

NOTES

An earlier version of this essay appeared as "The Fractures of Desire" in *Psychoanalytic Review* 70 (1983), pp. 241–267.

1. Harvey R. Greenberg, *The Movies on Your Mind* (New York: Saturday Review Press/Dutton, 1975), p. 198.

2. Greenberg, p. 204.

3. Robin Wood, "The Return of the Repressed," *Film Comment* (August 1978), pp. 25–32.

4. Wood, p. 32.

5. Special *Alien* issue, *Cinéfantastique* 9, no. 1 (1979).

6. Daniel Dervin, "The Primal Scene in Film Comedy and Science Fiction," *Film/Psychology Review* 4, no. 1 (1980), pp. 115–147.

7. See the *Alien* issue of *Cinéfantastique*.

8. Dervin, p. 131.

9. Walter H. Abell, *The Collective Dream in Art; A Psycho-Historical Theory of Culture Based on Relations Between the Arts, Psychology and the Social Sciences* (Cambridge, MA: Harvard University Press, 1957).

10. Wood, p. 32.

11. Abell.

12. Lyn Davis and Tom Genelli, "*Alien*: A Myth of Survival," *Film/Psychology Review* 4, no. 2 (1980), p. 240.

13. Ibid.

14. Wood, p. 32.

15. For a more extensive Marxist critique, the reader is referred to the Science Fiction Studies Symposium on *Alien*, Jackie Byars, Moderator, *Science Fiction Studies* 7 (1980), pp. 278–305. See also Douglas Kellner, "*Blade Runner*, a Diagnostic Critique," *Jump Cut* 29 (1984), pp. 6–8.

Alien, drawing by H.R. Giger

Edison's phonographic talking doll (1890)

Ideal Hadaly
Raymond Bellour

> The New Eve, an electro-human machine
> (almost an animal! . . .), offering a replica
> of the world's first love, by the astonishing
> Thomas Alva Edison, the American engineer,
> Father of the Phonograph.
>
> Villiers de l'Isle-Adam, "Le Traitement du Doc-
> teur Tristan," *Contes cruels*, 1877

What, exactly, does *The Future Eve*[1] have to say?

In this story about a sublime robot, Villiers offers us an image which both pacified and exhilarated the imagination of his century, a sort of Woman-Computer. When the nineteenth-century writer was called upon to choose a sex for the machine, it was feminine. This choice, and the assumptions behind it, raise interesting questions: What conditions made such a choice possible? On what grounds does the narrative justify it? What does it tell us about the desire to write and to love? Why does Villiers luxuriate, to the point of excess, in this particular image, an image which he creates by including Thomas Alva Edison (still alive at the time) in the fantasy of his narrative?[2]

1.

The beginning of *The Future Eve* strikes a peculiar note. Five chapters (1, 2, 4, 7, 8) are devoted to introducing the characters, directly or indirectly. Five other chapters (3, 5, 6, 9, 10) show us Edison alone, meditating. Each of the two series is obviously strengthened by this overlapping. But the second, which has no follow-up, also forms a sort of prologue to the whole of the novel and is worth dwelling upon.

"The father of the Phonograph," "The man who took Echo prisoner," is quietly lamenting to himself: if only he (and consequently his invention) "could have been one of the first-born of our species! . . . I could have recorded all the important sayings of the gods and man through the ages . . . so that by now there could be no doubt concerning their authenticity"(9-10). Edison stages in his mind the capture of History, recorded through these voices, and stored in these never-ending archives; he thereby becomes its privileged spokesman. Here Villiers evokes one of the grand obsessions of his century: the fantasy of the Whole, and the work which would be its echo. It is an unscrupulous obsession because it uses the slightest excuse to drift from a simple utopian gesture to wholesale digression, and from the retrospective to the prospective. As if to emphasize the megalomania and madness at the core of this obsession, Edison blames the phonograph "for its incapacity to reproduce, say, the *sound* of the Fall of the Roman Empire"(10). Neither can it record the sound of rumors, eloquent silences, the voice of conscience, the voice of the blood, or unspoken innuendo. And so he concludes, significantly, that he would have to invent "a machine which would speak before spoken to"(10).

. This reverie about sound quickly moves on to images. Like the Phonograph, Photography's arrival on the historical scene was too late. But Edison manages to bring them together in a collaboration which could replicate reality ("The Camera, aided by the Phonograph")(52). Here again is the dream of the interminable parade of "Snapshots of World History": great scenes from the Bible and classical mythology, portraits of the most beautiful women, from Venus to Lady Hamilton. Here again the utopian vision expands: "And of course we'd have all the gods as well, and all the goddesses, down to and including the goddess of Reason, without neglecting Mr. Supreme Being!"(23). And here again Edison-Villiers stops at God. God is at once the first and the last term, the term around which all others gravitate. Initially Edison had proclaimed, with a hint of irony, that he harbored no hopes for capturing God's first words—"Fiat Lux!"(6). A few pages later he concludes otherwise:

> Just think, if He would only allow the slightest, most humble photograph of Himself to be taken, or permit me, Thomas Alva Edison, American engineer, one of His own creatures, to make a simple phonographic record of His true Voice . . . *from that day there wouldn't be a single atheist left on earth*(24)!

This development leads us to the fantasmatic core of *The Future Eve*. On the one hand, God remains an absolute: He is the logical ground and originary source of enunciation. Because God exists, Man speaks, the scientist invents, the writer writes. So too, and in accordance with a logic dear to the nineteenth century, it is to compete with God that Villiers-Edison thinks of God as "the most probable of gods." The writer concealed within the scientist can fall back on this belief because he grants to himself the powers of a God whom he redefines at will. Edison thinks that God exists only in terms of the idea one has of him.

No one knows where illusion begins or what reality consists of. Thus, God being the most sublime of conceptions, and all conceptions existing only according to the particular spirit and the *intellectual* vision of each living creature, it follows that the man who dismisses the idea of God from his thoughts does nothing but deliberately decapitate his own mind(24).

Belief is purely internal to the subject's mind: it depends on his capacity for projection and on his need for the absolute. Paradoxically, it is the same with the machine. What would a machine be which could prove the existence of God? Would it not be God himself, in another form? But the machine becomes God only in and for the man who conceives it, insofar as he recognizes himself as God through the machine. In this respect, the machine's objectivity is merely an apparent dialectic of illusion. The external image, the simulacrum which it reproduces, depends on the internal, mental image which can alone make it true for the mind. Thus, only the utopia invested in the machine can enable it to attain the infinite of which God is the psychic model. And this way of thinking obliges Edison to dream of the exceptional case when "man will some day be able to recover, either by electricity or by some more subtle means, the eternal interstellar reverberations of everything that has occurred on earth"(22). This formulation is an equivalent of what could still be imagined, in the nineteenth century, as the perspective of a God who, self-alienated, transmutes himself in man and is there self-negated.

What is Villiers up to when he makes of Edison's technological power such an obvious metaphor of his own power to speak or write? What does he mean when he sets up this twofold equivalence, between God and the machine, and between God and the man whose mind creates the machine? On the one hand, he is acting out his century's dreams, given a new twist by the image of the machine. He predicts, for example, as did so many others of the period, the as-yet-to-be-invented cinema; Edison will in fact soon become one of its precursors. On the other hand, however, his work prepares the ground for the hegemony of metaphor, which will govern the novel and catalyze its enunciatory desire. He focuses on what is generated by the image of Woman: The Future Eve is at once the magical object of science and the transcendental subject of this fiction. When woman becomes the ideal machine invented by man, she takes the place of God. At the same time and by the same token, man transforms himself into God. Man and woman thus become God through each other, with all that this entails for their respective identities and the fantasies that it fuels.

2.

Woman presides over the passage from monologue to dialogue: her image gives substance to the debate between Edison and Lord Ewald (a wealthy English gentleman who, in the past, supported the scientist's research). This debate does not merely dominate the book, it is the narrative itself. Villiers's book is not easy to summarize, and so the novel's rare events are immediately understood as either themes or symbols, and seen as moments in a discourse rather than as markers in a plot. The language is often obscure, convoluted, improbable, and always evocative, but it does not prevent this novel of style and ideas from making free with the structural ruses of serial fiction. In his inimitable style, Mallarmé sums it up thus: "Un jeune lord mourait que sa maîtresse contînt une imperfection, quelque vulgarité, inaperçue du monde, pas de lui . . . .Edison, par un automate, de sa fabrication, requérant un ingéniosité, la remplace . . . ." ["A young lord was pained that his mistress had an imperfection, some commonness unperceived by society, but not by him . . . . Edison, using an automaton of his own making, calls upon his own ingenuity to replace her . . . ."][3] How does Villiers choose to speak of Lord Ewald's disillusionment?

Ewald sums up Alicia's "defect" this way: she is a "bourgeois Goddess"(36). More specifically: "The sole misfortune afflicting Miss Alicia is reason. If she were deprived of all reason, I could understand her. The marble *Venus*, after all, *has nothing to do with reason*"(41). This image of the statue of Venus, triggered by the unique beauty of his mistress, is a pure projection; like all works of art, it exists only in the mind of its beholder. By contrast, Lord Ewald deplores his bourgeois Goddess's blend of conformism, vanity, egoism, and frivolity. A witty woman, or rather one who aspires to be witty, and a virtuoso (she is a singer), Alicia is, at best, talented. But her mimicry of the outward appearance of Art and Genius only serve to heighten the effects of this sham. Lord Ewald makes it quite clear: foolish she may be, stupid she is not.

In Lord Ewald's description of Alicia, we see emerge another image of femininity familiar to the nineteenth century: the foolish woman, or the *femme un peu bête*, who, unlike the *femme d'esprit*, is half worshipped for her very mediocrity. Collected, religious, and passive, she has, Ewald says, the "marvelous" ability to be able to "divine the true sense of a phrase as if through a veil of light"(39). Ewald will return to this idea; woman is the lens which refracts, magnifies, and is transparent all at once. But she does not achieve this through real understanding, or inspiration proper (these are beyond her), but rather through a mysterious property of her "nature." A nature whose thoughts, as Lord Ewald puts it, a man's love must be able to shape wilfully until they mirror his own. The plasticity of the feminine nature will guarantee that she reflects and feeds the thoughts of the man whom she mirrors, and will do so according to the shape of his whims and inclinations. This is what Villiers, through Lord Ewald, calls "the true communion of love," and it is a communion which dissolves the perverted nature of Alicia. Ewald's words are quite precise. Her radiance, he says (the fire of her look, the luster of her thoughts) "strikes a wall where it is shattered"; it cannot reflect back upon itself, or focus its "radiant power" into his own eyes—instead, it returns weakened, enhanced, or illuminated by the look of the other. "My look," Lord Ewald points out, "as it captures more and more of these returning rays, will be the Sisyphean rock of my eyesight." Instead of acting as a mirror, and "naturally" refracting everything, Alicia becomes this "creature of death" who destroys both look and thought "in her horrible *camera obscura*." This unexpected metaphor completes the image of the wall: either Lord Ewald's look is returned to him excessively, overflowing with light, or else it is lost in an excessively dark place—he can never locate himself at the optimum distance where he would be reflected by the mirror-body of the love object.

So Lord Ewald cannot be happy with this woman who *"would be the absolute feminine ideal for three-quarters of modern humanity"*(44). His disillusionment prevents him from feeling any desire for her. His senses have become "distant and numb. . . . She is the radiant obsession of my spirit. That is all there is to it"(49). But this "all" is immense, consuming. For Alicia has awakened in him an impossible idealism. Her beauty is so remarkable that it prompts him to conceive a unique relation between the physical and the artistic, the perceived and the nameable. Alicia's existence thus prevents Lord Ewald from even imagining another love (one of those simple, elementary, quiet loves that he speaks of to her with nostalgia. If Alicia cannot be what he wants her to be, no one else could be this in her place. Hence his mad wish ("Ah! who will remove this soul from this body?"(44)).

3.

Edison responds to this wish: "I will realize your dream in full." He promises Ewald that in 21 days, Alicia Clary will appear to him, transfigured, and endowed with a sort of immortality: "the present gorgeous little fool will no longer be a woman, but an angel; no longer mistress but a lover; no longer reality, but the IDEAL!"(54). Edison's argument, briefly, is as follows. Since you prefer an image to reality, since this image is constantly threatened by the dissonances of reality, I shall raise this image to its point of perfection and then show you how to be satisfied with the image, since it is the quality of the image which corresponds to the deepest nature of your desire.

While Lord Ewald agrees to go along with Edison's astounding proposal, he persists in raising objections of two types. They serve both to construct the object offered up to his desire and to elucidate the nature of this desire, its deepest resistances and compulsions. His first objections are of a material sort: how can Edison create a physical equivalent of real life? Describing in minute detail all the procedures whereby science (a most fictional science) can produce the illusion of life, Edison skillfully tempers the appeal of his technical revelations with touches of didactic and poetic seriousness. Increasingly, from then on, Lord Ewald (and the reader) is persuaded to "believe" in Edison.

Hadaly, for example, is shown to have two golden phonographs in place of lungs. They will record, in addition to Alicia's voice, a sixty-hour "program" whose effect constitutes "precisely the miracle, and also the hidden peril" which the Android inspires. Edison explains that they are made of virgin gold because it is the only metal which does not oxidize, but that he was obliged to use iron for the joints ("it's one of the important elements making up our own blood"). He does so because "in Hadaly's structure, the socket is a magnet powered by electricity; and as the metal on which magnetism works best . . . iron . . . is what . . . I have had to use." But, objects Lord Ewald, "won't the joints rust?" Certainly not, replies Edison: "Here on my shelf is a bottle of oil of roses, heavily perfumed, tightly stoppered, which will lubricate the joint as well as any sinovial membrane." Besides, perfumes, says Edison, are "appropriately feminine." "Once a month, he continues, "you'll slip about a teaspoonful between Hadaly's lips while she seems to be napping (as you would with an attractive invalid). You will see, she's Humanity incarnate." Hadaly breathes, but without burning oxygen. Her usual state is a dreamy half-sleep. "To rouse her to her mysterious existence" one need only take her by the hand while "activating the fluid in one of her rings." "One of her rings?" Lord Ewald asks. "Yes," replies Edison, "the one on her index finger; it's her wedding band." A slight pressure on the ring of her right hand will make her rise. "The pressure on the ring should be light and natural, as if you were pressing gently and tenderly the hand of the original model. But such nuances are necessary only for the sake of the illusion." Such rings are on all of Hadaly's fingers. For example, "Touch ever so gently the turquoise on her ring finger and she will sit down." Besides all these rings, she wears a necklace, "every pearl of which corresponds to a function" and "will serve as your guide to the subtleties of her character." This "semi-living" creature bathes "every day, *naturally!*" As for nourishment, she needs only some lozenges and little pills that she takes once or twice a week

Galaxy Science Fiction, September 1954

when one brushes the pearls in her necklace. The lozenges are made of zinc, bichromate of potassium, and lead peroxide. She drinks only distilled water, filtered through charcoal, and mixed with some salts. This is necessary to dispel the

> harsh metallic odor that the stale water of her organic crystal flagon would have . . . . You must remember to infuse the first mouthful of her drink with the various reagents for which you will find the formulas and the dosage in the Manuscript . . . . And there she is again as alive as you or me, ready to obey all her rings and all the pearls of her necklace just as we respond to all our impulses.

Lord Ewald has noted that she wears a dagger at her waist. This is for her self-protection. When required, the blade is put in contact with a powerful current.

> So that the merry rake . . . who tries, for example, to "snatch a kiss" from this Sleeping Beauty will find himself rolling on the floor, his face blackening, his limbs broken . . . beneath Hadaly's feet, before his hands even reach her dress. She's a faithful mistress . . . .Ah, that's right! So it would be!, murmurs Lord Ewald impassively. The seducer's kiss would intercept the current(74-84).

These explanations, still random, come to an end when the two men confront the "First Instance of the Machine in Human Form" in Hadaly's underground dwelling. Disconnected by the engineer, the Android is stretched out "like a corpse on the dissecting table of an amphitheater"(125). Edison opens up her "feminine armature" and unties the "black veil at her waist." The Android, he says impassively, is divided into four parts: the living system of the interior, the equivalent of the soul; the plastic mediator or skeleton; the artificial flesh which covers it; and the epidermis, or human skin, which includes, among other things, the individuality of the Look(129).

The demonstration goes on this way, increasingly precise and improbable. It literally exhausts, point by point, the mechanical body of the Android while prefiguring the incarnate body of the Future Eve. In the course of this dissection, the cold precision of science is balanced by the seduction of its metaphors. Villiers perpetuates here the very old tradition of *blasons* or emblems describing the woman's body. He brings the tradition up to date, however, by displacing and radicalizing it. Nothing is overlooked, nothing hidden in this transformation of nature into artifice: what Villiers is giving us is Scève rewritten by Condillac and La Mettrie. By dismembering, and by naming the parts, he makes of the female body an experimental field, an object exposed to generalized sadism. The corrosive materialism is, however, marked by an increased idealism. Woman ("abominable because she is natural," Baudelaire said) is blown up to proportions hitherto unthinkable. Each parallel established between copy and model has the effect of raising by a notch the process of idealization. Scève's Délie was no more *idée* than Hadaly.

Lord Ewald's second set of objections is addressed to this very problem. He is not content to ask of Edison merely, "How can you reproduce the identity of a woman?" but, "How can I believe in this reproduction? . . . What devious subtleties will you use to convince *me* of the *reality* of this new Eve?"(66).

Edison gives a two-part answer.

1. First of all he challenges Lord Ewald's rhetorical duplicity when

the latter asks him whether this creature, lacking a soul, will possess consciousness. Edison reminds him of the terms of their contract:

Isn't that exactly what you asked for when you cried out, "WHO WILL RE-MOVE THE SOUL FROM THIS BODY?" You called for a phantom, identical to your young sweetheart but MINUS *the consciousness with which she seemed to be afflicted.* Hadaly has come in answer to your call. It's as simple as that(85).

But this "minus" is a plus, and something else besides; it is what Edison promised Lord Ewald. Hadaly is in any case more than a woman; she is of an abstract, complex, virtual nature, irreducible to simple Humanity. "Will you breathe into her an intellect? *An* intellect? No. IN-TELLIGENCE? Yes." So too when Lord Ewald is astonished that the inventor seems to think that his Android has a notion of the Infinite, Edison replies, "Not much more than a notion of it"(158).

2. But Edison must do more than this. He must prove to Lord Ewald that Hadaly's concrete form corresponds to Ewald's desire for Alicia. Since Lord Ewald's consuming despair is basically a result of his vision of the ideal, this vision becomes Edison's target when he very precisely points out that

the creature whom you love, and who for you is the *sole* REALITY is by no means the one who is momentarily embodied in this transient human figure, but a creature of your desire . . . . This illusion is the one thing that you struggle against all odds to VITALIZE in the presence of your beloved, despite the frightful, deadly, withering nullity of Alicia. What you love is this *phantom* alone; it's for the *phantom* that you want to die. That and that alone is what you recognize as unconditionally REAL. In short, it's this objectified projection of your own mind that you call on, that you perceive, that you CREATE in your living woman, *and which is nothing but your own mind reduplicated in her*(68).

These last words, underlined by Villiers, speak volumes. The "ideal-double" whose possibility Edison suggests to Lord Ewald is none other than the ideal-double of himself, projected through Alicia. We shall call this encompassing of doubles the Narcissistic double. It is born from the subject's concern for his own image, and for the conditions necessary for its formation. Edison seeks to exteriorize an image which has remained captive in Lord Ewald's mind. It is an image without which he does not and cannot see himself, an image denied by the real Alicia. In her and through her, replacing what Lord Ewald calls her "horrible *camera obscura*," Edison wants to create an echo chamber.

Not content with this, Lord Ewald appeals for his freedom in the name of his love itself. Edison answers by invoking the reality of his dream. He shows him to what degree the freedom he demands is illusory; it is from this freedom that he most suffers in his imaginary appeal to Alicia, because this freedom is victim to the unanswerable logic of his desire. Lord Ewald asks: but wouldn't such a dialogue mean my learning by heart both questions and answers? This is partly true, says Edison, but isn't that what you do in ordinary life when you anticipate an answer which is never the one you would expect? With Hadaly, the beauty of the answer will depend on what you yourself suggest. "Her 'consciousness' will no longer be the negation of yours, but rather will become whatever spiritual affinity your own melancholy suggests to you"(133). So it's play-acting you expect of me? objects Lord Ewald. Edison asks him whether he has ever acted otherwise with the living woman, from whom he felt obliged to hide his real thoughts. And how is it any different in the case of passionate love, in which each of the two lovers loves the phantom he or she has formed of the other? And in which illusion is essential to the preservation of an emotion which would vanish if one could see the other as he or she really is, or, even worse, see oneself as imagined by the other? Furthermore, says Edison, parrying a final objection by Lord Ewald, "I contend that when two persons love one another, every alteration of appearance can only involve loss of devotion; it can only alter the flow of passion and dissipate the dream . . . . The Android . . . is nothing but the first hours of love, immobilized, the hour of the Ideal made eternal prisoner!"(135). "You contradict yourself," he tells Lord Ewald, in being frightened of "the monotony of your wish fulfilled"(136).

It should be clear already that Edison's game with Lord Ewald (like Villiers's with his reader) is to string him along, the better to convince him. He has not yet explained to him (and will not, until the end) who the Android is, nor how this artificial creature can have the "naturalness" of a real woman. He has not told him that in her there are two parts. One of these is the "programmed" part whose "interactive" capacity he wishes to develop so that she can seem to respond to her interlocutor's desire. The other is the unknown part, half unknown to Edison himself, and this part is the contribution of Sowana, a woman whose soul speaks in Hadaly. In this way Edison himself can be surprised by what he himself controls, and Lord Ewald seduced by what he does not understand. Hadaly's duality proves the validity of Edison's reasoning by persuading Lord Ewald to cathect the object offered up to him. Sowana's involvement, however, by virtue of its nature and hers, presupposes a "true" Hadaly, and necessitates a choice among the different versions of the "program" Edison has composed.

If we are to understand this truth and this choice, we must come back to the Android's genealogy, which Edison gives us indirectly through the tragic story of his friend Edward Anderson, a model husband and father who is seduced by a dancer, Evelyn Habal. He neglects his wife, family, and business, and kills himself when his mistress abandons him. Edison finds Mrs. Anderson sick, and cures her through hypnosis, which awakens in her supernatural powers of clairvoyance. When he decides to create the Android as an antidote to passions like those of Anderson, Sowana helps him complete the Hadaly project in order, as she puts it, "to be able . . . TO EMBODY HERSELF THEREIN, ANIMATING IT WITH HER OWN SUPERNATURAL STATE if occasion required." His reasoning is as follows. If, he says, women are capable of producing, physically as well as morally, such a degree of artificiality that men who take this for reality are consumed by an unquenchable passion of a destructive sort, then let us spare women this task of replacing themselves with the artificial by deliberately creating the Android for which woman provides us with the model. Edison wants to "obtain from Science an equation for Love [which] *will not have the evil effects which are inevitable* without this sudden new addition to the human species, an equation which will circumscribe the danger"(168). He adds:

> *it's a normal property of the Android to be able to neutralize within a few hours any low and degrading desires for the original model that may exist in the most inflamed of hearts; and this is accomplished by saturating it with a profound awe hitherto unknown, the irresistible effect of which I do not think anyone can possibly imagine who has not experienced it*(123).

When he portrays the Android, he describes it as possessing the "model's sexuality." Nothing of this sexuality appears, however, in the detailed explanation of how the model was replicated. Villiers plays a tricky game with sex. The model's sex is neither copied nor transposed, unless by Hadaly herself in a general sense when she became Alicia. While she may be equipped with a sublime body, Hadaly remains completely ideal. Her overwhelming sensual attraction, borrowed from Alicia's beauty, is immediately spiritualized. She is an angel of fire and of light (the metaphor supported by her electro-magnetic nature(124)). How is the transubstantiation managed?

The idea is in one respect a simple one: Hadaly is a bodiless body. Genitality and the capacity to procreate are impossibilities for a machine. Something more subtle is at work, however: Sowana, who inhabits this bodiless body, chooses to be in Hadaly that woman whom Lord Ewald must love. What she asks of him is that he ignore all the other potential women in her, women so numerous that "no harem could hold them all," but who can be made to appear by merely pressing one of her rings (199). How should we interpret this restriction? It is clearly a way of staging a typical passion between Hadaly and Lord

Ewald, by making her into a woman who wants to be loved for herself. But Hadaly's desire has the deeper implication that she wants Lord Ewald to dismiss any image she might project which does not correspond to the incarnation of Sowana's soul, for example, any feature belonging to Evelyn Habal or to the real Alicia.[4] To summon other women to this shadowy existence would be to possess their image rather than to recognize in Hadaly, through her persistent presence in an illusory body, the "Unpossessible," as she calls herself. This would be to use the image in a sensual way, à la Don Juan, rather than to accept "THE IMAGINARY" in its pure incarnation. In this sense the wholly sublimated body of Hadaly serves to transpose the sex it lacks, in order to annihilate it more effectively. The intoxicating but chaste kiss which unites the lovers transforms sex into breath, flesh into spirit. Such is the paradox which Hadaly embodies. "Don't touch the forbidden fruit in my garden"(199). Her designation as the future Eve is thus fully justified. She reverses the meaning of her ancient namesake's example, transforming the symbol of carnal temptation into that of spiritual temptation. When Lord Ewald yields to Hadaly at the end, it is to a body which has become the image of a soul.

Here we reach the ultimate in that idealization for which Hadaly provides the pretext. Villiers is in his own way quite close to Freud at this point. Describing the mechanisms of idealization in the chapter of *Group Psychology and the Analysis of the Ego* entitled "Being in Love and Hypnosis," Freud distinguishes between that half of love which is sensual and earthly and that which is non-sensual and heavenly. Intercourse between these halves depends on the degree to which sensual impulses have been repressed. It may thus happen, says Freud, that "the illusion is produced that the object has come to be sensually loved on account of its spiritual merits, whereas on the contrary these merits may really only have been lent to it by its sensual charm." We note how precisely this description corresponds to Lord Ewald's situation, (even though it is obviously expressed in other terms: while Villiers establishes a moral division between the "sensual" and the "celestial," Freud's view is that there is a sexual overvaluation at the origin of any psychological one). Initially Lord Ewald was attracted sensually to Alicia and felt through this desire a strong psychic attraction which he could not satisfy. He then lost all physical desire for her and in the end, despairing, could not think of her as anything other than the "radiant illusion" of his mind. The lack is writ large in Hadaly. As with Freud's description of the idealized woman, the Android fixes the man's narcissistic libido on the woman and absorbs his ego; she restores and metamorphoses his lost narcissism by occupying the "place of the ego-ideal." It is a move which, as Freud explains, relates the state of love to hypnosis. In the case of love, the temporarily inhibited sexual tendencies remain in reserve, latent, ready to reemerge. Thus, when they are satisfied, they bring about a reduction in sexual overvaluation, and this itself weakens the idealization of the love object. Inversely, in hypnosis, "the total absence of sexual tendencies . . . contributes . . . to the extreme purity of the phenomena." Requiring that sexual satisfaction be excluded, the hypnotic relation is a "limitless yielding to love."[5]

It is now clear what Edison is proposing to Lord Ewald: a blend of hypnosis and love, or rather, a state of love under hypnosis. Freed from all sexuality, fixing love in the heat of its first moment, the Android induces a transcendental form of "erotic subjection." In a state of self-purified feeling, the love object comes to occupy, once and for all, the place of the ego-ideal. This is why Edison says that in Persian (a way of shrouding this evidence with mystery), the name Hadaly "means the 'IDEAL'"(76).

There is a whole series of hypnoses to be reckoned with. Edison hypnotizes Mrs. Anderson, thus revealing Sowana. He subsequently hypnotizes Alicia, and Sowana in turn hypnotizes Alicia in order to bring about the transformations which produce Hadaly. As for the latter, it is no exaggeration to say that the effect she produces on Lord Ewald is comparable to hypnosis, for she makes him accept the pure Ideal that she has become as the only reality possible.

In this experiment pushed to its limits, Lord Ewald is the hero of this Ideal and Edison its purveyor. But what is there to say about Edison's own relationship to the Ideal? What are we to understand by his declaration, "Because the two of us are in this experiment together"(63) and by the two men's collusion and dialogue throughout the novel?

It is important, in other words, to see that they are both involved in defining this multiple image of woman. By placing this image between his two heroes in this way, Villiers reaffirms the power of autonomy over his writing and imagination.

4.

During their second debate, Edison expresses a doubt (he has Alicia in mind) concerning the degree of "consciousness" with which women are supposedly endowed. Lord Ewald replies: "Unhappy as one woman has made me, I still think you talk of women with a great deal of severity"(86). Edison's answer to this is to distinguish, on the one hand, "lovers," who are in the "sphere of carnal desire," and on the other, "the true world of Love"(87). He honors those women who are, as he says, "fully inspired by some principle more lofty than Pleasure," and those "who freely and gladly allow their wombs to be torn apart repeatedly,

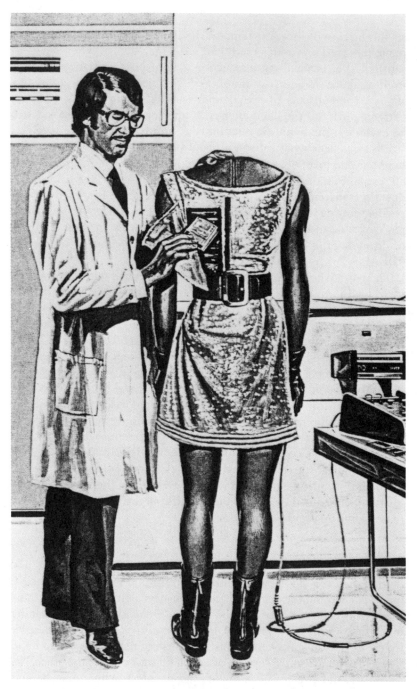

The World of Robots by Jonathan Rutland (New York: Warwick Press, 1979)

so that we may be allowed a life of the mind"(86-87). The distinction is clear-cut, as is the place assigned to women in each instance.

In the sphere of lovers, of passionate love, man is subject to a desire which oscillates between the satisfaction of a drive and its opposite—idealization. He finds himself in the realm of the illusory, with its various threats of destruction. In true love, on the other hand, illusion is mastered or at least restrained: Villiers evades carnal desire, using the child to mediate it. Marriage and maternity give thinking life to man, abetted by those "good lifetime companions" of whom man asks neither too much nor too little. Edison is thus shown at the outset, though discretely, to be a father. He telephones his children twice, the first time alone, the second in the presence of Lord Ewald, who is visibly troubled by Edison's words: "Will you pardon me while I say goodbye to my children, for one's children are really something"(73). Mrs. Edison does not appear in the book, but she is given her symbolic place. This is done—and it is one of the novel's master strokes—by overlapping two couples and two families (the homophony Edison/Anderson can suggest this). Mrs. Anderson is an unhappy double of Mrs. Edison. The scientist's moral genius counterbalances his friend Anderson's weakness, while the latter's destructive passion for Evelyn Habal inspires Edison to create the Android.

Should we conclude that Edison asks less of his own wife than he does of women in general? Despite his reproach to Lord Ewald, does he not himself desire that woman be "different from what she must be"? Does he himself not ask "too much of her, or expect her to achieve the impossible"? Is he too not tempted "to rely on his idea of what a woman thinks"? When he cures Mrs. Anderson through hypnosis, he produces Sowana. Without realizing it he thus causes the appearance of a second, different woman, hidden in the first.

> She used to be a simple woman, perfectly honorable, even intelligent, but, after all, of very limited views—and so I knew her. But in the depths of her slumber another person is revealed to me, completely different, many-sided, and mysterious. So far as I can tell, the enormous knowledge, the strange eloquence, and the penetrating insight of this somnambulist named Sowana . . . are logically inexplicable(210).

As was customary in the wake of Mesmer, the mystery of the psychic unconscious is described here with terms like "nervous fluid" and "clairvoyance." Henceforth this force, combined with electricity, will nourish the inventor's genius. Using two iron rings with an enormous charge of magnetic energy, he is able to enter into telepathic communication with Sowana, transmit to her his wishes, and see what she sees. Sowana's power, obscure and prodigious, increases Edison's many times over. Villiers emphasizes the clairvoyant's role in the conception and realization of the Android. Hadaly is their co-creation. She is more, however, than just another of Edison's thousand-and-one inventions. She is at the very source of his capacity to invent:

> When I need solitude, I go to visit this sorceress who dispels all cares. Above all, when the fire dragon of a discovery is beating his invisible wings within my head, I come here where only she will hear me if I speak aloud. After a while, I return to the surface of the earth, my problem solved. She is my own private nymph, my Egeria(88).

Her mysterious presence enhances Edison's ability to hear himself; she is a muse, an echo. Like Edison, I use the name Hadaly; properly speaking, one should say Sowana-Hadaly, for it is Sowana's soul which speaks in the Android. As we see, Edison's inspiration comes to him from a woman, but she is also as little a woman as it is possible to be since she has as yet neither face nor body, nor is she even a woman's image. In this respect she becomes, as a creation and as the inspiration of creative work, the absolute ideal. As a pure machine haunted by an external soul, the Android is also the abstract and conceptual counterpart of the reassuring (and desexualized) maternal body of Mrs. Edison.

Nevertheless, Edison is well aware that the Android makes sense as a work to be realized only if she is actually incarnated. The ideal machine must become a woman's body, even if that body is an evanescent one. It is not enough that she inspire creation: to come into being as a created work she must escape her creator. Here Villiers's subtle interlocking of Edison and Lord Ewald manifests itself. For Edison, Hadaly may incarnate the absolute, but she represents a limited investment (he already has a wife and children). She may illuminate the whole of his creative work, but she is still a creation in the literal sense, independent of him, and to be treated with caution. This is why, when Lord Ewald asks him which choice he, Edison, would make between submitting to the proposed experiment or death, Edison replies without hesitation: "I would blow out my brains"(71). Conversely, what he proposes to Lord Ewald admits of no such divisiveness. The proposed transfiguration of love involves a continuous creation based on an indivisible image of woman. It will be an intimate, poetic kind of creative process, unpredictable from one day to the next and requiring unconditional submission to chance and to a passion of the sort that exists between Narcissus and Echo. The Woman-Masterwork, in a word, is what is in Edison's mind when he says to Lord Ewald (obeying the radical impulse of the feelings he delegates to his alter-ego: "Ah the task that is ahead! If you could conceive! If you . . ."(62). Oscillating between the two men, Hadaly is in turn and all at once, Work and Object.[6]

Hadaly: the desire of a work, the desire of an object, doubly ideal.

What, then, is the Ideal? It is God himself ("the most sublime conception possible"). God is thus understood as the ground of the Ideal that woman replaces and which permits man to be. Edison shrewdly points out to Lord Ewald that our prayers to God are formulaic, as are our declarations to the woman we love. Let us take another look at this web woven around God, but this time at the thread which passes through Hadaly. In the early chapters the powers ascribed to the machine were such that they suggested some kind of mediation between God and Edison, making the latter God's true spokesman. Shortly thereafter, God is invoked to introduce a qualification in Edison's unprecedented project. I can, he tells Lord Ewald, make emerge from the clay of present-day human science a creature *made in our image* and who, accordingly, will be to us WHAT WE ARE TO GOD"(64). Two pages later Lord Ewald remarks: "but to undertake the creation of such a creature . . . it seems to me that would be challenging . . . *God*"(65). Still later, imagining Lord Ewald's future life with the Android in his castle in Scotland, Edison reminds him that he will have to "accept the perpetual challenge of two risks: madness and God"(78). The conflict thus postulated between man and God facilitates the shift from the idea of imitation to the idea of substitution. To convince Lord Ewald that he should accept the superior truth of the simulacrum, Edison tells him: "You must feel like a god completely, and let the devil take it, when you DARE WILL *what is under discussion here*"(68). The words convey both the similarities and the differences between the two men: Edison, the demiurge, takes God's place to tempt Lord Ewald; the latter, tempted, must be willing to consider himself God in order to get what he wants. When he finally meets Hadaly-Alicia, his impulse is to recoil: "Since when did God permit machines to speak?"(193). He then yields to the Android in the following terms: "I submit my resignation from the living"(204). Because the Ideal takes God's place, it is deadly. For those who are its aspirants, the Ideal displaces death's zone of action. Hadaly, a sovereign machine, becomes God by forcing man to suppose himself God. The new Ideal inherits that idea of the absolute whose symbol was God, even as it incarnates his death. This is why the name of Hadaly, signifying Ideal in Persian, is engraved on the coffin in which the Android will "make the [sea] crossing as a dead person"(76), just like Nosferatu. Lord Ewald says, in effect: I am willing to think of myself as God; I will inhabit the imaginary space of death because nothing is now left to me of the ideal except this image of myself. It is an image which I invent through the image I conceive of woman, and through the work which I construct, with her, in her, through her. I thus enter into the space of the work, transmuting in myself that death which she now both negates and assures.

This is the way in which the Woman-Masterwork is created for Villiers: she is verbalized by Edison, embodied in Lord Ewald, produced as a virtual fact by the two men and, between them, by Hadaly, who is her incarnation.

5.

All of this suggests that Hadaly is, in effect, a "writing machine." For Edison, however, she is "in the first place a superlative machine for creating visions"(84). What assumptions about woman, work, and image are involved here?

We have seen that the two golden phonographs which are the Android's lungs contain sixty hours of a program recorded by Alicia under Sowana's direction. The program—Lord Ewald is invited to admire its "infinite complexities"—was conceived by Edison, but its words are those "composed by the greatest poets, the most subtle metaphysicians, the most profound novelists of this century"(131). In other words, it is a work made out of language, incorporating and combining all the levels of writing—poetry, philosophy, novels—in a synthetic and superior form which abolishes every distinction of mode or of genre. Edison points to the "wonderful verbal condensations composed by those whose trade is speech, whose habit is thought, and who alone can express the feelings of all Humanity!"(138). In this way Hadaly makes language speak in the form of a Work, one which strives to fuse, mentally and culturally, the real along with the possible, thereby holding in check the infinite expansiveness of language. And in its materiality, this work is a book. Hadaly's body mimes the process of its material fabrication: the two golden phonographs "exchange between one another tapes of those harmonious—or I should say, *celestial*—conversations: the process is rather like that by which printing presses pass from one roller to another the sheets to be printed"(131). A moving book of sorts, and a place of interaction. *Post partum*, its author becomes both its printer and its reader. Here again, it is not hard to rationalize the distribution of dramatic roles, nor the mediating circuit established between Edison and Lord Ewald. Nor must we forget the importance of Sowana in the book. For she is the engineer of all this: it is she who rehearses with Alicia the texts which Edison assembled. In a deeper sense, however, she is the book's provision of the virtual or potential once she enters the body of Alicia, animating in her a supernatural state. Artfully, Villiers offers us a glimpse of this shortly before the end of the book. What had been merely possible before is here actualized: Hadaly-Alicia talks like a book. (Or like an inspired woman. It amounts to the same. As Edison puts it: "It's like a game of chess; the possibilities are limitless. Like a woman"(206).)

There are certain parallels to be drawn here with Mallarmé's work at this time: the idea of the "Book." Villiers's novel proposes a set of ideas close those Mallarmé attacked head on in a meditation on the ultimate historical, philosophical and artistic consequences of the Book. Although Villiers says less about the Book as such, he does suggest something only enigmatically present in Mallarmé's text, something which needs to be interpreted (in the manner, say, of Jean-Pierre Richard's *Univers imaginaire de Mallarmé*). Villiers tells us this: the Book is Woman; the idea of the book and the image of woman are consubstantial. The same utopia informs both. The sentence I quoted earlier expressing Lord Ewald's ultimate submission to the Android clearly echoes Mallarmé's distinction between general and restricted action. On the one hand we have History, society, and life, as they unfold in time; on the other, the Imaginary, death and its transfiguration, and the Book (for which the Woman-Fantasy is the sign, substitute, and the guarantee), all withdrawn in the name of a truth and a desire which cannot otherwise be assuaged.

The Future Eve is one of the culminating moments in the development of Romantic idealism. In fact, Edison's pact with Lord Ewald follows the curve of this cultural development. It leads, via woman, from German Romanticism to the Germanic equivalent of French Symbolism: "I shall endow this shade with all the songs of Hoffmann's *Antonia*, all the passionate mysticism of Poe's *Ligeia*, all the ardent musical seductions of Wagner's potent *Venus*!"(64). All women in one woman, like all books in one book. But more than that, for Woman and Book have become interchangeable. *The Future Eve* could well be the last word on Romantic idealism.

It would be easy to travel further along a descending curve in the French literary tradition. In Surrealism, for example, the kind of apotheosis of Woman we have seen is presupposed; the difference is that she is also highly sexualized. But psychic overvaluation (to use Freud's language) stemming from sexual overvaluation produces Surrealistic effects which are ultimately very similar to those we have seen in Villiers. In the transfigured body depicted by Villiers, woman becomes a sort of echo; as a narcissistic double she plays the role of muse. At least one Surrealist text allegorizes this in a strikingly comparable, idealized way. Breton's "Nadja" is such a woman, discovered and made to speak by the power of this writer's genius. His inspiration is heightened by her bewitching example, and by her own strange genius (she is, as he says, both "inspiring and inspired"). In short, *Nadja*, the book, owes itself to her inspiration.

So too there is something similar at work in the more secret play of metaphors, phantoms, and myths that we find in Maurice Blanchot's writing, the most extreme literary strategy of modern times. Conjured up as she who holds the image in sway, and who is the source of writing, the Mother is brought to the threshold of "literary space." She is that same withdrawn presence, both sovereign and non-entity, pursued in vain by Orpheus, because in Hell (another form of "underground Eden," the term Villiers uses for Hadaly's dwelling place) he made the mistake of turning to look at Eurydice. Her voice is the Siren Song heard by Ulysses tied to his masthead. The voice and the image, coming to Villiers from afar (that they are not very Greek is of no great importance) are, in effect, what Villiers calls "Hadaly."

6.

Let us not forget that the writing machine is also an image machine. Villiers continually draws connections and correspondences between three image-registers: psychic, verbal, and visual. Hadaly's language is made up of literary images. She transforms speech into visions for the mind. But her vision machine is called "superlative" because she provides a tangible foundation for the image's power to fascinate, building up its appeal to materiality. Hadaly transfigures the mental image by offering at once the surface on which it is projected and the requisite substantial volume. The Phonograph and the Camera are not only linked within her as twin instruments to reproduce the real; they operate together in such a way as to transform the real. What is interesting here is not so much the way in which this anticipates the talking film; rather, it paves the way towards a much wider understanding of the meaning of simulacra, parallel to the utopian incarnation of the Book. This equation—the simulacrum or the book as woman—helps us to understand how sexual difference operates here. This in turn helps us to see how the operation of *mise en scène* (or in other words, of the simulacrum, male or female, and how this sexual difference is to be produced) underpins the abstract idea of the machine and historicizes it.

In this respect the interest of *The Future Eve* lies in the way it bridges two periods. At the end of the nineteenth century the representation of sexual difference was still for the most part dominated by a bourgeois-Romantic view-point and hence strongly asymmetrical. The simulacrum has its first heyday with the development of photography, the invention of the phonograph, and the (imminent) birth of the cinema. Villiers interprets these developments by projecting his Android into a future which his century could by and large accept. With the appearance of "new images," of the holograph, of cybernetics, and automation (not to mention new theories in biology), an environment takes shape in which the copy tends to rival the model—the theme has become commonplace today—the difference between the two threatens to disappear.

Recent films like *Blade Runner* or *Liquid Sky* are in their way typical of this state of things. And both films re-stage, in modern terms, the archetypal representation of *Metropolis*, a fact which reminds us of how close we have remained to Villiers's book.

There is one thing in particular which I would emphasize. Why, when transposed to the screen, is the construction of the Android found to be so gripping, whether in *Metropolis* or in *The Bride of Frankenstein*? Why do the films dwell on this scene in particular? It pertains, I think, to the nature of the medium. The actual process of substituting a simulacrum for a living being directly replicates the camera's power to reproduce automatically the reality it confronts. Every *mise en scène* of the simulacrum thus refers intrinsically to the fundamental properties of the cinematic apparatus. Villiers had a deep feeling for this. He understood, as had Baudelaire before him (his praise of makeup, of the fake, for example) that in the age of mechanical reproduction the artificial has become a determining condition for modernity. This he shows, as we have seen, in his own way: to limit the dangers of artifice, let us push it to its limits. The example he uses to illustrate this—the woman's gaze—is eloquent. His reasoning on this topic (a problem for the construction of the Android), touches directly on the material status of cinema, its most living core. "In our day," Edison explains, "carefully reared women have acquired a unique glance, sophisticated, conventional, truly charming (that's the word used) wherein everyone can find the expression he desires . . . . This glance can be photographed. After all, isn't it just a photograph itself?"(160). The scientist defies Lord Ewald to "find more living nullity in the glance of Miss Alicia than in that of her phantom"(160). What is the glance of the film star? Is it not the living photographic reproduction of the promise of love, tenderness or sex, the vast commercial gaze of shared desire? Villiers felt this so strongly that we can find in *The Future Eve* all the elements necessary for a consideration of the star as machine. To see the fully contoured image of Villiers's filmed body, we must first recall the phases of decomposition-recomposition described by Villiers as necessary for the transfer from Alicia's body to that of the Android, and then project the movement of this process onto a screen capable of capturing it in a complete illusion of reality.

Villiers went a long way towards giving us the full implications. He elaborated the institutional aspect of the fantasy which was at work in his own glance. It is true that Hadaly is portrayed as unique, as are Sowana, Edison, and Lord Ewald. And *The Future Eve*, with its praise of individualistic, aristocratic genius, is a self-enclosed book. But the Android is also, potentially, a mass product, infinitely multipliable. Her moral dimension implies a social mission, and Edison draws upon all of his powerful and precise rhetorical skills to persuade Lord Ewald of this. Consider again the remarkable powers of deduction Villiers gives to his character!

> I have come with this message: Since our gods and our aspirations are no longer anything but *scientific*, why shouldn't our loves be so, too? In place of that Eve of the forgotten legend, the legend despised and discredited by Science, I offer you a scientific Eve—the only one, I think, now worthy of those blighted visceral organs which you still—by a kind of sentimentality that you're the first to mock—call "your hearts" . . . . In a word, I have come, I, the "Wizard of Menlo Park," as they call me here, to offer the human beings of these new and up-to-date times to my scientific contemporaries as a matter of fact, something better than a false, mediocre, and ever-changing Reality(164).

This moral, scientific, and artistic program derives as much from a clearly worked-out industrial logic:

> Only the first Android was difficult. Once the general formula was written, all that remained was a kind of handicraft work. There's no doubt that within a few years, models like this one will be fabricated by the thousands; the first manufacturer who picks up this idea will be able to start the first factory for the production of Ideals(147).

A factory for the production of ideals. Using the utopia of the Book, has anyone outlined more vividly the institution of Cinema? And in its American version? Edison could easily be its prophet because he is the enunciator of Villiers's Book-of-Books.

7.

An unsubstantiated tradition has it that the Count Jean-Marie-Matthias-Philippe-Auguste de Villiers de l'Isle-Adam suffered severe distress, when he was seventeen, at the loss of a girl he loved too dearly. Her image filling his mind, Villiers's desire was fixed on three types of women. The first—and in this he resembled many men of his time—was the *demi-mondaine*. Louise Dyonnet was such, and though he was poor, as he always would be, he paid for her body as he paid her debts. His love for her, as he imagined it at least, was violent and passionate. He accused her (in a letter) of having made him live out an "accursed dream."

He was next attracted by the sweet calm of marriage. His choice fell upon Estelle Gautier, second daughter of Theophile Gautier, perhaps after having coveted the elder sister Judith (who remained friendly but preferred the poet Catulle Mendes). Villiers loved Estelle steadily and wholeheartedly, it seems. But his family, decadently and inflexibly aristocratic, threatened to cut off his income if he married the illegitimate daughter of a bourgeois who was anything but rich. Wretched, forced to live by his pen, he renounced the idea of marriage.

From then on he pursued a repetitive fantasy: an heiress whose wealth would permit him to restore his family's fortune and escutcheon. (Boasting that his lineage went back to the thirteenth century, he declared himself a candidate for several thrones). Three or four possible marriages were aborted because of this. On one occasion he even had the chance to realize this dream in the person of Anna Eyre Powell, a Scottish heiress whom he besieged in London, having first signed a contract with a marriage-broker. Enchanted by Anna, he wrote to Mallarmé and to Judith Gautier, calling her an "Angel" and "a dream out of Ossian." But his exuberance seems to have frightened the girl and he returned to Paris, disillusioned once more.

1878. Villiers is forty years old. He is starting to write *The Future Eve*. He is living in Paris in a poor neighborhood and a wretched house. He accepts the devoted service of a housekeeper, Marie-Elisabeth Dantine. She mends his worn clothing and in due time shares his bed. She has a son, Albert, from her first marriage. She is without charm or intelligence. In 1881 she gives birth to Villiers's son Victor, a son he is quite fond of. They live more or less together, but more as master and servant than as husband and wife or lover and mistress. With the irony and wisdom of despair, Villiers relinquishes a final hope for ideal love with Marie de Montifaud, woman of letters and adventurer.

1889. Villiers is even poorer, and seriously ill. Mallarmé initiates, discreetly, a *cotisation amicale*, a collection from Villiers's friends, to help with the writer's most pressing needs. Villiers worries about Victor's future: because of Marie's low social origins his son has remained illegitimate. He resolves himself to the obvious solution (to marry the mother and thus legitimate the child), on the condition that this humiliation not be inflicted on him until the last moment, when it would come to join "the supreme humiliation of death." It is a game he almost wins. Five days before his death, the Count Villiers de l'Isle-Adam marries Marie Dantine. The author of *The Future Eve* is joined to a woman who can neither read nor write, whose hand must be guided to sign the marriage contract, with Mallarmé as witness.

Translated by Stanley E. Gray

NOTES

1. *The Future Eve* was partially serialized in *L'Étoile française* (December 13, 1880 to February 4, 1881); later it was serialized in its entirety in *La Vie moderne* (July 18, 1885 to March 27, 1886). It appeared in book form in March, 1886.

   Edison's two patents on the phonograph were recorded in 1877 and 1878.

   I have respected the typographical markings used by Villiers for emphasis, in particular his use of italics and capital letters. See *L'Eve Future* in *Oeuvres de Villiers de l'Isle-Adam* (Club Français du Livre, 1957).

   [Translator's note: English quotations are taken from *Tomorrow's Eve*, trans. Robert Martin Adams (Urbana: University of Illinois Press, 1982). In some instances the translation has been modified for clarity and consistency. I have rendered the French title, *L'Eve Future*, as *The Future Eve*.]

2. In the course of writing this essay, I came across two other texts which share many of the same concerns: Max Milner's *La Fantasmagorie* (Paris: PUF, 1984) and Annette Michelson's "On the Eve of the Future: The Reasonable Facsimile and the Philosophical Toy," *October* 29, 1984.

3. Mallarmé, *Oeuvres complètes* (Paris: Gallimard (Pléiade), 1950), p.503.

4. In a first, and more naive, version of the great scene in which Lord Ewald encounters Hadaly, Lord Ewald was at first tempted to make Alicia appear through Hadaly. The Android makes him swear that he will tear off the metal ribbon which would make this transfiguration possible. This version is also of significant interest in that here Alicia is called Evelyn, a way of underlining the link between the two women. The linking is confirmed also by the title of the novella, *Miss Hadaly Habal*, whose date of composition is unsure but which contributed to the conception of *The Future Eve*.

5. This is why, Freud concludes, in the amorous state the object takes the place of the ego rather than that of the ego-ideal.

6. In technical language, we would say that Hadaly is for Edison an example of sublimation, whereas for Lord Ewald she is an idealization.

   Edison's final explanations of the Android clearly situate the overlap and the division shown by the two heroes. Before Hadaly becomes Alicia, she appears to Lord Ewald, by way of Sowana, through Edison. This explains the reason for the scene in which Hadaly gives a clairvoyant and minutely detailed description of Alicia in the train bringing her from New York to Menlo Park: all that was needed to make this clairvoyance possible was for Lord Ewald to touch the Android's hand. His own fluid, impregnated with Alicia's presence, thus enters into contact with that of Sowana and produces the required image. It also explains the "naturalness" of the dialogues between Lord Ewald and Hadaly: "And all I had to do was repeat, *but silently*, what you said, to have this spirit, unknown to both of us, hear what you had said, and then reply to it through the phantom"(212).

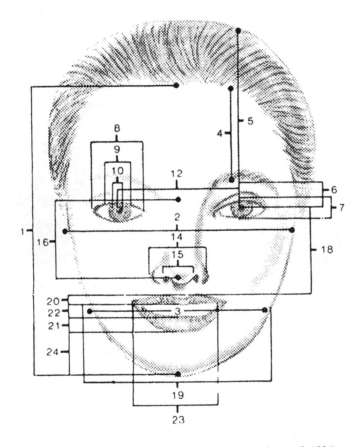

"Blueprint for Beauty," *The New York Times*, August 5, 1986

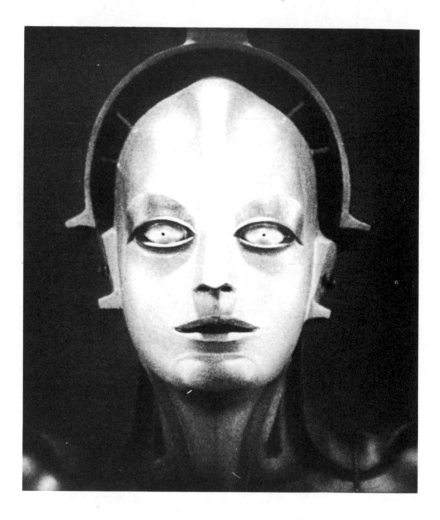

Metropolis
Mother-City—"Mittler"—Hitler
Roger Dadoun

> *I have never, if I may say so, been able to ask questions or think in any sense other than theological—precisely in keeping with the Talmudic precept concerning the forty-nine levels of meaning in every passage of the Torah.*
> Walter Benjamin, letter to Max Rychner

Metropolis is a German film made by Fritz Lang in 1926. It is commonly held to be a "classic" of cinema; some even call it a "masterpiece." Apart from the stylistic qualities that make it, for many viewers, one of the masterworks of expressionism, it is chiefly the film's moral, or ideology, that has been singled out for praise. The final sequence, a model of the "happy ending," depicts the emotional reconciliation of the employer with his workers, brought about by the employer's son, who, with the blessing of Maria, the pure young woman who is soon to become his wife, assumes the role of Mediator (*Mittler* in German). The film drew harsh words from some critics. H. G. Wells pronounced it "an amalgam of all the nonsense and platitudes we have ever heard, upon which is ladled a sentimental sauce like no other." More significantly, some critics have seen parallels with, not to say instances of, Nazi ideas, values, and fantasies. For Francis Courtade, "*Metropolis* is a fascist, pre-Nazi work." Siegfried Kracauer's analyses in *From Caligari to Hitler* provide valuable evidence in support of this judgment, in particular Lang's own statements to an American newspaper. When the Nazis came to power, Lang was summoned by propaganda chief Goebbels, who told him that he and Hitler had seen the film together some years earlier in a small provincial town. " . . . Hitler said [to Goebbels] at that time," Lang recounted, "that he wanted me to make the Nazis' pictures" (*New York World Telegram*, June 11, 1941, p.12). The theme of destiny being a recurrent favorite of Lang's, it is curious to note here the Nazi historical "destiny" of *Metropolis*. Before elaborating further on this point, I will briefly review the film's scenario. My main point, however, will be to demonstrate the need for, and pertinence of, psychoanalytic concepts in investigating the specifically filmic content of the work.

The Subject of *Metropolis*

Abbreviated to the bare minimum, the film's credits are as follows.

Producer: UFA, 1926. Director: Fritz Lang. Cameramen: Karl Freund, Günther Rittau. Special effects: Eugen Schüfftan. Set design: Otto Hunte, Erich Kettelhut, Karl Volbrecht. Music: Gottfried Huppertz. Cast: Brigitte Helm (Maria), Gustav Fröhlich (Freder), Alfred Abel (Joh Fredersen), Heinrich George (foreman), Rudolf Klein-Rogge (Rotwang the inventor), Theodor Loos (Joseph, Fredersen's secretary), Fritz Rasp (an employee of Fredersen), Erwin Binswanger, Heinrich Gotho, Margarete Lanner, Georg John, Walter Kuhle, Erwin Vater, Grete Berger, Olly Böheim, Helene Weigel, and Anny Hintze.

Briefly summarized, the story goes like this:

Metropolis is a gigantic city of the future, filled with enormous skyscrapers. Workers are housed below ground, along with factories and machinery. There they live a hellish existence as slaves subservient to the needs of mechanized production. Above ground, in the Upper City, are the vast offices of industrialist Joh Fredersen, master of Metropolis, who dictates his orders to squads of secretaries; complementing the office building is an Edenic Garden, where the masters' sons frolic.

Into this garden, which is protected by an imposing gateway, wanders Maria, the daughter of a worker, surrounded by a group of wretched children. She stares long and hard at Freder Fredersen, the employer's son, who stands transfixed, as though hypnotized. "These are your brothers," she says, pointing to the children. She is then driven out of the garden, but her visit has revealed to the son the horrible conditions in which workers live. As though walking in his sleep, Freder descends into the machine room. We see a tableau of workers on the job. An explosion takes place, killing some and injuring others. Freder then goes to see his father, who curtly informs him that class division is inevitable and that the worker must toil for his daily bread. The worker's place is "down below." A secretary, Joseph, is fired for not keeping an adequate guard. He contemplates suicide, but Freder prevents him from going through with it and they become friends.

Freder returns to the machine room and assumes the place of a worker. For ten long hours he submits to the torture of labor. Along with other worn-out laborers he then descends into the catacombs, where he finds Maria, immaculately white and gleaming, preaching patience and prophesying the coming of a "mediator." Meanwhile, the father, to whom a foreman has handed over plans found on the bodies of dead workers, turns for advice to the inventor Rotwang, who describes his masterpiece: a robot that never tires and never makes an error, designed to replace the human worker. The two go down into the catacombs and observe Maria's preaching from a hiding place. The father asks Rotwang to make the robot look like Maria. Thus disguised, the robot could be used to incite the workers to rebellion.

Rotwang, alone, continues to watch Maria. She approaches the kneeling Freder and kisses him. When Freder leaves, Rotwang pursues Maria and after a fierce struggle seizes her and carries her off. He ties her down and forces her to undergo a transformation. The mechanism of the robot is concealed beneath an outer shell that exactly resembles Maria. Thus the robot becomes her double. (I shall refer to the robot thus disguised as the False Maria, to distinguish it from the Real Maria.) Freder sets out in search of Maria but is caught and imprisoned in Rotwang's house, where he hears the girl's cries.

The False Maria is shown to the father. Fascinated by the resemblance, he takes her by the shoulders. The son arrives, witnesses the scene, and falls ill. The False Maria is presented to an audience of employers dressed in tuxedos and performs an extraordinary, erotic dance. She then returns underground and incites the workers to rebellion. A frenzied mob invades the machine room and wreaks havoc. There is fire and flooding. The Real Maria manages to escape and heads for the workers' city to save the children. Freder joins her in this task. The workers, suddenly aware of the situation, lay hold of the False Maria, tie her to a stake, and set her afire. The flames destroy her human covering but leave the inner mechanism intact. "Witch!" cries the mob. Rotwang pursues the Real Maria to the top of the cathedral, himself pursued by Freder. The two men fight and Rotwang falls. The father, on his knees, says, "Praise God!" On the porch of the cathedral the father advances, flanked by his son and Maria. Ahead of them a disciplined troop of workers in triangular formation also advances. The foreman steps out ahead and walks toward the boss. The son takes his father's hand and joins it to the foreman's. Thus the "heart" completes its mission of "mediating" between "hand and brain."

This summary, which may seem rather drawn out, is necessary for my purposes. Readers who have not seen the film need to know the main points of the plot. Those who have seen the film generally recall only brief snatches. Even the few who have seen *Metropolis* numerous times fail to recall all its details. Film criticism operates under an essential handicap: the raw material is evanescent. Fleeting images are lost forever (occasioning what has been called *le deuil cinématique*, or mourning of the lost image). When the substance of a film is rendered in words (as it must be in criticism), images are systematically eliminated. Hence the narration of a film plot always sounds like a rather tedious anecdote. The analogy with the psychoanalytic patient's account of a dream is obvious.

The Production of *Metropolis*: UFA

No film is unaffected by the material and ideological conditions under which it is produced. This is especially true of *Metropolis*, a film that played an important part in the ambitious plans of UFA (Universum Film Aktiengesellschaft, "one of the most powerful political filmmaking trusts that Europe has ever known." The corporation was set up with government capital made available by Ludendorff, a proponent of pan-Germanist policies for whom the war had amply demonstrated "the power of images and film as a means of educating and influencing the masses," and with private capital provided by a number of well-known trusts: Krupp Steel, I.G. Farben (chemicals), A. E. G. (electrical equipment), and Deutsche Bank, to name a few. The firm's mission was to produce films that would distract attention from reality ("escapist pictures," or *Traumfilms*) and in various ways cast doubt on the prospects for revolution. Later, under the Nazis, the film industry carried this policy even further, producing a mix of love comedies, elaborate production numbers, and Viennese operettas, apparently with great success: the *Encyclopédie du cinéma* reports that "in 1942 more than a billion movie tickets were sold in Hitler's Greater Reich." At the time *Metropolis* was made, the president of UFA was a publishing magnate by the name of Alfred Hugenberg, who was also the leader of the extreme right-wing "Steel Helmets" group and a financial contributor to Hitler's Nazi Party. Lang's wife, Thea von Harbou, approved of the Nazis's ideas; after Lang's departure in 1933, she remained active, making films for the Nazis.

UFA wanted *Metropolis* to be "the greatest film of all time." Advertising for the picture (which should be taken with a grain of salt) underscored the colossal character of the project: 310 days and 60 nights of shooting, from 22 March 1925 to 30 October 1926; 6 million marks; 750 actors; 26,000 male extras, 11,000 female extras, and 750 children; 1,300,000 meters of positive film and 620,000 meters of negative film; as well as 2,000 pairs of shoes, 75 wigs, 50 automobiles, and so on. The film followed the *Nibelungen*, an ambitious vehicle for traditional mythological themes, written and directed by Lang and Thea von Harbou in 1923-1924. The gargantuan size of the *Metropolis* project, in keeping with its overall ideological aims, could hardly fail to elicit a certain "gigantism" not only in the treatment of scenery and architecture and the use of extras but even more in the nature of the filmic discourse that was developed—a discourse of the paranoid type. To put the point in somewhat different terms, there is a certain accord or unity or interaction between the historical, political, financial, and existential or personal circumstances in which a film is made and the fantasy materials that shape or enter into the composition of the filmic text. In other words, the various elements that make up the film (characters, situations, forms, technical procedures, and so on), though in a sense circumscribed by history and politics, cannot be adequately articulated and organized except in terms of the unconscious processes and fantasy structures discovered by psychoanalysis. This, at any rate, is what I shall attempt to show in the remainder of this essay.

The Mother-City Metropolis and Its Inner Divisions

Etymologically *Metropolis* means "mother-city" (from the Greek *meter*, mother + *polis*, city). This historical residue of meaning is structurally embodied in the title, with all its cultural overtones; these overtones are marshalled into waves of meaning that animate the film as a whole (making it literally a "moving picture").

Metropolis is, superlatively, the City. The ranks of massive skyscrapers in the opening frames make this quite clear (these images were supposedly suggested to Lang by his first sight of New York City). Yet the masses of stone punctuated by square black openings in cold, geometric patterns do not stand erect like the Empire State Building in *King Kong*, for example, where the image of phallic erection is driven home by the lengthy scene in which the ape laboriously climbs the tower. In *Metropolis*, by contrast, oblique spotlights play over the buildings' naked facades and seem to lift or remove their skin; the moving spotlights weave the fabric of the city and, from the film's opening moments, suggest a stripping, skinning, or peeling away.

The city is sealed, closed in on itself, like a womb. The only movement we see (apart from the symmetrical, sublimating ascent in the cathedral) proceeds along tortuous, bowel-like passageways into the lower depths, the catacombs, to the central, altar-like structure where the two Marias stand and preach. Nature is almost totally absent; it is alluded to twice, once in the story of Babel, which is retold in the film (through a gray and barren landscape endless columns of slaves haul huge building stones—nature is thus petrified in myth and in stone), and again in two brief sequences. One of these depicts the Edenic garden, which is treated in painterly fashion with a pool, fountains, vegetation, and great white birds. But this garden stands behind an imposing gateway; it is a hothouse, an *objet d'art*, an artificial production. The second sequence reinforces this interpretation of nature: the sumptuous room occupied by the son, Freder, has walls covered with stylized plant motifs. Nature is reduced to a decorative sign, crushed and flattened against the surface of stone. These motifs (in all senses of the word) of petrifaction establish a complex of fantasies that plays an important part in the film's libidinal economy.

The film's opening frames consist of long, static shots of building models. These are immediately followed by more dynamic, animated shots, with impressive close-ups of machines, or, more precisely, of parts and pieces of machines, partial objects, cogs and complex mechanisms that throb, churn, reciprocate, or rotate. Looking at the image from close up, one might say: it is moving, it is turning within. One point should be made at once, before these images are subsumed in subsequent social and technological totalities: within this city of surfaces, this tissue of stone, there is something—the id (*ça*)—moving, working mechanically, like a machine. And since there is nothing in these frames but pieces of machines working without either raw materials or finished products, we can say: it (*ça*) is working on itself. Now, the usefulness of theory is that it enables us to transform this last statement as follows: the id (*le Ça*), the unconscious, asserts itself as a productive drive or mechanism; it is formed by or takes the form of machinery, a complex, repetitive, articulated interaction of various operations and processes. These quick opening images make it perfectly clear what the film's ideological and cultural position concerning mass production, exploitation, and alienation will be. More than that, they give the key to the production and development of images and signifers; we might even say that they reveal the film's id: together, the work of the id and the work of the film are intertwined, as cinematographic technique and unconscious processes cooperate in the animation, development, deployment, and organization of figures and forms.

The first and perhaps the primordial operation is the division of the city into two radically different parts, which are kept separate by edict of the father/owners. This hierarchical division is strongly influenced by mythological and religious tradition (God began the creation of the world by separating the "upper" from the "lower" waters). The Upper City is that of the masters and owners, the superior place of supreme and total authority. Here, thought is magisterial. (Fredersen's huge office reflects the enormous size of his brain, which is indicated in the film by pointing: in one frame he is shown lying on his back, and before continuing with his speech he moves two fingers close to his head.) Here pleasure is as readily available as it was in the Garden of Eden (not unlike the garden in which the sons of the owners cavort). This is the "good" city. "Good" means that it is the owners who establish the law and name all things; we are reminded, too, of the Kleinian notion of the "good" mother.

The Lower City, where the workers work and reside, lies in the "lower depths." It is composed of three rather different layers, one lying more or less above the next: the machine room, the vast territory of labor, suffering, and death (which appears as Moloch in a hallucination experienced by Freder, the son); the workers' dwellings, which are seen, briefly, only from the outside, densely packed around an empty central square; and finally the catacombs, decorated with skeletons and bones. This is clearly the "bad" part of the city.

The spatial division of the city is mirrored in various ways, including the striking, indeed frightening and spectacular division of the Maria character into two quite distinct, indeed antagonistic, parts (the same actress, Brigitte Helm, plays both). Maria is clearly a maternal figure in two senses: the Real Maria is the "good" mother, and the False Maria is the "bad" mother.

In her first appearance, when she enters the garden of the sons after hurdling, as if by miracle, all the obstacles, Maria—the Real Maria, the Good Maria—is surrounded by a host of small children over whom she extends her arms, creating a sheltered zone outlined by the placenta-like veil that hangs from her shoulders. When she points to the children and says to Freder, "They are your brothers," he is so thunderstruck that he stops his lovemaking and places his hand on his heart, a gesture that will be repeated throughout the film; Maria thus turns him into a "child," an "infant." He becomes, in a sense, one of "her" children. Maria's maternal protective function is clearly in evidence in the catastrophe near the end of the film. She saves the children from the flood, rescues them from the water. A deliberately theatrical image, elaborate and decorative, shows her standing on a sort of pedestal in the small square at the center of the workers' city, surrounded by clusters of children who clutch her body. The central object, the gong that she sounds to give the alarm, is circular in shape with a protrusion at the center, exactly like a breast. What is more, Maria occupies, or is identified with, yet another central space that obviously resembles a uterus: the cave at the bottom of the catacombs, reached at the end of a laborious and somber "descent into the underworld." There stands a sort of altar, bristling with tall crosses and candles, a typical place of meditation. Maria's name here takes on its full religious significance. Like Mary she is an immaculate virgin all dressed in white, a virgin mother with arms extended in a cross as she raises her veil, and her evangelical speech soothes the pain of the workers and announces the coming of a messiah, the Mediator (*Mittler*). In this closed, mystical space, Maria's speech evokes and opens up, through a fantastic process of infinite regression, another, still deeper region, a more primordial mythical space, built around the story of the Tower of Babel. This provides Fritz Lang with the opportunity to indulge in (or reveal himself in) various fantastic, large-scale directorial effects: huge, crushing blocks of stone, endless staircases rising toward infinity, gray, antlike slaves emerging in interminable columns from the gray earth, great circles of light that swallow up the sky. In this hallucination, however, the Tower of Babel itself is nothing but a scale model, a paltry thing, a humble erection around which the masters gather to meditate. To all this colossal imagery Lang attaches, in grandiose letters as on an advertising billboard, the principle of a spectacularly inflated religious humanism: "Great is the Creator and Great is Man!"

A clearly more complex, extraordinary, and disturbing figure than the Real Maria, the False Maria (the robot disguised beneath Maria's skin and sharing her appearance) stands out immediately as an imago of the "bad" mother, flaunting herself as a de-naturation of the "good" Maria with her lascivious winks and smiles, her stiff arm, and so forth. Significantly, it is the False Maria, far more than the would-be terrifying gestures of Rotwang, who frightens children aged five or six who see *Metropolis*. The False Maria systematically repeats in the "wicked" mode all that the Real Maria does in the "good" mode. She occupies the same key points in space and enters into relations with the same objects (Rotwang, Freder, the mob, etc.), each time inverting or subverting the system of values, that is, turning them upside down so as to reveal an archaic and repressed layer. We, too, must subvert this figure, turn it over, in order to discover its primordial meaning. The appearance will turn out to be the deeper meaning: the human skin that covers the metallic robot is precisely what the robot is trying to hide. The progress of the narrative itself suggests another reversal of this figure: born a mechanical contrivance wreathed in the prestige of science, a science fiction robot, the False Maria ends up a witch, burned at the stake.

The distressing and horrifying primitive maternal dimension of the False Maria is established chiefly in the various primal scenes that occur at intervals throughout the film. Before examining them, let me point out the notable absence of any individualized, homogeneous, and named maternal figure. Freder, the hero of the film, has no mother that we know of. When he falls ill, it is always his father that we see at his side. The fact that the institution of motherhood is so thoroughly expunged from the film makes it clear that the whole burden of maternity is carried by the two Marias, and that the maternal dimension underlies (*fonde*) and merges into (*se fond dans*) the totality of Metropolis, the mother-city.

The Underlying Structure of *Metropolis*: The Primal Scene

Fusion, diffusion, and scrambling of figures, forms, and values beneath apparently solid, one-dimensional entities: therein lies part of the wealth and originality of *Metropolis*. So complex are the displacements and overdeterminations that there is scarcely an image in the film that cannot occupy the most surprising positions at any of the forty-nine levels of Talmudic interpretation. Yet the unusual abundance of signifiers is powerfully polarized by an organizing structure: the primal scene, which through a series of frequent reiterations occupies nearly the entire film. The most typical sequence occurs near the middle, as if in the center or "heart" of the film, and it brings into play a cinematographic rhetoric of rare virtuosity. Rotwang, the scientist, has made a robot that looks like Maria and sends it off to be examined by Fredersen. The latter is struck, moved, and seduced by the resemblance. He stares hard at the young woman, moves closer to her, places his hands on her shoulders. The woman plays the seductress with eyes, smile, and body. At that moment the son, looking for Maria, bursts into his father's office. He sees his father and Maria locked in a quasi-embrace. Dumbfounded, he feels the ground fall away; he staggers, and to his eyes, deluded by madness, the couple seems to draw together and begins to whirl about. The two figures—two parents now—are linked together in a rotation, caught up in a blur in which dark and light lines seem to merge. This geometry, these crossed and rotating figures create—do they not?—a swastika: two entwined bodies with four arms. Transfixed as by the sight of Medusa, the son sees an immense, expanding black hole dotted with glowing spots of light (phantasms in the strict sense) and experiences a sense of falling into a void, a loss of consciousness or, better, of a loss of the unconscious, as horror takes refuge in illness: Freder falls ill. After the spectacular image of the fall, we return to Freder lying in bed, racked by fever and hallucinations.

Furthermore, these hallucinations, indicated by Freder's haggard look of fright and horror, establish a link to another version of the primal scene, which is characterized not by traumatic effects but by an extreme, frantic voyeurism, lavishly filmed. The father leaves the room of his sick son to attend the dinner given by Rotwang. We see a crowd of employers, masters, all wearing tuxedos. All are men, who can be considered doubles of the son, because a very effective parallel montage alternates between, and hence identifies, the son and the guests, portraying their common vision of the scene. The purpose of the dinner is to introduce the False Maria, to present her to the public. In a very precise sense, therefore, she is re-presented. A large, glowing object, a sort of basin or cup, slowly rises. An enormous cover is raised, and the False Maria, splendidly dressed, slowly emerges. She spreads her veils, exhibits her almost naked body, and begins to dance. Her whole body revolves at a dizzying rate, turning faster and faster until all that can be seen is a moving, sinuous, serpentine line. Intensely, totally absorbed in voyeurism, the audience is all eyes, all stares—quite literally (or, since it is an image that is involved, iconically): a repeated frame shows a series of huge eyes, a mosaic of fascinated stares, of eyes popping out of heads. Plucked from their sockets, these eyes leave the spectators' tense bodies and voluptuously attach themselves to the spectacle. This is a hallucinatory voyeurism in two senses: it is a hallucination created by the technical means of the cinema, with the shot of a mosaic of eyes, and it is a psychological hallucination of the son, who, lying unconscious in his bed, follows the action. What this complex scene of the dancer watched by voyeurs reveals is that the False Maria is more than just a simple figuration of the "bad" mother. The choreographic rotation, which confuses the feminine shapes of the body and links belly, breasts, thighs, shoulder, and head in a brilliant serpent-like coil, together with the sumptuous display of the hot and smoking cup or basin, suggests that the False Maria should be seen as a condensed, pantomime representation of the primal scene. Recall that the False Maria is in fact composed of two radically different parts, joined together and perfectly fused (and the crucial importance of the process of fusion in the primal scene can hardly be overstated): a rigid metallic form, the robot, and a soft, feminine envelope of lovely flesh, extorted by Rotwang from Maria's body. In other words—to reduce it to the simplest possible conceptual terms—the robot is part phallus, indeed a sort of phallic principle. I say phallic principle because it cannot be clearly defined as either father or son: after the coupling with the father, he and the robot separate, and the robot goes off to serve as provocateur, sowing discord. At one point, when the mob believes that it has won a victory, the robot is even brandished like a trophy, a totem erected on the shoulders of all the sons, workers and bourgeois alike, joined together in communion. The robot is also the object in which the socio-political paternity of Fredersen couples and combines with the technological-scientific paternity of Rotwang. Thus the robot assumes the paternal functions of tyranny, repression, and punishment. But it also assumes the filial functions of criticism, accusation, resistance, and rebellion. (Here the robot is like the severed phallus of Rotwang, who has been symbolically castrated, his hand cut off, for having dared to lay hands on Mother Nature, for having "had" her, to use a slang term [French: entuber] that suggests the tubular machinery that fills his laboratory. The Promethean nature of Rotwang's enterprise is underscored by the shot that shows him, in the presence of the frightened Fredersen, claiming victory by raising his stump covered with a glove whose black color links it to the black shell of the Robot that stands motionless behind him. Like the liver of Prometheus eternally regenerating itself, the black form of the robot, which the hysterical crowd has accused of witchcraft, survives the flames at the stake, cackling with the witch's blasphemous phallic laughter. The son's phallus is structurally heretical; no hell can annihilate it, and no mutilation, castration, or Inquisition can do away with it. Neither the robot nor Rotwang really dies in the film, as we shall see.) Thus the robot is in part the phallus, a mobile, inner core. But it is also—the second aspect of the construct known as the False Maria—the primordial maternal skin, the placenta, the hot, protective envelope, swollen by the heat, engorged as Hermann would say, and detached from Maria's body: pure intumescence, then, which returns to the bonfire in the ritual consummation of the burning forest (to borrow again from Hermann). This montage of mother-upon-phallus is a traditional but always impressive and fecund condensation, source of monsters from the Sphinx to the Gorgon: the False Maria is a monster of this type, a splendid mythological creation of cinema, baby sister of the formidable King Kong and a woman who no doubt seduced and aroused her own creator, Lang himself, who was able to find the precise shot to express his fascination: a montage of dazzled eyes exploring as a louse might the voluptuous woman's skin (voluptuous and—if the reader will permit—*volutueuse*, or curvaceous, flesh; the latter word, through its Latin roots *volvere*, *volutum*, suggests *vulva* or *volva*, vulva or womb). The primal dance, which the son hallucinates in his neonatal bed while his doubles, the men at the dinner, look on as voyeurs, is wonderfully amplified by the scenery. The vast smoking tub —pelvis of what phylogenetic mother?—from which the False Maria emerges (inwardly armed, one might say) is one of many circular shapes, along with its cover and the circle that surrounds Maria's head, and the curves of the veils and the hairdo and the woman's body. The tub itself is decorated with a motif of hydra-headed serpents upon which the dancer rests her body. The polymorphic sensuality of the dance and the use of redundant signifiers produce a powerful image of the primal scene. (It is not without interest to note that the spectator can easily miss various shots in the sequence just described, particularly the guard of hydra-headed serpents that surrounds the False Maria. In analyzing a film, what was not seen is just as important as what was.)

For the unconscious, of course, no amount of repetition is enough, nor can the variety of repetition be exhausted. In the major scenes analyzed above, sight and its hallucinatory representation of reality are the key elements. This is perfectly consistent with the rest of the film, in which eyes and gazes are powerfully omnipresent. In yet a third version of the primal scene, we are given highly dramatic "shots" of auditory perceptions. (I do not think that it is a misnomer to speak of "shots" of sound in this silent film, because the pantomime and gesticulations are so eloquent, not to say piercing.) These shots accompany, or more precisely herald, a sumptuous technological and "scientific" treatment of the fantasy. As further evidence of the film's innovative style and depth of comprehension of fantasy, primitive memories of the primal scene are given material embodiment in a very theatrical way: an unusual architectural form, a sort of curved or swollen triangle, like a grubby wart grown up, oddly (and insolently) enough, in the vicinity of the great cube-like workers' dwellings and the cathedral. The text says: "In the midst of the city stood an old house." Meaningful paradox: this old building houses the futuristic laboratory of Rotwang, "the genius inventor." Redundancy always multiplies the meanings of an image. Here, the notions Old, Ancient, Primal are emblematically inscribed in what we see as the label or trademark of occultism and the esoteric tradition, the five-pointed star or pentacle, which appears on the entrance to the house, on various inner doors, and, in a more monumental way, on the wall against which the robot's seat is placed; the head of the robot seems to fit inside the star's lower triangular cavity.

Freder hears Maria's cries as Rotwang drags her through the dark corridors of his house, which, given his predatory behavior and the nature of his victim, might also be called his den or lair. The son enters the house in a strange way. Rage and magic mingle and alternate as all doors resist Freder's blows only to open and close suddenly of their own accord—an imperious determinism that suggests both the omnipotent magic of infantile thought and the perfectly ordered structure of fantasy, which here requires a son caught in a trance and trapped in an enclosed room entombed in stone, petrified, while all around the alchemist continues with his work.

In a technological forest bristling with tubes swollen with black sap, with throbbing balloons, quivering levers, thermometers, measuring devices, and rotating coils (serpentins), Rotwang bustles about, rapidly moving his hands—the black and the white—over all his "gadgets." This energetic overexcitation centers on and culminates in a sort of glowing white sphere, a sun-like globe mounted high up in the room, which its radiant energy makes "fertile." Maria lies in a glass coffin, her body girded or encircled by black metal rings which create around it something like a space of pregnancy. Waves or rays or filaments of nervous electricity traverse this region and penetrate the body of the passive victim. The other Maria, the robot, mirrors this composition exactly. Motionless in a seated position, the robot is connected to the Real Maria by numerous filaments that slither across the floor like serpents. Large, glowing, white rings circle the robot's body and rotate around it, rising and falling as they turn in an accelerated masturbatory motion. Merely by changing the sign, we can view the black robot as engaged in frenzied copulation, moving rapidly in and out of its hot white sheath. Excitation reaches its peak in the orgiastic atmosphere of the laboratory. Rotwang, after his period of intense activity, is nothing but a gaze contemplating the miraculous impregnation. The robot acquires vessels, nerves, and organs and begins to move; a human skin now covers its structure. Maria, drained, lets her head fall to one side, in a primal gesture suggesting both orgasm and death. The creative act is done. A door opens, freeing the son and allowing the story to proceed.

This is a scene of remarkable density, and it is instructive to compare it with a similar sequence, also depicting the creation of a woman, in *The Bride of Frankenstein*, where the same battery of signifiers is used: electrical charges and discharges, light waves, ringlike forms, mechanical motions of the robot gradually changing to more supple human movements, and so on. In *Metropolis* a subtle movement and interplay of forms makes the scene unusually arresting. Inventor, creator, and impregnator, Rotwang is single, double, and multiple all at once: he is the paternal and divine One, symbolized by the solar globe from which all energy emanates (a globe heated until it glows red, suggesting the inventor's very name—Rot-wang, or red cheek; *Wange* also designates clay and hands). He is sovereign over the empirical realm as well as the realm of reproduction. Yet he is a man who not only desires, conceives, orders, and carries out the experiment but also contemplates it: after conceiving it and then carrying it out, he follows its progress with his eyes, in a state of anxious fascination. Thus he assumes the role of the voyeuristic son, the passive witness of the scene. He is the double (in both senses of the word) of the excluded and banished son. Prostrate, the son is castrated; his entire body fails to achieve erection. Rotwang takes on this aspect of castration. His severed hand is punishment for his filial curiosity and establishes a female component of his personality, clearly indicated by his black gown. Finally, Rotwang is multiple in that he disintegrates into the innumerable objects that he manipulates and operates; he is one with his devices (for it is these that we contemplate in his laboratory-lair). The mother herself is double, Maria and the robot. This split is pregnant with sexual dualities, moreover: both figures exhibit a phallic rigidity (Maria in her catatonic state and the robot with its stiff black metal structure, which also allows the phallic axis to be inscribed on the anal register) while the rings and circles suggest feminine and maternal curves. Add to this the plethora (of energy as well as forms) evident in the wires and filaments that fill the zone of copulation with waves and rings, which one cannot fail to recognize as the nerve rays imagined by Judge Schreber in his paranoid fantasy of sexual action at a distance.

Rotwang's dual function—as paranoid father and creator and as rebellious rival son—is also apparent in two more or less symmetrical sequences, one of which ends in triumph, the other in failure. The first precedes and lays the groundwork for the great technological primal scene analyzed above: Maria, having finished her sermon and bestowed her kiss upon Freder, is left alone when Freder departs. Nearby, Rotwang, having concluded his alliance with Fredersen, is left alone when Fredersen departs. In the dark, primitive depths of a cavern, he follows Maria by focusing the beam of his lamp on her. Lang's stylistic virtuosity is given free rein to indulge the expressionist taste for effects of light and shadow, for contrasts of black and white that set off, engulf, or heighten actual forms. In her flight Maria runs into jagged walls, gazes in horror upon skulls and skeletons, and finally succumbs to Rotwang's attack. Duration is here an important part of the meaning: the scene clearly lasts longer than is required by the narrative or the representation of a fantasy. The insistence on these effusions of the imagination is more than just aesthetic license. A principle is laid down, made explicit by images of pursuit, confinement, and death: psychic mechanisms are inflexible, overwhelming, and inexorable. Indeed, I would call the whole sequence principled. It establishes, first, the principle that fantasies are causal, which governs the progress of the entire film. Second, it lays down a general principle of fate (pursuit, confinement, death), which is so important an element in all of Lang's work and which is masterfully expressed in the psychopath's confession scene in *M*. Maria stands with her back to a wall as Rotwang slowly and almost sensually raises the beam of his lamp over her body. In a close-up her face appears to be divided in two: the dark upper portion endures the hypnotic power of Rotwang's sparkling eyes, while the lower portion gleams white in the light cast by Rotwang's lamp, held at mouth level. Maria is thus the object of a hypnotic stare and the focus of a rigid beam of light. Both touch her and hold her still, cover or penetrate her. Sexual action at a distance takes place thanks to an upward displacement of the phallic power. Rotwang's barred phallus (*phallus barré*) moves off (slang: *se barre*) in two directions at once, establishing Rotwang's extreme ambivalence. Intellectual sublimation invests the eyes with a power of penetration-fascination of a hypnotic type, which literally holds the object at a distance: this is the scientist's expert gaze. On the other hand, a process of regression tends to polarize and structure various libidinal investments around the mouth, producing a sexual syncretism (mouth as anus, urethra, phallus, etc.) characteristic of Hitler's libidinal structure (as we shall see in a moment). The sadistic element implicit in this displacement (piercing eyes, mouth spewing forth its luminous jet) is underscored by several shots of skeletons and finally triumphs in the aggressive posture of Rotwang, who dominates Maria and brutally holds her against and beneath him in an embrace-rape that is almost a preliminary take of the great scene of impregnation that follows.

In the final part of the film, Rotwang revives his aggression against Maria, but now every effort ends in failure. The triumphal birth of the False Maria is offset by the robot's immolation at the stake. The depths of the cave in which Maria was caught are countered by the heights of the cathedral to which she escapes. The alliance with Fredersen that was sealed in the cave is broken off. Above all, the lonely, diabolical work of the scientist now gives way to public confrontation with the hero Freder. For this battle a mythological atmosphere is created by a striking low-angle shot. This, together with gargoyles and a Manichaean handling of shapes, confirms Maria's maternal function by distinguishing, in that complex of forms named Rotwang, the grimacing figure of a "wicked," incestuous son, diabolical brother of the "good," angelic Freder, who is set up as the protector of the "good" mother. Rotwang, the "bad" son, symbolizes the "bad" mother with his black gown and black robot. The whirl of images is dizzying: the "bad" son engenders the "bad" mother as much as she engenders him. The themes are Hitlerian: "bad" sons—intellectuals, homosexuals, rebels, Semites, and so forth—have created a bad Germany. Purification will come through extermination and fire.

The "good" son triumphs as Rotwang plunges into the abyss. The father, on his knees, says "Praise God!" This suggests that Rotwang's fall is to be interpreted as the fall of Lucifer. Indeed, in the glowing globe and the beams and coils of light we have seen Rotwang as *luci-fer*, bearer of light; hence he is cast out of Heaven, where God reigns. But the images tell the story: the "wicked one" is not destroyed. The flames may destroy the False Maria's outer covering of flesh, but they leave the robot's inner structure intact. Rotwang falls, but we know not where. The "black nakedness of wickedness" (Michaux) regains the shadows, where it may carry on with its evil work. To track him down, the "good" sons dress in black and, as they set out to eradicate evil amid the sound of bonfires and marching boots, tirelessly repeat that the battle is never-ending, that the extermination of the wicked knows no respite or remission or end. If "wickedness" can assume the guise of the "good" mother herself, it can hide anywhere. But here I am extrapolating in terms of known history the unconscious tendencies that Lang's film obscures, precisely with regard to Rotwang's fall. The slate must be wiped clean before the supreme displacement can occur: once the figures of fantasy are gone, the subjects of ideology can make their entrance—theater of representation, elevation of the Representatives.

The Mediator: From "Mittler" to Hitler

The final sequence is shot in a theatrical way. We first see a deserted, empty space in front of the cathedral, a stage waiting for the play to begin. Then an audience arrives: the army of workers, in close triangular formation, moving forward in disciplined ranks (or rows), rises from the bottom of the screen. The cathedral serves as backdrop, frame, and enclosure of the final scene. Fredersen, Freder, and Maria pass through a narrow door and are somewhat surprised to find themselves at the dawn of a new day, so to speak, beneath the maternal arch of the porch. The foreman steps out ahead of the group of workers, brawny and awkward in his respect for authority. A pantomime (with movements of the arms, looks, hesitations, and signs of awkwardness and embarrassment) makes it clear that something seeks to be represented, and that the characters do not yet perfectly embody their roles. Perhaps this scene should be called a "super-representation": before us we see not mere circumstantial characters playing to a passive audience, but well-defined socio-economic and ideological entities identified by name. The foreman represents labor (the hand); Fredersen represents capital (the brain). Freder, along with his double, the white shadow of Maria, represents mediation (the heart). Thus the heart, composed, as in sentimental postcards, of two curves, links capital to labor. Hands that had groped tentatively toward one another join in a handshake, and linked arms stretch horizontally across the frame in a composition now in a sense egalitarian, all angles, volumes, and vertical differentiations having been eliminated in the general leveling. Such is the ideological platitude of this happy ending in the form of a handshake; the vast, heterogeneous, contradictory spaces explored by the film are relegated to a place somewhere behind the screen. But they can be brought back in full delirium, by a mere squeeze of the hand: Hitler's manacles, brutally applied, will give the madness a new lease on life.

The triangular structure of the final scene repeats the triangles and diagonals that delimit figures and movements throughout the film. (To meet Maria in the triangular hollow of the catacombs, for example, the workers descend along a left-to-right diagonal, while Rotwang and Fredersen follow a right-to-left diagonal.) Particularly spectacular is the black triangle formed by the army of workers as it moves into center screen; heads lowered, the workers move in lock-step, a black sea of slaves. The robot, seated on its chair with wires coming down diagonally on both sides, also formed a black triangle, repeated once more in the pyramid of the bonfire and in certain of Rotwang's attitudes. Rotwang, the robot, and the workers are thus parts of the same triangle, which rises from below (energy rises into the robot's body, just

as the flames of the bonfire mount the stake and the workers' formation moves up toward the cathedral). This lower triangle is the "bad"
triangle, as is indicated by stiffness and blackness—in a sense phallic,
as we have seen. And just as the robot's head penetrated the lower triangular cavity of the pentacle, so, too, do the square workers' platoons
penetrate Moloch's wide-open mouth, and Rotwang the inventor raises
his black hand to begin the impregnation of the robot. But this interpretation conflicts with too much of the evidence: the femininity of Rotwang, the castrated male dressed in a black gown; the fact that the
robot's head does not so much penetrate the cavity of the star as reinforce it; the robot's female flesh, destroyed by the flames; and so on.
Accordingly, the phallic interpretation of this hardware seems rather
misleading to me, valid and pertinent though it may be in some respects.
It is a smokescreen, an overestimation, intended to conceal a more fundamental truth, something especially frightening, indeed truly horrifying, which can now be revealed simply by inverting the form or relation:
turned upside down, belly up, the black triangle turns out to be the V
shape of the female genitals. Recall that the False Maria consists of two
parts, internal and external. A feminine skin, a swollen womb, materi-
ally covers the robot's phallic metal structure. But we can now say, at
an even deeper level, in fantasy, that it is the phallic robot that hides
and covers the female sex organ in the very act of exhibiting it. Rotwang's complex figure also requires reinterpretation: his spectacular
powers as impregnator and father, his aggressive virility, are mere
pretenses designed to distract our attention from such less visible or
striking signs as his black gown and missing hand-phallus. These signs
point to a rich vein of hidden femininity in this highly ambivalent figure.
Hence it follows that the black triangle stands primarily for the female
genitals, and that the determination to deny, denigrate, camouflage,
repress, and destroy it (by crushing the workers, crushing Rotwang,
burning the robot, and so on) indicates horror of the female organ, and,
since the female organ stands for sex in general, horror of sexuality.
This is perhaps both a primal level of the film and an important piece
of information for understanding the Nazi imagination.

Apart from the oppressive, destructive context of the primal scene,
sexuality is depicted in the film several times as amusement or recreation. In the masters' lovely garden, Freder laughingly skips around a gay
fountain in pursuit of a cavorting damsel decked out with jewels,
flowers, and feathers. In general, however, the black sexual triangle is
crushed: it is always pushed into the depths, the abyss of Moloch, the
void, or the flames by a symmetric and antagonistic triangle—white,
placed higher up, and opening upwards. This is evident in the final
scene: while the black triangle of workers penetrates from below, from

the bottom of the screen, the upper portion of the screen is occupied by the cathedral porch, on which two symmetrical rows of saints' statues converge toward a vanishing point, or vertex, where the Fredersen trio makes its appearance, as though it were a holy family sent from on high. The sublime, transcendental, angelic nature of this holy triangle is evident (from the cathedral, whiteness, goodness, and so forth); it reminds us of the spectacularly white and glowing triangle formed in the black depths of the catacombs by Maria's angelic figure, flanked by a fan-shaped array of candles and crosses. The purpose and composition of the structure are further highlighted by Maria's gesture as she raises her arm and spreads her veil—her wings. The kiss that she then bestows on Freder's face can only be an extension of this sexual "whiteness," this chastity; later, Maria herself falls victim to Rotwang's black aggression.

The first thing that makes Freder stand out is his white clothing, and Lang exploits this in a systematic and even brutal way by contrasting the son's glaring white garb with the black suit worn by Joseph the secretary, the gray fumes and huge black bulks in the machine room, the black uniforms worn by the workers, and so on. When Freder rejoins his "brother" workers, he trades his white clothing for a black uniform, since whiteness is now superlatively embodied in Maria (who appears to be radiantly white). In a third stage, we see Freder recovering from his illness (the whiteness of the bed and the sickroom represent the digestive process, the catabolism of the blackness and evil that accompany disease) and again putting on his white clothes, which will henceforth survive every adversity. This three-part chromatic composition (white-black-white) is by itself sufficiently strict and homogeneous to distinguish the three major segments of the film. If the primal scene is the fundamental and motivating structure of the film, then the son's role as mediator can be seen as the primary axis of the narrative and the key to the elaboration of an ideology.

Freder becomes aware of his vocation as mediator in a revelation of messianic type: Maria assumes the role of inspired Annunciatrix. Obviously this has Christ-like overtones, not only in the quasi-osmotic relationship between Freder and the Virgin-Maria (light is transferred osmotically through the gaze, among other things) but also in an image that occurs at a particularly dramatic moment in the film: when Freder is crucified on the needles of an electrical gauge of some sort (like the hands of a clock) and, in the midst of his torture, invokes the name of the Father. But beneath the reference to Christ lies a rich lode of mythological material. The biblical Babel in the background points to still deeper images (from the architecture of the tower to the huge gray furrows of human beings excreted by the earth). The narrative structure is based on traditional mythological models, in which certain sequences occur in a fairly constant order: annunciation of the mission, vocation, trial, failure, symbolic death and rebirth, confrontation with the monster, triumph and resurrection. In terms of manifest content, composed primarily of elements of narrative and ideological messages, the film essentially follows the actions of the mediator. Indeed, Freder is the only character who appears in all the spaces represented in the film (the Edenic garden, the father's office, the machine room, the catacombs, Rotwang's house, workers' city, cathedral, and so on). He is also the only character who touches (to the point of grabbing or embracing) all the major characters (Fredersen, Maria, Rotwang, Joseph, and so on). Freder's trajectory is one of circular or cyclic totalization rather than a dialectical one of mediation or mediatization. Adversity is seen not as a historical or present contradiction but as an accursed survival of archaic material (the pentacle, the witch) or a sudden unleashing of natural forces (the flood). When Freder encounters Rotwang's opposition, he is immediately forced to take evasive action or to rely on magic to refuse and flee the challenge. Recall, in particular, the spectacular sequences in which Rotwang orchestrates first the technological primal scene and then the choreographic one, thereby in a sense causing Freder to fail to perform. We see him first lying prostrate in a dark room in Rotwang's house and then lying on his bed hallucinating in his sickroom. The contradiction is neither analyzed nor pondered, and no response is made that would exploit its dynamic; it is simply abandoned, hidden, and if possible crushed in a burst of feverish activity that might be classed as activism.

The mediator's mission is accomplished when he reunites Capital and Labor, Brain and Hand, in holy wedlock in the holy church (and recall that re-uniting, re-tying, comes from *religare*, the probable root of the word religion). He brings the opposing parties together and unites what has been separate, fragmented, and antagonistic by placing himself in the middle, in between, that is, by acting as intermediary: in German, the word is *Mittler*, which means "mediator" but is also the comparative of *Mittel*, meaning middle, central, intermediate. (*Mittel* is also the word for "means," in the sense of "means and ends," which suggests a cultural and economic instrumentalism characteristic of Nazism.) Freder's position is crucial in the strict sense of the word: he is at the center, the crossroads, the crossing, the crux. He encounters (*croise*) everyone in the film; in his hallucination he believes that he has witnessed the copulation (*croisement*) of his parents; he is crucified on the cross formed by the hands of the factory's time clock; he is the crusader (*croisé*) who confronts the heretic Rotwang; and finally he is the one who effects salva-tion by joining (in a *croisement*, a crossing of hands) capital and labor in the final reconciliation-resurrection. Freder is also the one who believes [in French: *celui qui croit—croit*, the third person singular of *croire*, to believe, being a homonym of *croix*, cross—Trans.]. Freder believes in his father, in the "good" Maria, and in his revealed mission. And I would add, freely associating in a manner inspired by the frenetic history of the times, that after 1926 he also became the person who would grow (*croitre*: with the Nazi victory in the 1933 elections) as well as crow (*croasser*), as Hitler crowed in his speeches.

At this point it should be noted that Hitler was enthusiastic about *Metropolis* and a great admirer of Fritz Lang. Superficially, the reason for his interest is easy to see: the film's ideology coincides with the Nazi vision (set forth by Hitler in *Mein Kampf*, the book he finished in the same year, 1926, in which the film was made) of a national and cultural harmony transcending class divisions. This explanation is no doubt correct as far as it goes. To see the film as an apology for class harmony, a constant of conservative and reactionary thought, can no doubt account for some of Hitler's pleasure, but it is not really likely to elicit the deep and passionate commitment we know he felt (a commitment so passionate that he was prepared, we are told, to overlook Lang's Jewish background and put him to work making Nazi films). But the essence of the film's power lies not in its rather tiresome didactic themes (apparently a specialty of Thea von Harbou, Lang's wife and collaborator) but in the images that Lang created and constructed, produced and directed (to use film jargon that is perfectly appropriate here) —images rich in libidinal investment and fantasy and capable of seducing or horrifying the viewer. Ideological allusions and references cannot by themselves win a film a special and highly significant place in history and politics. For these references must themselves be carried, traversed, weighted down, interpenetrated by work that informs and figures—that is, gives form and figure to—the unconscious. And that is what Lang achieved. Perhaps this work of informing form is the much-sought place where history and fantasy meet.

To explore this meeting place would, I suspect, require considerable multidisciplinary and interdisciplinary effort aimed at drawing together analyses of style, rhetoric, historical pressures, social and economic data, politics, psychoanalysis, and so on—nothing less than a program for a new anthropology, one possible model of which has been outlined in the journal *Psychoanalysis and the Social Sciences*, founded by Geza Roheim in New York. My purpose here is much more modest: by bringing together the figures of Hitler and *Metropolis*, I want to draw out some parallels, which prove nothing but suggest areas for further research; in this I am indebted to Walter C. Langer, whose book *The Mind of Adolf Hitler* (Basic Books, 1972) collects many useful documents. One is immediately struck by the similarity between the name

Hitler and the title *Mittler*, which is attached to the hero of the film. Although the process by which identification through names, or even through the letters of names, takes place remains rather obscure, it has been shown to occur in too many, often quite spectacular cases to be ignored as a major factor in the shaping of the imagination. Hitler may have been especially likely to see himself or read himself into the *Mittler* of *Metropolis* because his own name was (according to Langer) a subject of uncertainty, frustration, and confusion. Early party documents were signed *Hittler*; Adolph's father, Alois Hitler, was an illegitimate child who until age forty, when he was recognized by his father Johann Georg *Hiedler*, used the name of his mother, Maria Anna Schicklgruber. Yet owing to a common ancestor, Hitler's maternal grandmother was also named *Hitler*. The nominal foundations are even more severely shaken (just as Freder feels the ground give way under him as he sees the figures of his parents whirl about) by the suggestion that Alois was actually the son of a Rothschild. (Maria Anna Schicklgruber became pregnant while working in Vienna in the home of the Austrian branch of the Rothschilds.) Whatever the basis for this theory (which seems rather farfetched), the important fact is that Hitler was aware of it, and that it may have stamped his paternal line with a sign of infamy extending far back into the past (just as the diabolical image of Rotwang is marked as ancient by the sign of the pentacle). Hitler's feeling that his ownership of his last name was fragile was compounded by the fact that his father's various marriages were to women of widely varying ages. Alois's first wife was thirteen years his elder; she died in 1883 without having given birth. His second wife, Franziska, died in 1884, leaving two children: Alois, born in 1882, and Angela, born in 1883. His third wife was his own cousin, Klara Poetzl, who had earlier been adopted by the couple and was twenty-three years younger than Alois. Of six children born to her, four died in early childhood. The only survivors were Adolph Hitler and a sister named Paula, who was apparently slightly retarded. What is more, Adolph's half-sister Angela, the manager of a Jewish student restaurant in Vienna, married a man named Raubal and had a daughter, Geli, with whom Adolph had a long and tortured affair that ended when Geli died in 1930, killed by a bullet fired from her uncle's pistol. This confused family history, frequently punctuated by death, may have heightened Hitler's sensitivity to the primal scenes in *Metropolis*, in which confusion of the figures plays such an important role. Death appears in Freder's hallucination (the same one in which the choreographic primal scene occurs) as a statue moving against a background of the seven deadly sins; to Hitler, death must have been a familiar figure, and he was to ensure that it would enjoy a triumphal future.

There are rather remarkable similarities in the early experiences of Lang and Hitler. Both were born in Austria, Lang in Vienna in 1890, Hitler in Braunau in 1889. Both later moved to Germany, indeed to Munich. Both aspired to become architects; Lang actually studied architecture, but Hitler, who lacked a diploma, could not. Subsequently, both became painters in a minor way, selling postcards and watercolors in order to live, Lang in Brussels in 1910 and Hitler in Vienna from 1908 to 1913. When war was declared in 1914, both felt a surge of patriotism. Both were passionate about the movies, cinephiles in the full sense of the word, and both were attracted to women who worked in theater or film: Thea von Harbou and Eva Braun were former actresses. For our present purposes, the most important similarity is the almost obsessive interest in architecture: in terms both of concrete accomplishments, political in the one case and aesthetic in the other, and of the formation of the imagination, the aptitude for projection, for turning fantasies into spatial constructions and architectonic volumes, is manifest in the two men. As many people have pointed out, *Metropolis* is an architect's film; I earlier alluded to the etymological sense of the word, mother-city. Hitler, Langer writes, "believes himself to be the greatest of all German architects and spends a great deal of his time in sketching new buildings and planning the remodeling of entire cities"(30). Thus the "modeling" of the maternal figure as the mother-city in *Metropolis* corresponds to Hitler's desire to "remodel" his mother, to remake or repair (*Mittler* also means "one who repairs") her damaged body, dismantled by a violent and brutal father (just as the "good" Maria is dismantled, taken apart, by Rotwang). In *Metropolis* the "bad" part of the father is almost entirely invested in the figure of Rotwang. The real, social father, Fredersen, while always good to his son, remains an ambivalent figure (he plots with Rotwang, lays hands on the False Maria, and plays with fire by toying with the destructive rage of the workers) until the son's heroism and Rotwang's fall enlighten and purify him, liberating his essential "goodness" and thereby safeguarding the paternalist social model, the basis of order and discipline. The conclusion of the film, in a milky discharge of "goodness" by father, mother, and son on the cathedral porch, seems to correspond to (and therefore to satisfy) a syncretic vision of Hitler's in which he attempted to combine the maternal figure with a dominant father imposed by German tradition (as well as by western paternalism in general). In this connection, Langer notes that "although Germans, as a whole, invariably refer to Germany as the "Fatherland," Hitler almost always refers to it as the "Motherland"(153).

Freder rescues Maria from Rotwang's clutches. He saves the children from the catastrophic flood. All in all, then, he saves the entire city, the mother-city, as the final, summary image of universal marriage suggests. The story of the film is obviously one of salvation, and no word better describes Hitler's political and historical vocation. Thus communication and correspondences between the film's images and various aspects of Nazi ambition are permanent. The sequence that shows the rescue of the children from the flooded workers' city readily lends itself to "Hitlerian" political interpretation. In the small square at the center or heart of the city the waters rise (mounting perils menace the victim Germany); Maria sounds the alarm and calls for help (Hitler, we know, felt that he had a calling, that he was merely responding to the appeal, the voice, of the mother country—his vocation); the children, abandoned by their unworthy parents (compare Hitler's attraction to children; his anti-familial feelings; his ability to address the childlike populace and shape their behavior; etc.), unite (as the populace united around Hitler, ending "partisan" divisions) around Maria, toward whom they extend their arms in a gesture of supplication (did not Hitler see the innumerable outstretched arms, the Heil Hitlers, as a gesture of supplication addressed to him, expressing a desire to be saved?); at the height of danger, Freder arrives in the role of savior; he clasps Maria to his bosom (Hitler declared that he was "wedded" to Germany) and leads Maria and the children (Germany and her people) out of danger; he is their guide, their *Führer*.

Those responsible for the disaster have already been identified: Rotwang, the "ingenious inventor," whom Hitler must have numbered among those whom he denounced as "overeducated, stuffed with knowledge and intelligence yet devoid of all healthy instincts," representing "the intellect [which] has swollen to the point of becoming autocratic" (the troubling autonomy of Rotwang's house) and which "now resembles a disease" (the morbid hypertrophy of Rotwang's intellect, indicated by his huge forehead and vast library); to some extent Fredersen himself, the father and industrialist who pays too little heed to his son's voice and who (at Rotwang's gala party) is associated with a decadent, soft, and effeminate bourgeoisie symbolized by the revelers in tuxedos and evening gowns who, while dancing, allow themselves to be led into the abyss by the False Maria; the working class, too, is guilty of impatience, of having heeded agitators (the False Maria) who incited rebellion—the mob is impulsive, irresponsible, "feminine" in a word ("the mob is a woman," Hitler said, and "the vast majority of people are so feminine"). Like Maria, Hitler comes to "possess" the mob through oratory and leads it back to the straight and narrow: rectitude is nothing less than an obsession in *Metropolis*. Behind all these figures of guilt and sin (the statues of the seven deadly sins) looms the False Maria. It is in fact quite correct to say that she looms, and looms constantly: over the shoulders of Rotwang as he shows her to Fredersen; above the luminous cup from which she emerges; above the crowd of workers and bourgeois who carry her in triumphal processions; and even above the flames of the bonfire that consumes her. If, as I have suggested, she is, above and beyond her various avatars, sexuality itself, seen or treated as a profound, ultimate power, as danger, anguish, and horror; then omnipresent and ubiquitously reborn she becomes something that cannot be tolerated, that must be tracked down, eradicated, annihilated, and burned—the interminable Nazi extermination.

Many other traits typical of Hitler find counterparts in *Metropolis*. "I move forward with the infallible accuracy of the sleepwalker," Hitler wrote; in the film we see Freder receiving Maria's revelation and then proceeding toward his destiny with both arms outstretched in the manner of a sleepwalker. The Christ-like aspect of *Metropolis* has its parallel in the history of Hitler and the Nazi movement, which for a time had a quasi-religious dimension; according to Langer, Hitler cited the Bible and drew "comparisons between Christ and himself"(35). The obsession with architecture that we find in *Metropolis* has its counterpart in Hitler's construction of the "eagle's nest" at Berchtesgaden, reached through "a long underground passage . . . enclosed by a heavy double door of bronze. At the end of the underground passage a wide lift, panelled with sheets of copper, awaits the visitor. Through a vertical shaft of 330 feet cut right through the rock, it rises up to the level of the Chancellor's dwelling place . . . . The visitor finds himself in a strong and massive building containing a gallery with Roman pillars, an immense circular hall with windows all around . . . . It gives the impression of being suspended in space, an almost overhanging wall of bare rock rises up abruptly"(169). The first part of this description accords remarkably well with some of the images of the underground city in *Metropolis*, while the latter part describes the precipice from which the paranoid King Kong surveys his empire. In citing these lines by [then ambassador] François-Poncet, Langer notes that "Hitler often retires to this strange place to await instructions concerning the course he is to pursue"(169). The images of petrifaction that we noted in *Metropolis* (the Tower of Babel, the enormous blocks of stone dragged by the slaves, Freder immured in stone during the impregnation scene), along with the constant presence of eyes and intense stares (Freder staring at his father embracing Maria, Freder hallucinating the erotic dance of the False Maria), were associated with the figure of the "bad" mother and its primal sexual dimension, both represented by the head of Medusa. I therefore find the following note by Robert Waite (from the epilogue to Langer's book) particularly striking: "He was infatuated with the head of the Medusa, once remarking that in von Stuck's painting the flashing eyes that turned men to stone and impotency reminded him of the eyes of his mother"(218). As Hitler watched *Metropolis*, how could he not have been fascinated and hypnotized by the repeated hypnotic stares (of Fredersen and Rotwang and Maria and Freder), so like his own gaze, filled with the magical and paranoiac omnipotence of the stare that petrifies, engulfs, and penetrates, the gaze that wishes it were a disembodied orgasm, which in a frightening reversal injects its venom and like a vampire sucks the blood of its victim in an ersatz of displaced and dis-figured sexuality. Langer speaks accurately of the "diffuse sexual function" of Hitler's eyes and notes: "When he meets persons for the first time he fixates his eyes on them as though to *bore through* them. There is a peculiar *glint* in them on these occasions that many have interpreted as an *hypnotic* quality"(201; my italics).

Moloch: Hitler's Mouth and the World's Anus

The Führer's speeches shaped the Nazi imagination, which ultimately produced the crematoriums of Auschwitz: from Hitler's mouth to the "world's anus." Hitler's mouth, all observers agree, was capable of casting a spell over multitudes, producing what Langer, citing Axel Heyst, calls a "veritable orgasm": "In his speeches we hear the suppressed voice of passion and wooing which is taken from the language of love; he utters a cry of hate and voluptuousness, a spasm of violence and cruelty"(204). Auschwitz, anus of the world, enjoys the dubious honor of symbolizing the extremity of horror. In *Metropolis* these images are fused in a layer of destructive and sadistic anality, concretely and compactly expressed in Freder's hallucination of Moloch. As human operators fail to watch over their machines, a series of explosions takes place in the machine room. Liquids and gases are set free, bursting forth with destructive energies. Injured workers roll about on the ground or plunge into the void, so much dark debris. On a buckled, melted screen Freder's hallucination of Moloch's head takes shape. He sees an enormous, fiery mouth framed by huge teeth, into which diabolic creatures toss human beings with their pitchforks. But this fiery fantasy of consumption—the "bad" mother with her tongue of flame swallowing her young, the head of Medusa (flames as serpents) leaving Freder petrified —is further complicated, indeed contorted, into an anal scene of sadistic domination: if we reverse the motion, the unbending black columns of workers who climb toward the mouth-hole become streams of fecal matter expelled or excreted from the anal orifice. A hallucinatory fusion of organs and functions gives rise to a monstrous chiasm, which the Nazis put into practice: the mouth excretes ("filth" flowed from Hitler's mouth) and the anus devours (Auschwitz).

The head of Moloch can serve as emblem for a reinterpretation of the signifiers in *Metropolis* in anal terms: the corridors and labyrinths are like viscera; the blacks and whites are expressive (expressionist) of filth (the material of the walls, partitions, ground, and clothing); the glossy blackness and mechanical rigidity (relative sublimation) of the robot and of Rotwang's prosthetic hand; the character structure of Fredersen; the explosions and destructions by gas, smoke, liquids, and so on. The phallic organization of *Metropolis*, which serves to cover the primal scenes and, in my view, to mask the horror of sexuality, incorporates this strong anality and thereby reinforces itself (as one says of concrete, but also of billy clubs) with fecal power in order to enclose the libidinal economy (the walls of the mother city are more visceral than uterine) within a rigid structure and orient it toward destruction.

P.S. If we view *Metropolis* as primarily a "spatialization," a shaping and figuration of fantasy, then we may speak of a Langian traversal or exploration of the unconscious, whose existence is recognized in aesthetic terms through an intuitive elaboration and construction of concrete forms, yielding a specific type of ecstasy (*jouissance*) in which knowledge of the unconscious remains trapped. The author plays on (*joue*), and takes pleasure from (*jouit de*), a magical commutability of differences (the two Marias). The Hitlerian exploration is quite different: the existence of the unconscious is recognized, but it is constantly displaced and exploited through active, activist miscognition (*méconnaissance*) of structures, of the intrinsic productivity and lawfulness of the unconscious, all mixed in with the ideological pap (along with a parallel political-economic fusion of social differences—bourgeois, petit bourgeois, workers, peasants—through an outpouring of nationalism and racism). Instead of knowledge we have "acting out," on a historical scale. The imaginary architecture of *Metropolis* becomes Berchtesgaden, Nuremberg, Berlin, Auschwitz. The nation wants all differences to be effaced. Radically different is the Freudian exploration: here the existence of the unconscious is recognized for the first time as a field open to the understanding, to the elaboration of theories and concepts; Freud envisioned a science, a critical rationality, and attempted to establish a praxis for liberating otherness. Here differences are spelled out and called forth (childhood, neurosis, arts, etc.) in order to be articulated.

It may be of some interest to point out that all three explorations, divergent as they are in many respects, start, along with innumerable other explorations of other realms, from the same place: another rich* but identical mother-city, Vienna.

Translated by Arthur Goldhammer

[*_Autre riche_: the author is punning on _Autriche_, French for Austria—Trans.]

This article was first published in the *Revue Française de Psychanalyse* 1 (January, 1974); it was reprinted in a collection of articles by Dadoun, *Psychanalyse entre chien et loup* (Paris: Editions Imago, 1984). We would like to thank the author for permission to present the article in English translation.

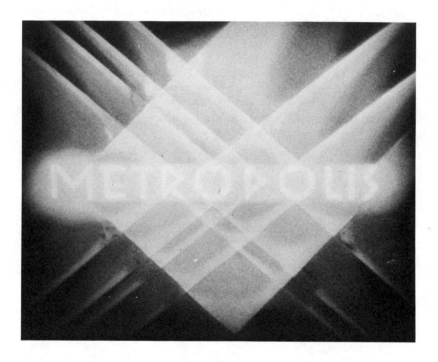

Metropolis, Scene 103
Enno Patalas

You may remember:

> "Within easy reach of the city's guiding hand stood a strange house."
> "The man who lived there—Rotwang—had worked thirty years to bring true the great dream of John Masterman."

Next you see Rotwang, the inventor, at his desk. A hunchback servant, emerging from a spiral staircase through a trapdoor in the floor, announces:

> "John Masterman."
> *Let him wait* . . . , Rotwang gestures in response.

And this is how the scene continues in traditional prints. Rotwang, gesticulating wildly, his face distorted, cries out, according to the intertitles:

> "My work is done . . . !"
> "A machine that can be made to look like a man—or a woman—but never tires . . . never makes a mistake . . . !!!"
> "Now we can do without man!"
> "The dream that it might be possible to go a step beyond making machines of men—by making men of machines."
> "Isn't it worth the loss of a hand to have created a machine that can be made to look like a man—or a woman—but never tires—never makes a mistake—"[1]

Why does the inventor proclaim his good news with such desperate gestures and contorted expressions? A lapse on the part of the actor, Klein-Rogge? This is not the only inconsistency that will puzzle the attentive viewer of existing prints of *Metropolis*.

If Rotwang creates a robot to replace the workers, why does he make that robot female? Even recently, an ingenious essay on "Technology and Sexuality in Fritz Lang's *Metropolis*" takes the motivation of this femininity for granted: "Precisely the fact that Fritz Lang does not feel the need to explain the female features of Rotwang's robot shows that a pattern, a long-standing tradition is being recycled here, a tradition which is not at all hard to detect, and in which the *Maschinenmensch*, more often than not, is presented as a woman."[2]

The motivation of the robot's female features, as conceptualized by Thea von Harbou and Fritz Lang, remains a question that cannot be explained from existing prints, but only with the help of various documents. *Metropolis* has been thoroughly and irreparably destroyed, as few other films have been. On the other hand, very few films of the 1920s come with such a host of reliable and detailed source material. Thus we have the music that Gottfried Huppertz composed for the film, including not only parts of the orchestral score but also the director's cues for the pianist, together with instructions for the particular arrangement. This score contains 1,029 cues for the conductor, one for about every third bar, so as to synchronize the music with images and intertitles; the cues list almost every other shot and just about every intertitle.

In this score, the sequence which begins with the servant announcing the visitor is transcribed in the following way:

Curtain open—Fredersen close—base of monument—Fredersen—enter Rotwang—a brain like yours—only once in my life—Fredersen—let the dead rest—for me she is not dead—Rotwang's hand—do you think that the loss— would you like to see her?

Only the subsequent cues ("spiral staircase—Rotwang pulls the curtain—Fredersen—robot slowly rising") correspond to a scene of the film as we know it: after Rotwang's fierce outburst we see the inventor enter his laboratory from the staircase, accompanied by Joh Fredersen (John Masterman in the American version). They step in front of a curtain which Rotwang proceeds to open. And, as Fredersen watches tensely, the robot slowly rises and walks toward them.

In addition to the score, we have a second document that provides reliable information, although it concerns a limited aspect of the original version of *Metropolis*. This is the censorship card of the Film Censorship Office in Berlin which passed the film for release on November 13, 1926 at a length of 4,189 meters. These censorship cards were actually little notebooks made out of blue cardboard—the one for *Metropolis* was ten pages long. In addition to credits and the length of individual reels, they contained a complete list of intertitles without, however, distinguishing between explanatory and dialogue titles or identifying speakers.

At the beginning of the third reel (of nine), the censorship card lists the following intertitles:

1. In the center of Metropolis there was a strange house, forgotten by the centuries.

2. The man who lived there was Rotwang, the inventor.

3. Joh Fredersen . . . .

4. Hel, born to make me happy and a blessing to humanity, lost to Joh Fredersen, died when she gave birth to Freder, Joh Fredersen's son.

5. A brain like yours, Rotwang, should be able to forget . . .

6. Only once in my life, I forgot: that Hel was a woman and that you were a man . . .

7. Let the dead rest, Rotwang . . . She is dead, for you just as for me . . .

8. For me she is not dead, Joh Fredersen—for me she lives!

9. Do you think the loss of a hand is too high a price for the recreation of Hel?!

10. Would you like to see her?!

This explains six of the cues given in the score. "A brain like yours— only once in my life—for me she is not dead"—each quote the beginning of intertitles and refer to the dialogue between Rotwang and Fredersen.

Intertitle 4, however—"Hel, born to make me happy"—does not have a counterpart in the score.

A third source sheds light on this line. In the three albums of production stills from *Metropolis* which Fritz Lang donated to the Cinémathèque Française in 1959, there are three photographs showing a monument, or at least its base. Flanked by Fredersen on the left and Rotwang on the right, the monument carries an inscription which we can identify as the text of intertitle four of the censorship card. Another photograph shows Rotwang raving in front of the monument, and the camera crew standing on its base. A third shows the same scene, but with a woman's head on the base—a photomontage?—and to the left and right, parts of a curtain. Now the other cues from the score fall into place as well: "Curtain open—Fredersen close—base of monument— enter Rotwang."

Finally, there is a fourth source which helps us visualize the scene. For a long time, Thea von Harbou's script was believed to be lost, until one copy surfaced in the estate of the composer Huppertz; it now belongs to the Deutsche Kinemathek in West Berlin. If we compare this script with the censorship cards, with the score, and the existing parts of the film, we find that Lang departed from the script in numerous details, that he chose to discard entire scenes, even in the original version of the film. Of Lang's shooting script, only one page has survived—as a facsimile in an UFA promotional brochure. It represents Scene 13 (Stadium of the Club of the Sons), which is missing from the American version of the film and consequently from many prints. A comparison with the corresponding pages from Harbou's script would make an interesting seminar paper.

In the script, the scene between Rotwang and Fredersen corresponds to Scene 103, entitled "Hel's Room." We could imagine the scene as follows. After the intertitle "Joh Fredersen"—the announcement by the servant—we see the person who has been announced (very often in Lang a dialogue title provides the cue for the next shot) with his back to the camera, in a somber, almost empty room with high ceilings. He stands in front of a curtain that extends from ceiling to floor, "as if attracted by a magnet," according to the script; he pulls one of the curtain's heavy tassels, it opens, and behind him a monument appears with a gigantic head representing Hel. Fredersen stares, visibly moved, at the woman's head, then he reads "the words engraved on the base, which join Rotwang, Hel and Joh Fredersen in a common fate." Without a sound, Rotwang enters the room. Seeing the man who had robbed him of his beloved standing before her statue, he flies into a rage, plunges toward the monument, pulls the curtain closed behind him violently, and leans forward against Fredersen, who steps back slightly. Fredersen "becomes calmer, in the face of Rotwang's increasing rage," and speaks (intertitle):

"A brain like yours, Rotwang, should be able to forget . . ."

Then follows the dialogue we know from the censorship card.

> Rotwang: "Only once in my life, I forgot: that Hel was a woman and that you were a man . . ."
> Fredersen, gentler than usual: "Let the dead rest, Rotwang . . . . She is dead, for you just as for me . . ."
> Rotwang, in mad triumph: "For me she is not dead, Joh Fredersen—for me she lives!" And so on.

It is well known that *Metropolis* was produced by UFA under the terms of the Parufamet agreement of 1926. Paramount-Famous Players-Lasky and Metro-Goldwyn supplied a loan of 17 million marks in return for which UFA agreed to distribute forty Paramount and MGM films and to allocate to them half of the exhibition time available in UFA theaters. The American companies, for their part, agreed to distribute ten UFA films in the United States.

The Berlin premiere of *Metropolis* took place on January 10, 1927. At this point, an American version was already being prepared. On March 13, *The New York Times* published an article with the title "German Film Revision Upheld as Needed Here," in which a certain Randolph Bartlett justified the cuts and changes made for the American release.[3] The Germans' problem was either a "lack of interest in dramatic verity or an astonishing ineptitude. Motives were absent or were extremely naive." This could not be tolerated.

The German producers were quick to accept the American verdict.

As early as April 7, the UFA Board of Directors resolved to persuade Parufamet to release *Metropolis* in the provinces in the fall, and to re-release it in Berlin at the same time, "in the American version[4] after deleting as many intertitles as possible with a communist tendency."[5] The next day the distributor suggested withdrawing the film, and releasing the new version at the end of August, in Berlin first, after some of the "pietistic revisions[6] added by the Americans were removed." The UFA Board of Directors complied on April 27, and by August 5, the film was resubmitted to the Censorship Office in a version 3,241 meters long, in other words, cut by nearly a quarter. About half of approximately 200 original intertitles survived, more or less exactly, the other half were dropped; 50 new intertitles were added.

The cuts in the American and the second German version are largely the same, although the Americans cut 400 meters more than the Germans. They also took more liberties with reediting and intertitles. The formulation of new titles went hand in hand with a new montage that both shortened and rearranged the film, even breaking into individual sequences. Thus, changing the dialogue between Rotwang and Fredersen in Hel's Room into a monologue by Rotwang on the creation of the robot rendered all shots superfluous in which Fredersen is seen speaking. These shots were either eliminated or, as in the case of one shot, inserted at another point in the film, so as to give Fredersen a chance to remark about the robot: "It has everything but a soul."

Why the monument of Hel and thus the character of Hel and the motivation for Rotwang's behavior had to be sacrificed to the American censors, we learn from *The New York Times*:

> [The scene] showed a very beautiful statue of a woman's head, and on the base was her name—and that name was "Hel." Now the German word for "hell" is "Hölle," so they were quiet [sic] innocent of the fact that this name would create a guffaw in an English-speaking country. So it was necessary to cut this beautiful bit out of the picture, and a certain motive which it represented had to be replaced by another.

For Harbou and Lang, Rotwang's story was, as the song goes in *Rancho Notorious*, "a story of Hate, Murder and Revenge," with a complex motivation. In the amputated version of *Metropolis*, Rotwang, the genius inventor, is little more than a tool in the hands of Fredersen, at whose command he instructs the robot to instigate a self-destructive revolt among the workers. For Harbou and Lang, Rotwang had his own reasons for creating the robot as the "new Hel."

The women in *Metropolis* are the projections of male fantasies, authorized by Rotwang, Fredersen, and Lang—the spectator in front of the screen recognizes himself among the spectators on the screen: in

Freder, when the door to the Eternal Gardens opens and Maria, the virgin-madonna, appears surrounded by the children; in Fredersen, when Rotwang pulls open the curtain and the new Hel, the robot, arises; in the collective of men in tuxedos at Rotwang's party, as the new Hel, flesh incarnate, appears on a broad dish emerging from beneath the stage, her position fixed until she begins her dance. Invariably, the woman, virgin, mother, whore, witch, vamp[7] is constituted—and deconstituted—under the direction of one of the male characters, which in turn predicates the look of another, or many others, including the spectator. And Lang also presents these looks, in the "thousand eyes" of the spectator at Rotwang's party.

Rotwang presents Hel as a stone monument. As he had chiselled into stone, she "was born for him." She had refused him by marrying another for whose son she died—a son who should have been his, according to the law of her birth. He built a monument to her in his house and concealed it behind a curtain, as if he didn't want to share his grief with anyone, to keep the dead woman to himself. But his way of presenting Hel is also clearly motivated. Hel had to be born, had to betray him and die, so that Rotwang could turn her into a stone monument.

In this retrospective conception, Hel prefigures the new, artificial woman as her double. She would not merely be "born for him"; she would be born "of him"—daughter and lover in one. He gives this artificial woman the features of the girl with whom the dead woman's son has fallen in love, so as to have him be destroyed by her double. Thus he takes his revenge not only on his rival, but also on the son who denied himself to Rotwang when his mother conceived him by another. He fantasizes the desired son as the offspring of his lover's infidelity which in turn allows him to motivate and rationalize his sadistic lust.

The authors of the American version were not as naive as they pretended to be when they eliminated Hel. Their stale joke about "this hell of a woman" gives them away.

Translated by Miriam Hansen

Editors' note: This translation from the German appears by permission of the author. The article was originally published in French translation in *Metropolis, un film de Fritz Lang: Images d'un Tournage* (Paris: Centre National de la Photographie et Cinémathèque Française, 1985). We would like to thank Enno Patalas and Gerhard Ullmann of the Munich Film Archive, and the Cinémathèque Française for the photographs used in this article.

Enno Patalas has been responsible for the major part of the reconstruction of *Metropolis*. The version released by Giorgio Moroder in 1984 owes a great deal to this archival work. The sub-plot involving Hel would be known to readers who have seen Moroder's print; this, and several other "lost" scenes, were included through an inventive use of photographs and optical effects.

NOTES

1. Titles are from the American release version.

2. Andreas Huyssen, "The Vamp and the Machine: Technology and Sexuality in Fritz Lang's *Metropolis*," *New German Critique* 24-25 (Fall/Winter 1981-82), p.225.

3. Quoted in Paul M. Jensen, *The Cinema of Fritz Lang* (New York: A.S.Barnes, 1969), p.64.

4. Transcripts of the UFA Board of Directors meetings, Bundesarchiv, Koblenz.

5. The intertitles of Maria's inflammatory speech to the workers survived, almost literally, in the American version. They were toned down only in the second German version.

6. The American version added a number of interpretive intertitles and even completely new dialogue. Thus Freder (now called Eric) says to Joh Fredersen (now John Masterman): "Father, for centuries we've been building a Civilization of Gold and Steel—what has it brought us? Peace? Understanding? Happiness? Has it brought us nearer to God? . . ."

7. On the etymology of the name Hel—in the Old German *Edda*, the ruler of the underworld, the Goddess of Death—see Georges Sturm, "Für Hel ein Denkmal, kein Platz—un 'rêve de pierre'," *cicim* 9 (Munich, 1984).

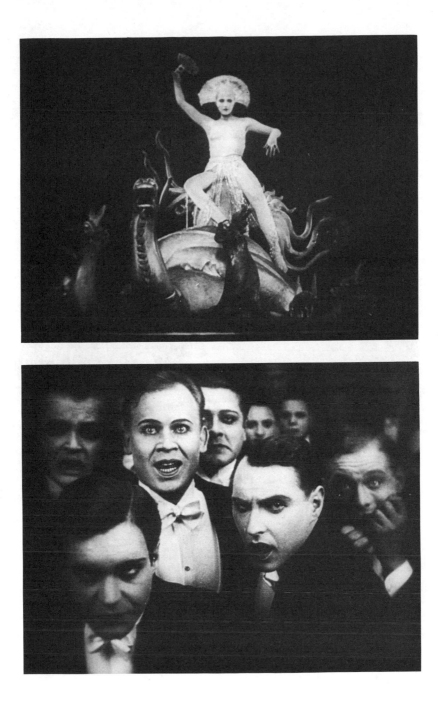

Star Trek Rerun, Reread, Rewritten:
Fan Writing as Textual Poaching
Henry Jenkins III

> *Suppose we were to ask the question: what became of the Sphinx after the encounter with Oedipus on his way to Thebes? Or, how did Medusa feel seeing herself in Perseus' mirror just before being slain?*
>
> *Teresa de Lauretis,* Alice Doesn't *(1982)*

> *How does Uhura feel about her lack of promotion, what does she try to do about it, how would she handle an emergency, or a case of sexual harassment? What were Chapel's experiences in medical school, what is her job at Starfleet headquarters, what is her relationship with Sarek and Amanda now . . . ?*
>
> *E. Osbourne,* Star Trek *fan (1987)*

In late December 1986, *Newsweek* marked the twentieth anniversary of *Star Trek* with a cover story on the program's fans, "the Trekkies, who love nothing more than to watch the same 79 episodes over and over."[1] The *Newsweek* article, with its relentless focus on conspicuous consumption and "infantile" behavior and its patronizing language and smug superiority to all fan activity, is a textbook example of the stereotyped representation of fandom found in both popular writing and academic criticism: "Hang on: You are being beamed to one of those *Star Trek* conventions, where grownups greet each other with the Vulcan salute and offer in reverent tones to pay $100 for the autobiography of Leonard Nimoy" (p. 66). Illustrated with photographs of a sixty-six-year-old bookstore worker who goes by the name of "Grandma Trek" and who loves to play with toy spaceships, of a balding and paunchy man in a snug Federation uniform, and of an overweight, middle-aged woman with heavy eyeshadow and rubber "Spock Ears," the article offers a lurid account of the program's loyal followers. Fans are characterized as "kooks" (p. 68) obsessed with trivia, celebrity, and collectibles; as social inepts, cultural misfits, and crazies; as "a lot of over-weight women, a lot of divorced and single women" (p. 68). Borrowing heavily from pop Freud, ersatz Adorno, and pulp paperback sociology, *Newsweek* explains the "Trekkie" phenomenon in terms of repetition compulsion, infantile regression, commodity fetishism, nostalgic com-placency, and future shock: "Like music, it appeals to man's love of repetition. The same characters do basically the same thing in each show; and the shows get repeated and . . . " (p. 66). Perhaps most telling, *Newsweek* consistently treats *Trek* fans as a problem to be solved, a mystery to be understood, rather than as a kind of cultural activity that many find satisfying and pleasurable.

Academic writers depict "Trekkers" in essentially the same terms. For Robin Wood, the fantasy film fan is "reconstructed as a child, sur-rendering to the reactivation of a set of values and structures [the] adult self has long since repudiated."[2] The fan is trapped within a repetition compulsion similar to that which an infant experiences through the fort/da game. A return to such "banal" texts could not possibly be war-ranted by their intellectual content but can only be motivated by a re-turn to "the lost breast," by the need for reassurance provided by the passive reexperience of familiar pleasures: "The pleasure offered by the *Star Wars* films corresponds very closely to our basic conditioning; it is extremely reactionary, as all mindless and automatic pleasure tends to be. The finer pleasures are those we have to work for" (p. 164). Wood valorizes academically respectable texts and reading practices at the expense of popular works and their fans: "It is possible to 'read' a film like *Letter from an Unknown Woman* or *Late Spring* twenty times and still discover new meanings, new complexities, ambiguities, possi-bilities of interpretation. It seems unlikely, however, that this is what takes people back, again and again, to *Star Wars*" (p. 163). Academic rereading produces new insights; fan rereading rehashes old ex-periences.[3]

As these two articles illustrate, the fan constitutes a scandalous cate-gory in contemporary American culture, one that calls into question the logic by which others order their aesthetic experiences, one that provokes an excessive response from those committed to the interests of textual producers. Fans appear to be frighteningly "out of control," undisciplined and unrepentant, rogue readers. Rejecting "aesthetic dis-tance," fans passionately embrace favored texts and attempt to inte-grate media representations within their own social experience. Like cultural scavengers, fans reclaim works that others regard as "worth-less" trash, finding them a source of popular capital. Like rebellious children, fans refuse to read by the rules imposed upon them by the schoolmasters. For the fan, reading becomes a kind of play, responsive only to its own loosely-structured rules and generating its own kinds of pleasure.

Michel de Certeau has characterized this type of reading as "poaching," an impertinent "raid" on the literary "preserve" that takes away only those things that seem useful or pleasurable to the reader: "Far from being writers . . . readers are travellers; they move across lands belonging to someone else, like nomads poaching their way across fields they did not write, despoiling the wealth of Egypt to enjoy it themselves."[4] De Certeau perceives popular reading as a series of "advances and retreats, tactics and games played with the text" (p. 175), as a kind of cultural bricolage through which readers fragment texts and reassemble the broken shards according to their own blueprint, salvaging bits and pieces of found material in making sense of their own social experience. Far from viewing consumption as imposing meanings upon the public, de Certeau suggests, consumption involves reclaiming textual material, "making it one's own, appropriating or reappropriating it" (p. 166).

But such conduct cannot be sanctioned; it must be contained, through ridicule if necessary, since it challenges the very notion of literature as a kind of private property to be controlled by textual producers and their academic interpreters. Public attacks on media fans keep other viewers in line, making it uncomfortable for readers to adapt such "inappropriate" strategies of making sense of popular texts. One woman recalled the negative impact popular representations of fandom had on her early cultural life:

> Journalists and photographers always went for the people furthest out of mainstream humanity . . . showing the reader the handicapped, the very obese, the strange and the childish in order to "entertain" the "average reader." Of course, a teenager very unsure of herself and already labeled "weird" would run in panic before finding out fandom is a lot like everywhere else with all sorts of human types and usually accepting everyone on individual terms.[5]

Such representations isolate potential fans from others who share common interests and reading practices, marginalize fan-related activities as outside the mainstream and beneath dignity. These same stereotypes reassure academic writers of the validity of their own interpretations of the program content, readings made in conformity with established critical protocols, and free them of any need to come into direct contact with the program's "crazed" followers.[6]

In this essay, I propose an alternative approach to fandom, one that perceives "Trekkers" (as they prefer to be called) not as cultural dupes, social misfits, or mindless consumers, but rather as, in de Certeau's terms, "poachers" of textual meanings. Behind the exotic stereotypes fostered by the media lies a largely unexplored terrain of cultural activity, a subterranean network of readers and writers who remake programs in their own image. Fandom is a vehicle for marginalized subcultural groups (women, the young, gays, and so on) to pry open space for their cultural concerns within dominant representations; fandom is a way of appropriating media texts and rereading them in a fashion that serves different interests, a way of transforming mass culture into popular culture.

I do not believe this essay represents the last word on *Star Trek* fans, a cultural community that is far too multivocal to be open to easy description. Rather, I explore aspects of current fan activity that seem particularly relevant to cultural studies. My primary concern will be with what happens when these fans produce their own texts, texts that inflect program content with their own social experience and displace commercially-produced commodities for a kind of popular economy. For these fans, *Star Trek* is not simply something that can be reread; it is something that can and must be rewritten to make it more responsive to their needs, to make it a better producer of personal meanings and pleasures.

No legalistic notion of literary property can adequately constrain the rapid proliferation of meanings surrounding a popular text. But there are other constraints, ethical constraints and self-imposed rules, enacted by the fans, either individually or as part of a larger community, in response to their felt need to legitimate their unorthodox appropriation of mass media texts. E. P. Thompson has suggested that eighteenth- and nineteenth-century peasant leaders, the historical poachers behind de Certeau's apt metaphor, responded to a kind of "moral economy," an informal set of consensual norms, that justified their uprising against the landowners and tax collectors in terms of a restoration of a preexisting order being corrupted by those who were supposed to protect it.[7] Similarly, the fans often cast themselves not as poachers but as loyalists, rescuing essential elements of the primary text "misused" by those who maintain copyright control over the program materials. Respecting literary property even as they seek to appropriate it for their own uses, these fans become reluctant poachers, hesitant about their relationship to the program text, uneasy about the degree of manipulation they can "legitimately" perform on its materials, policing each other for "abuses" of their interpretive license, as they wander across a terrain pockmarked with confusions and contradictions. These ambiguities become all too apparent when fan writing is examined as a particular type of reader-text interaction. My discussion will consequently have a double focus, first outlining the process by which the fans force the primary text to accommodate their own interests, and later, reconsidering the issue of literary property rights in light of the "moral economy" of the fan community.

Fan Readers/Fan Writers

The popularity of *Star Trek* has motivated a wide range of cultural productions, creative reworkings of program materials from children's backyard play to adult interaction games, from needlework to elaborate costumes, from private fantasies to computer programing and home video production. This ability to transform personal reaction into social interaction, spectatorial culture into participatory culture, is one of the central characteristics of fandom. One becomes a "fan" not by being a regular viewer of a particular program but by translating that viewing into some kind of cultural activity, by sharing feelings and thoughts about the program content with friends, by joining a "community" of other fans who share common interests. For fans, consumption naturally sparks production, reading generates writing, until the terms seem logically inseparable. In fan writer Jean Lorrah's words:

> Trekfandom . . . is friends and letters and crafts and fanzines and trivia and costumes and artwork and filksongs and buttons and film clips and conventions—something for everybody who has in common the inspiration of a television show which grew far beyond its TV and film incarnations to become a living part of world culture.[8]

Lorrah's description of fandom blurs all boundaries between producers and consumers, spectators and participants, the commercial and the home-crafted, to construct an image of fandom as a cultural and social network that spans the globe.

Many fans characterize their entry into fandom in terms of a movement from the social and cultural isolation doubly imposed upon them as women within a patriarchal society and as seekers after alternative pleasures within dominant media representations, toward more and more active participation in a "community" receptive to their cultural productions, a "community" within which they may feel a sense of "belonging." One fan recalls:

> I met one girl who liked some of the TV shows I liked . . . but I was otherwise a bookworm, no friends, working in the school library. Then my friend and I met some other girls a grade ahead of us but ga-ga over *ST*. From the beginning, we met each Friday night at one of the two homes that had a color TV to watch *Star Trek* together. . . . Silence was mandatory except during commercials, and, afterwards, we "dis-

cussed" each episode. We re-wrote each story and corrected the wrongs done to "Our Guys" by the writers. We memorized bits of dialog. We even started to write our own adventures.[9]

Some fans are drawn gradually from intimate interactions with others who live near them toward participation in a broader network of fans who attend regional, national, and even international science fiction conventions. One fan writes of her first convention: "I have been to so many conventions since those days, but this one was the ultimate experience. I walked into that Lunacon and felt like I had come home without ever realizing I had been lost."[10] Another remarks simply, "I met folks who were just as nuts as I was, I had a wonderful time."[11]

For some women, trapped in low-paying jobs or within the socially-isolated sphere of the housewife, participation within an (inter)national network of fans grants a degree of dignity and respect otherwise lacking. For others, fandom offers a training ground for the development of professional skills and an outlet for creative impulses constrained by their workday lives. Fan slang draws a sharp contrast between the "mundane"—the realm of everyday experience and/or those who dwell exclusively within that space—and fandom—an alternative sphere of cultural experience that restores the excitement and freedom that must be repressed to function in ordinary life. One fan writes, "Not only does 'mundane' mean 'everyday life,' it is also a term used to describe narrow-minded, pettiness, judgmental, conformity, and a shallow and silly nature. It is used by people who feel very alienated from society."[12] To enter fandom is to "escape" from the "mundane" into the marvelous.

The need to maintain contact with these new friends, often scattered across a broad geographic area, can require speculations and fantasies about the program content to take written form, first as personal letters, later as more public newsletters, "letterzines," or fan fiction magazines. Fan viewers become fan writers.

Over the twenty years since *Star Trek* was first aired, fan writing has achieved a semi-institutional status. Fan magazines, sometimes hand-typed, photocopied, and stapled, other times off-set printed and commercially bound, are distributed through the mail and sold at conventions, frequently reaching an international readership. *Writer's Digest* recently estimated that there were more than 300 amateur press publications that regularly allowed fans to explore aspects of their favorite films and television programs.[13] Although a wide variety of different media texts have sparked some fan writing, including *Star Wars, Beauty and the Beast, Wiseguy, Blake's 7, Battlestar Galactica, Doctor Who, Miami Vice, Road Warrior, Remington Steele, The Man from*

UNCLE, *Simon and Simon*, *The A-Team*, *The Professionals*, *Hill Street Blues*, and others, *Star Trek* continues to play the central role within fan writing. *Datazine*, one of several magazines that serve as central clearinghouses for information about fanzines, lists some 120 different *Star Trek*-centered publications currently in distribution. Although fan publications may take a variety of forms, fans generally divide them into two major categories: "letterzines," which publish short articles and letters from fans on issues surrounding their favorite shows, and "fictionzines," which publish short stories, poems, and novels concerning the program characters and concepts.[14] Some fan-produced novels, notably the works of Jean Lorrah and Jacqueline Lichtenberg, have achieved a canonized status in the fan community, remaining more or less in constant demand for more than a decade.[15]

It is important to distinguish between these fan-generated materials and commercially-produced works, such as the series of *Star Trek* novels released by Pocket Books under the official supervision of Paramount, the studio that owns the rights to the *Star Trek* characters. Fanzines are totally unauthorized by the program producers and indeed face the constant threat of legal action for their open violation of the producer's copyright authority over the show's characters and concepts. Paramount has tended to treat fan magazines with benign neglect so long as they are handled on an exclusively nonprofit basis. Producer Gene Roddenberry and many of the cast members have been known to contribute to such magazines. Bantam Books even released several anthologies showcasing the work of fan writers.[16]

Other producers have not been as kind. Lucasfilm initially sought to control *Star Wars* fan publications, seeing them as rivals to their officially sponsored fan organization, and later threatened to prosecute editors who published works that violated the "family values" associated with the original films. A letter circulated by Maureen Garrett, director of the official *Star Wars* Fan Club, summarized their position:

> Lucasfilm Ltd. does own *all* rights to the *Star Wars* characters and we are going to insist upon *no* pornography. This may mean no fanzines if that measure is what is necessary to stop the few from darkening the reputation our company is so proud of. . . . Since all of the *Star Wars* Saga is PG rated, any story those publishers do print should also be PG. Lucasfilm does not produce any X-Rated *Star Wars* episodes, so why should we be placed in a light where people think we do? . . . You don't own these characters and can't *publish* anything about them without permission.[17]

Such a scheme met considerable resistance from the fan-writing community, which generally regarded Lucas's actions as unwarranted interference in their own creative activity. Several fanzine editors continued to distribute adult-oriented *Star Wars* stories through an underground network of "special friends," even though such works were no longer publicly advertised through *Datazine* or sold openly at conventions. A heated editorial in *Slaysu*, a fanzine that routinely published feminist-inflected erotica set in various media universes, reflects these writers' opinions:

> Lucasfilm is saying, "you must enjoy the characters of the *Star Wars* universe for male reasons. Your sexuality must be correct and proper by my (male) definition." I am not male. I do not want to be. I refuse to be a poor imitation, or worse, of someone's idiotic ideal of femininity. Lucasfilm has said, in essence, "this is what we see in the *Star Wars* films and we are telling you that this is what you will see."[18]

C. A. Siebert's editorial asserts the rights of fanzine writers to consciously revise the character of the original texts, to draw elements from dominant culture in order to produce underground art that explicitly challenges patriarchal assumptions. Siebert and the other editors deny the traditional property rights of textual producers in favor of a right of free play with the program materials, a right of readers to use media texts in their own ways and of writers to reconstruct characters in their own terms. Once characters are inserted into popular discourse, regardless of their source of origin, they become the property of the fans who fantasize about them, not of the copyright holders who merchandise them. But the relationship between fan texts and primary texts is often more complex than Siebert's defiant stance might suggest, and some fans do feel bound by a degree of fidelity to the original series's conceptions of those characters and their interactions.

Gendered Readers/Gendered Writers

Media fan writing is an almost exclusively feminine response to mass media texts.[19] Men actively participate in a wide range of fan-related activities, notably interactive games and conference-planning committees, roles consistent with patriarchal norms that typically relegate combat—even combat fantasies—and organizational authority to the "masculine" sphere. Media fan writers and fanzine readers, however, are almost always female. Camille Bacon-Smith has estimated that more than 90 percent of all media fan writers are female.[20] The greatest percentage of male participation is found in the "letterzines," like *Comlink* and *Treklink*, and in "nonfiction" magazines, like *Trek*, that publish speculative essays on aspects of the program's "universe"; men may feel comfortable joining discussions of future technologies or military lifestyle, but not in pondering Vulcan sexuality, McCoy's childhood, or Kirk's love life.

Why this predominance of women within the media fan-writing community? Research suggests that men and women have been socialized to read for different purposes and in different ways. David Bleich asked a mixed group of college students to comment, in free-association fashion, on a body of canonized literary works. His analysis of their responses suggested that men focused primarily on narrative organization and authorial intent, while women devoted more energy to reconstructing the textual world and understanding the characters. He writes, "Women enter the world of the novel, take it as something 'there' for that purpose; men see the novel as a result of someone's action and construe its meaning or logic in those terms."[21] In a related study, Bleich asked some 120 University of Indiana freshmen to "retell as fully and as accurately as you can [William] Faulkner's 'Barn Burning,' " and again, noted substantial differences between men and women:

> The men retold the story as if the purpose was to deliver a clear simple structure or chain of information: these are the main characters, this is the main action, this is how it turned out. . . . The women present the narrative as if it were an atmosphere or an experience. (p. 256)

Bleich also found that women were more willing to enjoy free play with the story content, making inferences about character relationships that took them well beyond the information explicitly contained within the text. Such data strongly suggest that the practice of fan writing, the compulsion to expand speculations about characters and story events beyond textual boundaries, draws more heavily upon the types of interpretive strategies common to the "feminine" than to the "masculine."

Bleich's observations provide only a partial explanation as they do not fully account for why many women find it necessary to go beyond the narrative information while most men do not. As Teresa de Lauretis has noted, female characters often exist only in the margins of male-centered narratives:

> Medusa and the Sphinx, like the other ancient monsters, have survived inscribed in hero narratives, in someone else's story, not their own; so they are figures or markers of positions—places and topoi—through which the hero and his story move to their destination and through which they accomplish meaning.[22]

Texts written by and for men yield easy pleasures to their male readers yet may resist feminine pleasure. To fully enjoy the text, women are often forced to perform a kind of intellectual transvestitism — identifying with male characters in opposition to their own cultural experiences, or constructing unwritten countertexts through their daydreams or through their oral interaction with other women — that allows them to explore their own narrative concerns. This need to reclaim feminine interests from the margins of "masculine" texts produces endless speculation, speculation that draws the reader well beyond textual boundaries into the domain of the intertextual. Mary Ellen Brown and Linda Barwick have shown how women's gossip about soap opera inserts program content into an existing feminine oral culture.[23] Fan writing represents the logical next step in this cultural process: the transformation of oral countertexts into a more tangible form, the translation of verbal speculations into written works that can be shared with a broader circle of women. To do so, their status must change; no longer simply spectators, these women become textual producers.

Just as women's gossip about soap operas assumes a place within a preexisting feminine oral culture, fan writing adopts forms and functions traditional to women's literary culture. Cheris Kramarae has traced the history of women's efforts to "find ways to express themselves outside the dominant modes of expression used by men," to circumvent the ideologically-constructed interpretive strategies of masculine literary genres. Kramarae concludes that women have found the greatest room to explore their feelings and ideas within privately circulated letters and diaries and through collective writing projects.[24] Similarly, Carroll Smith-Rosenberg has discussed the ways in which the exchange of letters allowed nineteenth-century women to maintain close ties with other women, even when separated by great geographic distances and isolated within the narrow confines of Victorian marriage. Such letters provided a covert vehicle by which women could explore common concerns and even ridicule the men in their lives. Smith-Rosenberg concludes:

> Nineteenth-century women were, as Nathaniel Hawthorne reminds us, "damned scribblers." They spoke endlessly to one another in private letters and journals . . . about religion, gender roles, their sexuality and men's, about prostitution, seduction, and intemperance, about unwanted pregnancies and desired education, about their relation to the family and the family's to the world.[25]

Fan writing — with its circulation conducted largely through the mail, with its marketing mostly a matter of word of mouth, with the often collective construction of fantasy "universes," and with its highly confessional tone — clearly follows within that same tradition and serves

some of the same functions. The ready-made characters of popular culture provide these women with a set of common references that can help to facilitate discussions of their similar experiences and feelings with others with whom they may never have enjoyed face-to-face contact. They draw upon these shared points of reference to confront many of the same issues that concerned nineteenth-century women: religion, gender roles, sexuality, family, and professional ambition.

Why *Star Trek?*

While most texts within a male-dominated culture potentially spark some sort of feminine countertext, only certain programs have generated the kind of extended written responses characteristic of media fandom. Why, then, has the bulk of fan writing centered on science fiction, which Judith Spector has characterized as a "genre which . . . [has been until recently] hostile toward women," a genre "by, for and about men of action"?[26] Or around others like it (the cop show, the detective drama, or the western) that have represented the traditional domain of male readers? Why do these women struggle to reclaim such seemingly unfertile soil when there are so many other texts that more traditionally reflect "feminine" interests, and which feminist media critics are now trying to reclaim for their cause? In short, why *Star Trek?*

Obviously, no single factor can adequately account for all fanzines, a literary form that necessarily involves the translation of homogeneous media texts into a plurality of personal and subcultural responses. One partial explanation, however, might be that traditionally "feminine" texts—the soap opera, the popular romance, the "woman's picture"—do not need as much reworking as science fiction and westerns do in order to accommodate the social experience of women. The resistance of such texts to feminist reconstruction may require a greater expenditure of creative effort and therefore may push women toward a more thorough reworking of program materials than socalled feminine texts that can be more easily assimilated or negated.

Another explanation would be that these "feminine" texts satisfy, at least partially, the desires of traditional women yet fail to meet the needs of more professionally-oriented women. Indeed, a particular fascination of *Star Trek* for these women appears to be rooted in the way that the program seems to hold out a suggestion of nontraditional feminine pleasures, of greater and more active involvement for women within the adventure of professional space travel, while finally reneging on those promises. Sexual equality was an essential component of producer Gene Roddenberry's optimistic vision of the future. A woman, Number One (Majel Barrett), was originally slated to be the Enterprise's second-in-command. Network executives, however, consistently fought efforts to break with traditional "feminine" stereotypes, fearing the alienation of more conservative audience members.[27] "Number One" was scratched after the program pilot, but throughout the run of the series, women were often cast in nontraditional jobs, everything from Romulan commanders to weapons specialists. The networks, however reluctantly, were offering women a future, a "final frontier," that included them.

Fan writers, though, frequently express dissatisfaction with these women's characterizations within the episodes. In the words of fan writer Pamela Rose (1977), "When a woman is a guest star on *Star Trek*, nine out of ten times there is something wrong with her."[28] Rose notes that these female characters have been granted positions of power within the program only to demonstrate through their erratic emotion-driven conduct that women are unfit to fill such roles. Another fan writer, Toni Lay, expressed her mixed feelings about *Star Trek's* social vision:

> It was ahead of its time in some ways, like showing that a Caucasian, all-American, all-male crew was not the only possibility for space travel. Still, the show was sadly deficient in other ways, in particular, its treatment of women. Most of the time, women were referred to as "girls." And women were never shown in a position of authority unless they were aliens, i.e., Deela, T'Pau, Natira, Sylvia, etc. It was like the show was saying "Equal opportunity is OK for their women but not for our girls."[29]

Lay states that she felt "devastated" over the repeated failure of the series and the later feature films to give Lieutenant Uhura command duties commensurate with her rank: "When the going gets tough, the tough leave the womenfolk behind" (p. 15). She contends that Uhura and the other women characters should have been given a chance to demonstrate what they could do confronted by the same kinds of problems that their male counterparts so heroically overcome. The constant availability of the original episodes through re-runs and shifts in the status of women within American society throughout the past two decades have only made these unfulfilled promises more difficult to accept, requiring progressively greater efforts to restructure the program in order to allow it to produce pleasures appropriate to the current reception context.

Indeed, many fan writers characterize themselves as "repairing the damage" caused by the program's inconsistent and often demeaning treatment of its female characters. Jane Land, for instance, characterizes her fan novel, *Kista*, as "an attempt to rescue one of *Star Trek's* female characters [Christine Chapel] from an artificially imposed case of foolishness."[30] Promising to show "the way the future never was," *The Woman's List*, a recently established fanzine with an explicitly feminist orientation, has called for "material dealing with all range of possibilities for women, including: women of color, lesbians, women of alien cultures and women of all ages and backgrounds." Its editors acknowledge that their publication's project necessarily involves telling the kinds of stories that network policy blocked from airing when the series was originally produced. A recent flier for that publication explains:

> We hope to raise and explore those questions which the network censors, the television genre and the prevailing norms of the time made it difficult to address. We believe that both the nature of human interaction and sexual mores and the structure of both families and relationships will have changed by the twenty-third century and we are interested in exploring those changes.

Telling such stories requires the stripping away of stereotypically feminine traits. The series characters must be reconceptualized in ways that suggest hidden motivations and interests heretofore unsuspected. They must be reshaped into full-blooded feminist role models. While in the series Chapel is defined almost exclusively in terms of her unrequited passion for Spock and her professional subservience to Dr. McCoy, Jane Land represents her as a fiercely independent woman, capable of accepting love only on her own terms, prepared to pursue her own ambitions wherever they take her, outspoken in response to the patronizing attitudes of the command crew. C. A. Siebert has performed a similar operation on the character of Lt. Penda Uhura, as may be suggested by this passage from one of her stories:

> There were too few men like Spock who saw her as a person. Even Captain Kirk, she smiled, especially Captain Kirk, saw her as a woman first. He let her do certain things but only because military discipline required it. Whenever there was any danger, he tried to protect her. . . . Uhura smiled sadly, she would go on as she had been, outwardly a feminine toy, inwardly a woman who was capable and human.[31]

Here, Siebert attempts to resolve the apparent contradiction created within the series text by Uhura's official status as a command officer and her constant displays of "feminine frailty." Uhura's situation, Siebert suggests, is characteristic of the way that women must mask their actual competency behind traditionally "feminine" mannerisms within a world dominated by patriarchal assumptions and masculine authority. By rehabilitating Uhura's character in this fashion, Siebert has constructed a vehicle through which she can document the overt and subtle forms of sexual discrimination that an ambitious and determined woman faces as she struggles for a command post in Star Fleet (or for that matter, within a twentieth-century corporate boardroom).

Fan writers like Siebert, Land, and Karen Bates (whose novels explore the progression of a Chapel-Spock marriage through many of the problems encountered by contemporary couples trying to juggle the conflicting demands of career and family)[32] speak directly to the concerns of professional women in a way which more traditionally "feminine" works fail to do.[33] These writers create situations in which Chapel and Uhura must heroically overcome the same kinds of obstacles that challenged their male counterparts within the primary texts and often discuss directly the types of personal and professional problems particular to working women. Land's fan novel, *Demeter*, is exemplary in its treatment of the professional life of its central character, Nurse Chapel.[34] Land deftly melds action sequences with debates about gender relations and professional discrimination, images of command decisions with intimate glimpses of a Spock-Chapel marriage. An all-woman crew, headed by Uhura and Chapel, is dispatched on a mission to a feminist separatist space colony under siege from a pack of intergalactic drug smugglers who regard rape as a "manly" sport. In helping the colonists to overpower their would-be assailants, the women are at last given a chance to demonstrate their professional competence under fire, forcing Captain Kirk to reevaluate some of his command policies. *Demeter* raises significant questions about the possibilities of male-female interaction outside of patriarchal dominance. The meeting of a variety of different planetary cultures that represent alternative social philosophies and organizations, alternative ways of coping with the same essential debates surrounding sexual difference, allows for a far-reaching exploration of contemporary gender relations.

Genre Switching: From "Space Opera" to "Soap Opera"

If works like *Demeter* constitute intriguing prototypes for a new breed of feminist popular literature, they frequently do so within conventions borrowed as much from more traditionally "feminine" forms of mass culture as from *Star Trek* itself. For one thing, the female fans perceive the individual episodes as contributing to one great program text. As a result, fan stories often follow the format of a continuous serial rather than operating as a series of self-enclosed works. Tania Modleski has demonstrated the ways that the serial format of much women's fiction, particularly of soap opera, responds to the rhythms of women's social experience.[35] The shaky financing characteristic of the fanzine mode of production, the writers' predilections to engage in endless speculations about the program content and to continually revise their understanding of the textual world, amplifies the tendency of women's fiction to postpone resolution, transforming *Star Trek* into a "never-ending story." Fan fiction marches forward through a series of digressions as new speculations cause the writers to halt the advance of their chronicles to introduce events that "must have occurred" prior to the start of their stories or to introduce secondary plotlines that pull them from the main movement of the event chain. This kind of writing activity has been labeled a "story tree."

Camille Bacon-Smith explains:

> The most characteristic feature of the story tree is that the stories do not fall in a linear sequence. A root story may offer unresolved situations, secondary characters whose actions during the main events are not described or a resolution that is unsatisfactory to some readers. Writers then branch out from that story, completing dropped subplots, exploring the reactions of minor characters to major events. (p.26)

This approach, characteristic of women's writing in a number of cultures, stems from a sense of life as continuous rather than fragmented into a series of discrete events, from an outlook that is experience-centered, not goal-oriented: "Closure doesn't make sense to them. At the end of the story, characters go on living in the nebulous world of the not yet written. They develop, modify their relationships over time, age, raise families" (p.28).

Moreover, as Bacon-Smith's comments suggest, this type of reading and writing strategy focuses greater attention on ongoing character relationships than on more temporally-concentrated plot elements. Long-time fan writer Jacqueline Lichtenberg has summarized the difference: "Men want a physical problem with physical action leading to a physical resolution. Women want a psychological problem with psychological action leading to a psychological resolution."[36] These women express a desire for narratives that concentrate on the character relationships and explore them in a "realistic" or "mature" fashion rather than in purely formulaic terms, stories that are "true" and "believable" not "syrupy" or "sweet." Fan writers seek to satisfy these demands through their own *Star Trek* fiction, to write the kind of stories that they and other fans desire to read.

The result is a kind of genre switching, the rereading/rewriting of "space opera" as an exotic type of romance (and, often, the reconceptualization of romance itself as feminist fiction). Fanzines rarely publish exclusively action-oriented stories glorifying the Enterprise's victories over the Klingon-Romulan Alliance, their conquest of alien creatures, their restructuring of planetary governments, or their repair of potential flaws in new technologies, despite the prevalence of such plots in the original episodes. When such elements do appear, they are usually evoked as a background against which the more typical romance or relationship-centered stories are played or as a test through which female protagonists can demonstrate their professional skills. In doing so, these fan writers draw inspiration from feminist science fiction writers, including Joanna Russ, Marion Zimmer Bradley, Zenna Henderson, Marge Piercy, Andre Norton, and Ursula Le Guin, whose entry into the genre helped to redefine reader expectations about what constituted science fiction, pushing the genre toward greater and greater interest in "soft" science and sociological concerns and increased attention on interpersonal relationships and gender roles.[37] *Star Trek*, produced in a period when "masculine" concerns still dominated science fiction, is reconsidered in light of the newer, more feminist orientation of the genre, becoming less a program about the Enterprise's struggles against the Klingon-Romulan Alliance and more an examination of characters' efforts to come to grips with conflicting emotional needs and professional responsibilities.

Women, confronting a traditionally "masculine" "space opera," choose to read it instead as a type of women's fiction. In constructing their own stories about the series' characters, they turn frequently to the more familiar and comfortable formulas of the soap, the romance, and the feminist coming-of-age novel for models of storytelling technique. While the fans themselves often dismiss such genres as too focused on "mundane" concerns to be of great interest, the influence of such materials may be harder to escape. As Elizabeth Segel has suggested, our initial introduction to reading, the gender-based designation of certain books as suitable for young girls and others for young boys, can be a powerful determinant of our later reading/writing strategies, determining, in part, the relative accessibility of basic genre models for use in making sense of ready-made texts and for constructing personal fantasies.[38] As fans attempt to reconstruct the feminine "countertexts" that exist on the margins of the original series episodes, they have, in the process, refocused the series around traditional "feminine" and contemporary feminist concerns, around sexuality and gender politics, around religion, family, marriage, and romance.

Many fans' first stories take the form of romantic fantasies about the series' characters and frequently involve inserting glorified versions of themselves into the world of Star Fleet. A story by Bethann, "The Measure of Love," for instance, deals with a young woman, recently transferred to the Enterprise, who has a love affair with Kirk:

> We went to dinner that evening. Till that time, I was sure he'd never real-
> ly noticed me. Sitting across the table from him, I realized just what a
> vital alive person this man was. I had dreamed of him, but never im-
> agined my hopes might become a reality. But, this was real—not a
> dream. His eyes were intense, yet they twinkled in an amused sort of
> way. "Captain . . . "
>   "Call me Jim."[39]

Her romance with Kirk comes to an abrupt end when the young woman transfers to another ship without telling the Captain that she carries
his child because she does not want her love to interfere with his career.

Fans are often harshly critical of these so-called "Lt. Mary Sue" stories, which one writer labeled "groupie fantasies"[40] because of their
self-indulgence, their often hackneyed writing styles, their formulaic
plots, and their violations of the established characterizations. In
reconstituting *Star Trek* as a popular romance, these young women
have reshaped the series characters into traditional romantic heroes,
into "someone who is intensely and exclusively interested in her and in
her needs." [41] But many fan writers are more interested in what happens when this romantic ideal confronts a world that places professional duty over personal needs, when men and women must somehow
reconcile careers and marriage in a confusing period of shifting gender
relationships. Veteran fan writer Kendra Hunter writes, "Kirk is not
going to go off into the sunset with anyone because he is owned body
and soul by the Enterprise." [42] *Treklink* editor Joan Verba comments:
"No believable character is gushed over by so many normally level-
headed characters such as Kirk and Spock as a typical Mary Sue." [43]
Nor are the women of tomorrow apt to place any man, even Jim Kirk,
totally above all other concerns.

Some, though by no means all, of the most sophisticated fan fiction
also takes the form of the romance. Both Radway and Modleski note
popular romances' obsession with a semiotics of masculinity, with the
need to read men's often repressed emotional states from the subtle
signs of outward gesture and expression. The cold logic of Vulcan, the
desire to suppress all signs of emotion, make Spock and his father Sarek
especially rich for such interpretations. Consider this passage from
Lorrah's *Full Moon Rising*:

> The intense sensuality she saw in him [Sarek] in other ways suggested a
> hidden sexuality. She [Amanda] had noticed everything from the way he
> appreciated the beauty of a moonlit night or a finely-cut sapphire to the
> way his strongly-molded hands caressed the mellowed leather binding of
> the book she had given him. . . . That incredible control which she
> could not penetrate. Sometimes he deliberately let her see beyond it, as

he had done earlier this evening, but if she succeeded in making him lose control he would never be able to forgive her.[44]

In Lorrah's writings, the alienness of Vulcan culture becomes a metaphor for the many things that separate men and women, for the factors that block total intimacy within marriage. She describes her fiction as the story of "two people who are different physically, mentally, and emotionally, but who nonetheless manage to make a pretty good marriage" (p.2). While Vulcan restraint suggests the emotional sterility of traditional masculinity, their alien sexuality allows Lorrah to propose alternatives. Her Vulcans find sexual inequality to be "illogical," allowing very little difference in the treatment of men and women, an assumption shared by many fan writers. Moreover, the Vulcan mindmeld grants a degree of sexual and emotional intimacy unknown on earth; Vulcan men even employ this power to relieve women of labor pains and to share the experience of childbirth. Her lengthy writings on the decades-long romance between Spock's parents Amanda and Sarek represent a painstaking effort to construct a feminist utopia, to propose how traditional marriage might be reworked to allow it to satisfy the personal and professional needs of both men and women.

Frequently, the fictional formulas of popular romance are tempered by women's common social experiences as lovers, wives, and mothers under patriarchy. In Karen Bates's novels, Nurse Chapel must confront and overcome her feelings of abandonment and jealousy during those long periods of time when her husband, Spock, is totally absorbed in his work. Consider this passage from *Starweaver Two*:

> The pattern had been repeated so often, it was ingrained. . . . Days would pass without a word between them because of the hours he labored and poured over his computers. Their shifts rarely matched and the few hours they could be together disappeared for one reason or another. (p.10)

Far from an idyllic romance, Bates's characters struggle to make their marriage work in a world where professionalism is everything and the personal counts for relatively little. Jane Land's version of a Chapel/Spock marriage is complicated by the existence of children who must remain at home under the care of Sarek and Amanda while their parents pursue their space adventures. In one scene, Chapel confesses her confused feelings about this situation to a young Andorian friend: "I spend my life weighing the children's needs against my needs against Spock's needs, and at any given time I know I'm shortchanging someone" (p.27).

While some male fans denigrate these kinds of fan fiction as "soap operas with Kirk and Spock,"[45] these women see themselves as constructing "soap operas" with a difference—"soap operas" that reflect a feminist vision. In C. A. Siebert's words, "I write erotic stories for myself and for other women who will not settle for being less than human."[46] Siebert suggests that her stories about Lt. Uhura and her struggle for recognition and romance in a male-dominated Star Fleet have helped her to resolve her own conflicting feelings within a world of changing gender relations and to explore hidden aspects of her own sexuality. Through her erotica, she hopes to increase other women's awareness of the need to struggle against entrenched patriarchal norms. Unlike their counterparts in Harlequin romances, these women refuse to accept marriage and the love of a man as their primary goal; rather, these stories push toward resolutions that allow Chapel or Uhura to achieve both professional advancement and personal satisfaction. Unlike almost every other form of popular fiction, fanzine stories frequently explore the maturing of relationships beyond the nuptial vows, seeing marriage as continually open to new adventures, new conflicts, and new discoveries.

The point of contact between feminism and the popular romance is largely a product of these writers' particular brand of feminism, one that, for the most part, is closer to the views of Betty Friedan than to those of Andrea Dworkin. It is a feminism that urges a sharing of feelings and lifestyles between men and women rather than radical separation or unresolvable differences. Fan writing is a literature of reform, not of revolt. The women still acknowledge their need for the companionship of men, for men who care for them and make them feel special, even as they are asking for those relationships to be conducted in different terms. Jane Land's Nurse Chapel, who in *Demeter* is both fascinated and repelled by the feminist separatist colony, reflects these women's ambiguous and sometimes contradictory responses toward more radical forms of feminism. In the end, Chapel recognizes the potential need for such a place, for a "room of one's own," but sees greater potential in achieving a more liberated relationship between men and women. She learns to develop self-sufficiency, yet chooses to share her life with her husband, Spock, and to achieve a deeper understanding of their differing expectations about their relationship. Each writer grapples with these concerns in her own terms, but most achieve some compromise between the needs of women for independence and self-sufficiency on the one hand, and their needs for romance and companionship on the other. If this does not constitute a radical break with the romance formula, it does represent a progressive reformulation of that formula that pushes toward a gradual redefinition of existing gender roles within marriage and the workplace.

"The Right Way": The "Moral Economy" of Fan Fiction

Their underground status allows fan writers the creative freedom to promote a range of different interpretations of the basic program material and a variety of reconstructions of marginalized characters and interests, to explore a diversity of different solutions to the dilemma of contemporary gender relations. Fandom's IDIC philosophy ('Infinite Diversity in Infinite Combinations," a cornerstone of Vulcan thought) actively encourages its participants to explore and find pleasure within their different and often contradictory responses to the program text. It should not be forgotten, however, that fan writing involves a translation of personal response into a social expression and that fans, like any other interpretive community, generate their own norms, which work to ensure a reasonable degree of conformity among readings of the primary text. The economic risk of fanzine publishing and the desire for personal popularity ensure some responsiveness to audience demand, discouraging totally idiosyncratic versions of the program content. Fans try to write stories to please other fans; lines of development that do not find popular support usually cannot achieve financial viability.

Moreover, the strange mixture of fascination and frustration characteristic of fannish response means that fans continue to respect the creators of the original series, even as they wish to rework some program materials to better satisfy their personal interests. Their desire to revise the program material is often counterbalanced by their desire to remain faithful to those aspects of the show that first captured their interests. E. P. Thompson has employed the term "moral economy" to describe the way that eighteenth-century peasant leaders and street rioters legitimized their revolts through an appeal to "traditional rights and customs" and "the wider consensus of the community," asserting that their actions worked to protect existing property rights against those who sought to abuse them for their own gain.[47] The peasants' conception of a "moral economy" allowed them to claim for themselves the right to judge the legitimacy both of their own actions and those of the landowners and property holders: "Consensus was so strong that it overrode motives of fear or deference" (pp. 78–79).

An analogous situation exists in fandom: the fans respect the original texts yet fear that their conceptions of the characters and concepts may be jeopardized by those who wish to exploit them for easy profits, a category that typically includes Paramount and the network but excludes Roddenberry and many of the show's writers. The ideology of fandom involves both a commitment to some degree of conformity to the original program materials, as well as a perceived right to evaluate the legitimacy of any use of those materials, either by textual producers or by textual consumers. The fans perceive themselves as rescuing the show from its producers, who have manhandled its characters and then allowed it to die. In one fan's words, "I think we have made *ST* uniquely our own, so we do have all the right in the world (universe) to try to change it for the better when the gang at Paramount start worshipping the almighty dollar, as they are wont to do." [48] Rather than rewriting the series content, the fans claim to be keeping *Star Trek* "alive" in the face of network indifference and studio incompetence, of remaining "true" to the text that first captured their interest some twenty years before: "This relationship came into being because the fan writers loved the characters and cared about the ideas that are *Star Trek* and they refused to let it fade away into oblivion."[49] Such a relationship obliges fans to preserve a certain degree of "fidelity" to program materials, even as they seek to rework them toward their own ends. *Trek* magazine contributor Kendra Hunter writes, "*Trek* is a format for expressing rights, opinions, and ideals. Most every imaginable idea can be expressed through *Trek*. . . . But there is a right way."[50] Gross "infidelity" to the series' concepts constitutes what fans call "character rape" and falls outside of the community's norms. In Hunter's words:

> A writer, either professional or amateur, must realize that she . . . is not omnipotent. She cannot force her characters to do as she pleases. . . . The writer must have respect for her characters or those created by others that she is using, and have a full working knowledge of each before committing her words to paper. (p.75)

Hunter's conception of "character rape," one widely shared within the fan community, rejects abuses by the original series writers as well as by the most novice fan and implies that the fans themselves, not program producers, are best qualified to arbitrate conflicting claims about character psychology because they care about the characters in a way that more commercially motivated parties frequently do not. In practice, the concept of "character rape" frees fans to reject large chunks of the aired material, including entire episodes, and even to radically restructure the concerns of the show in the name of defending the purity of the original series concept. What determines the range of permissible fan narratives is finally not fidelity to the original texts but consensus within the fan community itself. The text they so lovingly preserve is the *Star Trek* they created through their own speculations, not the one that Gene Roddenberry produced for network airplay.

Consequently, the fan community continually debates what constitutes a legitimate reworking of program materials and what represents a violation of the special reader–text relationship that the fans hope to foster. The earliest *Trek* fan writers were careful to work within the framework of the information explicitly included within the broadcast episodes and to minimize their breaks with series conventions. In fan writer Jean Lorrah's words, "Anyone creating a *Star Trek* universe is bound by what was seen in the aired episodes; however, he is free to extrapolate from those episodes to explain what was seen in them."[51] Leslie Thompson explains, "If the reasoning [of fan speculations] doesn't fit into the framework of the events as given [on the program], then it cannot apply no matter how logical or detailed it may be."[52] As *Star Trek* fan writing has come to assume an institutional status in its own right and therefore to require less legitimization through appeals to textual "fidelity," a new conception of fan fiction has emerged, one that perceives the stories not as a necessary expansion of the original series text but rather as chronicles of "alternate universes," similar to the program world in some ways and different in others:

> The "alternate universe" is a handy concept wherein you take the basic *Star Trek* concept and spin it off into all kinds of ideas that could never be aired. One reason Paramount may be so liberal about fanzines is that by their very nature most fanzine stories could never be sold professionally. (L. Slusher, personal communication, August 1987)

Such an approach frees the writers to engage in much broader play with the program concepts and characterizations, to produce stories that reflect more diverse visions of human interrelationships and future worlds, to overwrite elements within the primary texts that hinder fan interests. But even "alternate universe" stories struggle to maintain some consistency with the original broadcast material and to establish some point of contact with existing fan interests, just as more "faithful" fan writers feel compelled to rewrite and revise the program material in order to keep it alive in a new cultural context.

Borrowed Terms: Kirk/Spock Stories

The debate in fan circles surrounding Kirk/Spock (K/S) fiction, stories that posit a homoerotic relationship between the show's two primary characters and frequently offer detailed accounts of their sexual couplings, illustrates these differing conceptions of the relationship between fan fiction and the primary series text.[53] Over the past decade, K/S stories have emerged from the margins of fandom toward numerical dominance over *Star Trek* fan fiction, a movement that has been met with considerable opposition from more traditional fans. For many, such stories constitute the worst form of character rape, a total violation of the established characterizations. Kendra Hunter argues that "it is out of character for both men, and as such, comes across in the stories as bad writing. . . . A relationship as complex and deep as Kirk/Spock does not climax with a sexual relationship" (p. 81). Other fans agree but for other reasons. "I do not accept the K/S homosexual precept as plausible," writes one fan. "The notion that two men that are as close as Kirk and Spock are cannot be 'just friends' is indefensible to me."[54] Others struggle to reconcile the information provided on the show with their own assumptions about the nature of human sexuality: "It is just as possible for their friendship to progress into a love affair, for that is what it is, than to remain status quo. . . . Most of us see Kirk and Spock simply as two people who love each other and just happen to be of the same gender."[55]

Some K/S fans frankly acknowledge the gap between the series characterizations and their own representations but refuse to allow their fantasy life to be governed by the limitations of what was actually aired. One fan writes, "While I read K/S and enjoy it, when you stop to review the two main characters of *Star Trek* as extrapolated from the TV series, a sexual relationship between them is absurd."[56] Another argues somewhat differently:

> We actually saw a very small portion of the lives of the Enterprise crew through 79 episodes and some six hours of movies. . . . How can we possibly define the entire personalities of Kirk, Spock, etc., if we only go by what we've seen on screen? Surely there is more to them than that! . . . Since I doubt any two of us would agree on a definition of what is "in character," I leave it to the skill of the writer to make the reader believe in the story she is trying to tell. There isn't any limit to what could be depicted as accurate behavior for our heroes.[57]

Many fans find this bold rejection of program limitations on creative activity, this open appropriation of characters, to be unacceptable since it violates the moral economy of fan writing and threatens fan fiction's privileged relationship to the primary text:

> [If] "there isn't any limit to what could be depicted as accurate behavior of our heroes," we might well have been treated to the sight of Spock shooting up heroin or Kirk raping a yeoman on the bridge (or vice-versa). . . . The writer whose characters don't have clearly defined personalities, thus limits and idiosyncrasies and definite characteristics, is the writer who is either very inexperienced or who doesn't have any respect for his characters, not to mention his audience.[58]

But as I have shown, all fan writing necessarily involves an appropriation of series characters and a reworking of program concepts as the

text is forced to respond to the fan's own social agenda and interpretive strategies. What K/S does openly, all fans do covertly. In constructing the feminine countertext that lurks in the margins of the primary text, these readers necessarily redefine the text in the process of rereading and rewriting it. As one fan acknowledges, "If K/S has 'created new characters and called them by old names,' then all fandom is guilty of the same."[59] Jane Land agrees: "All writers alter and transform the basic *Trek* universe to some extent, choosing some things to emphasize and others to play down, filtering the characters and concepts through their own perceptions."[60] If these fans have rewritten *Star Trek* in their own terms, however, many of them are reluctant to break all ties to the primary text that sparked their creative activity and, hence, feel the necessity to legitimate their activity through appeals to textual fidelity. The fans are uncertain how far they can push against the limitations of the original material without violating and finally destroying a relationship that has given them great pleasure. Some feel stifled by those constraints; others find comfort within them. Some claim the program as their personal property, "treating the series episodes like silly putty," as one fan put it.[61] Others seek compromises with the textual producers, treating the original program as something shared between them.

What should be remembered is that whether they cast themselves as rebels or loyalists, it is the fans themselves who are determining what aspects of the original series concept are binding on their play with the program material and to what degree. The fans have embraced *Star Trek* because they found its vision somehow compatible with their own, and they have assimilated only those textual materials that feel comfortable to them. Whenever a choice must be made between fidelity to their program and fidelity to their own social norms, it is almost inevitably made in favor of lived experience. The women's conception of the *Star Trek* realm as inhabited by psychologically rounded and realistic characters ensures that no characterization that violated their own social perceptions could be satisfactory. The reason some fans reject K/S fiction has, in the end, less to do with the stated reason that it violates established characterization than with unstated beliefs about the nature of human sexuality that determine what kinds of character conduct can be viewed as plausible. When push comes to shove, as Hodge and Tripp suggest, "Non-televisual meanings can swamp televisual meanings" and usually do.[62]

Conclusion

The fans are reluctant poachers who steal only those things that they truly love, who seize televisual property only to protect it against abuse from those who created it and who have claimed ownership over it. In embracing popular texts, the fans claim those works as their own, remaking them in their own image, forcing them to respond to their needs and to gratify their desires. Female fans transform *Star Trek* into women's culture, shifting it from space opera into feminist romance, bringing to the surface the unwritten feminine countertext that hides in the margins of the written masculine text. Kirk's story becomes Uhura's story and Chapel's and Amanda's as well as the story of the women who weave their own personal experiences into the lives of the characters. Consumption becomes production; reading becomes writing; spectator culture becomes participatory culture.

Neither the popular stereotype of the crazed Trekkie nor academic notions of commodity fetishism or repetition compulsion are adequate to explain the complexity of fan culture. Rather, fan writers suggest the need to redefine the politics of reading, to view textual property not as the exclusive domain of textual producers but as open to repossession by textual consumers. Fans continuously debate the etiquette of this relationship, yet all take for granted the fact that they are finally free to do with the text as they please. The world of *Star Trek* is what they choose to make it: "If there were no fandom, the aired episodes would stand as they are, and yet they would be just old reruns of some old series with no more meaning than old reruns of *I Love Lucy*."[63] The one text shatters and becomes many texts as it is fit into the lives of the people who use it, each in her or his own way, each for her or his own purposes.

Modleski recently, and I believe mistakenly, criticized what she understands to be the thrust of the cultural studies tradition: the claim that somehow mass culture texts empower readers.[64] Fans are not empowered *by* mass culture; fans are empowered *over* mass culture. Like de Certeau's poachers, the fans harvest fields that they did not cultivate and draw upon materials not of their making, materials already at hand in their cultural environment, but they make those raw materials work for them. They employ images and concepts drawn from mass culture texts to explore their subordinate status, to envision alternatives, to voice their frustrations and anger, and to share their new understandings with others. Resistance comes from the uses they make of these popular texts, from what they add to them and what they do with them, not from subversive meanings that are somehow embedded within them.

Ethnographic research has uncovered numerous instances where this occurs. Australian schoolchildren turn to *The Prisoner* in search of insight into their own institutional experience, even translating schoolyard play into an act of open insubordination against the teachers' authority.[65] American kindergartcners find in the otherness of Pee-wee Herman a clue to their own insecure status as semi-socialized beings.[66] British gay clubs host *Dynasty* and *Dallas* drag balls, relishing the bitchiness and trashiness of nighttime soap operas as a negation of traditional middle-class taste and decorum.[67] European leftists express their hostility to Western capitalism through their love–hate relationship with *Dallas*.[68] Nobody regards these fan activities as a magical cure for the social ills of postindustrial capitalism. They are no substitute for meaningful change, but they can be used effectively to build popular support for such change, to challenge the power of the culture industry to construct the common sense of mass society, and to restore a much-needed excitement to the struggle against subordination.

Alert to the challenge such uses pose to their cultural hegemony, textual producers openly protest this uncontrollable proliferation of meanings from their texts, this popular rewriting of their stories, this trespass upon their literary properties. Actor William Shatner (Kirk), for instance, has said of *Star Trek* fan fiction: "People read into it things that were not intended. In *Star Trek*'s case, in many instances, things were done just for entertainment purposes."[69] Producers insist upon their right to regulate what their texts may mean and what kinds of pleasure they can produce. But such remarks carry little weight. Undaunted by the barking dogs, the "no trespassing" signs, and the threats of prosecution, the fans have already poached those texts from under the proprietors' noses.

An earlier draft of this essay was presented at the 1985 Iowa Symposium and Conference on Television Criticism: Public and Academic Responsibility. I am indebted to Cathy Schwichtenberg, John Fiske, David Bordwell, and Janice Radway for their helpful suggestions as I was rewriting it for publication. I am particularly indebted to Signe Hovde and Cynthia Benson Jenkins for introducing me to the world of fan writing; without them my research could not have been completed. I have tried to contact all of the fans quoted in this text and to gain their permission to discuss their work. I appreciate their cooperation and helpful suggestions.

NOTES

1. Charles Leerhsen, "*Star Trek*'s Nine Lives." *Newsweek* (Dec. 22, 1986), p. 66.
2. For representative examples of other scholarly treatments of *Star Trek* and its fans, see Karin Blair, "Sex and *Star Trek*," *Science Fiction Studies* 10 (1983), pp. 292–297; Harvey Greenberg, "In Search of Spock: A Psychoanalytic Inquiry," *Journal of Popular Film and Television* 12 (1984),

pp. 53–65; Robert Jewett and John S. Lawrence, *The American Mono-myth* (Garden City, NY: Anchor Press, 1977); and William B. Tyre, "*Star Trek* as Myth and Television as Myth Maker," *Journal of Popular Culture* 10 (1977), pp. 711–719. Attitudes range from the generally sympathetic Blair to the openly hostile Jewett and Lawrence.

3. Robin Wood, *Hollywood: From Vietnam to Reagan* (New York: Columbia University Press, 1986), p. 164.

4. Michel de Certeau, *The Practice of Everyday Life* (Berkeley: University of California Press, 1984), p. 174.

5. Jean Ludlow, letter to *Comlink* 28, p. 17.

6. No scholarly treatment of *Star Trek* fan culture can avoid these pitfalls, if only because making such a work accessible to an academic audience requires a translation of fan discourse into other terms, terms that may never be fully adequate to the original. I come to both *Star Trek* and fan fiction as a fan first and a scholar second. My participation as a fan long precedes my academic interest in it. I have sought, where possible, to employ fan terms and to quote fans directly in discussing their goals and orientation toward the program and their own writing. I have shared drafts of this essay with fans and have incorporated their comments into the revision process. I have allowed them the dignity of being quoted from their carefully crafted, well-considered published work rather than from a spontaneous interview that would be more controlled by the researcher than by the informant. I leave it to my readers to determine whether this approach allows for a less mediated reflection of fan culture than previous academic treatments of this subject.

7. E. P. Thompson, "The Moral Economy of the English Crowd in the 18th Century," *Past and Present* 50, pp. 76–136.

8. Jean Lorrah, Foreword to *The Vulcan Academy Murders* (New York: Pocket, 1984).

9. P. L. Caruthers-Montgomery, letter to *Comlink* 28 (1987), p. 8.

10. Linda Deneroff, "A Reflection on the Early Days of *Star Trek* Fandom," *Comlink* 28 (1987), p. 3.

11. Toni Lay, letter to *Comlink* 28 (1986), p. 15.

12. Elizabeth Osbourne, letter to *Treklink* 9 (1987), pp. 3–4.

13. Carolyn Cooper, "Opportunities in the 'Media Fanzine' Market," *Writer's Digest* (Feb. 1987), p. 45.

14. The terms "letterzine" and "fictionzine" are derived from fan discourse. The two types of fanzines relate to each other in complex ways. Although there are undoubtedly some fans who read only one type of publication, many read both. Some letterzines, *Treklink* for instance, function as consumer guides and sounding boards for debates about the fictionzines.

15. Both Lorrah and Lichtenberg have achieved some success as professional science fiction writers. Many more science fiction writers emerged from the literary fanzine community. Marion Zimmer Bradley and C. J. Cherryh have been particularly instrumental in helping fan writers gain initial professional publications. For an interesting discussion of the relation-

ship between fan writing and professional science fiction writing, see Marta Randall, "Conquering the Galaxy for Fun and Profit," *Words in Our Pocket*, Celeste West (Paradise, CA: Dustbooks, 1985), pp. 233–241.

16. Sondra Marshak and Myrna Culbreath, *Star Trek: The New Voyages* (New York: Bantam Books, 1978).

17. Maureen Garrett, "Open Letter to *Star Wars* Zine Publishers" (August 1981), circulated informally.

18. Catherine A. Siebert, "By Any Other Name," *Slaysu* 4 (1982), p.44.

19. Media fan writing builds upon a much older tradition of "zine" publication within literary science fiction culture, dating back to the mid-1930s. For discussions of this earlier tradition, see Lester Del Rey, *The World of Science Fiction* (New York: Ballantine, 1979); Harry Warner, *All Our Yesterdays* (New York: Advent, 1969); and Sam Moskowitz, *The Immortal Storm* (New York: ASFO Press, 1954). These earlier fanzines differ from media fanzines in a number of significant ways: they were dominated by male fans; they published primarily essays or original fiction that borrowed generic elements of science fiction but not specific characters and situations; they were focused upon literary rather than media science fiction; they were far fewer in number and enjoyed smaller circulation than media zines. Media fans borrow traditional formats from these earlier zines, but give them a new focus and a new function; they were met with considerable hostility by the older literary science fiction community, though a number of media fans participate in traditional zine publishing as well as media-oriented ventures. Roberta Pearson has suggested to me that an interesting parallel to media fanzine publication may be the fan writings surrounding Sherlock Holmes, which date back to the beginning of this century. I do not at this time know enough about these publications to assess their possible relationship to *Trek* fan publishing.

20. Camille Bacon-Smith, "Spock Among the Women," *The New York Times Book Review* (Nov. 16, 1986), pp. 1, 26, 28.

21. David Bleich, "Gender Interests in Reading and Language," *Gender and Reading: Essays on Readers, Texts and Contexts*, eds. Elizabeth A. Flynn and P. P. Schweickart (Baltimore: Johns Hopkins University Press, 1986), p. 239.

22. Teresa de Lauretis, *Alice Doesn't: Feminism, Semiotics, Cinema* (Bloomington: Indiana University Press, 1982), p. 109.

23. Mary Ellen Brown and Linda Barwick, "Fables and Endless Generations: Soap Opera and Women's Culture." Paper presented at a meeting of the Society for Cinema Studies, Montreal (May, 1987).

24. Cheris Kramarae, *Women and Men Speaking* (Rowley, MS: Newbury House, 1981).

25. Carroll Smith-Rosenberg, *Disorderly Conduct: Gender in Victorian America* (New York: Alfred A. Knopf, 1985), p. 45.

26. Judith Spector, "Science Fiction and the Sex War: A Womb of One's

Own," *Gender Studies: New Directions in Feminist Criticism*, ed. Judith Spector (Bowling Green, OH: Bowling Green State University Press, 1986), p. 163.

27. S. E. Whitfield and Gene Roddenberry, *The Making of Star Trek* (New York: Ballantine Books, 1968).

28. Pamela Rose, "Women in the Federation." In *The Best of Trek 2*, eds. W. Irwin and G. B. Love (New York: New American Library, 1977).

29. Lay, letter to *Comlink*, p. 15.

30. Jane Land, *Kista* (Larchmont, NY: Author), p. 1.

31. Catherine A. Siebert, "Journey's End at Lover's Meeting," *Slaysu* 1 (1980), p. 33.

32. Karen Bates, *Starweaver Two* (Missouri Valley, IA: Ankar Press, 1982); *Nuages One* and *Nuages Two* (Tucson, AZ: Checkmate Press, 1982 and 1984).

33. Although a wide range of fanzines were considered in researching this essay, I have decided, for the purposes of clarity, to draw my examples largely from the work of a limited number of fan writers. While no selection could accurately reflect the full range of fan writing, I felt that Bates, Land, Lorrah and Siebert had all achieved some success within the fan community, suggesting that they exemplified, at least to some fans, the types of writing that were desirable and reflected basic tendencies within the form. Further, these writers have produced a large enough body of work to allow some commentary about their overall project rather than localized discussions of individual stories. I have also, wherever possible, focused my discussion around works still currently in circulation and therefore available to other researchers interested in exploring this topic. No slight is intended to the large number of other fan writers who also met these criteria and who, in some cases, are even better known within the fan community.

34. Jane Land, *Demeter* (Larchmont, NY: Author, 1987).

35. Tania Modleski, *Loving with a Vengeance: Mass-Produced Fantasies for Women* (Hamden, CT: Archon Books, 1982).

36. Jacqueline Lichtenberg, personal communication, August 1987.

37. I am indebted to K. C. D'Alessandro and Mary Carbine for probing questions that refined my thoughts on this particular issue.

38. Elizabeth Segal, "Gender and Childhood Reading," *Gender and Reading*, pp. 164–185.

39. Bethann, "The Measure of Love," *Grup* 5, p. 54.

40. Kendra Hunter, "Characterization Rape," *The Best of Trek 2*, p. 78.

41. Janice Radway, *Reading the Romance: Women, Patriarchy and Popular Literature* (Chapel Hill: University of North Carolina Press, 1984), p. 149.

42. Hunter, *The Best of Trek 2*, p. 78.

43. Joan Verba, "Editor's Corner," *Treklink* 6, p. 2.

44. Jean Lorrah, *Full Moon Rising* (Bronx, NY: Author, 1976), pp. 9–10.

45. Tim Blaes, letter to *Treklink* 9 (1987), p. 6.

46. Siebert, "By Any Other Name," pp. 44–45.
47. Thompson, p. 78.
48. Shari Schnuelle, letter to *Sociotrek* 4 (1987), p. 9.
49. Hunter, p. 77.
50. Hunter, p. 83.
51. Lorrah, introduction to *The Vulcan Academy Murders.*
52. Leslie Thompson, "*Star Trek* Mysteries—Solved!," *The Best of Trek*, eds. Walter Irwin and G. B. Love (New York: New American Library, 1974), p. 208.
53. The area of Kirk/Spock fiction falls beyond the project of this particular paper, raising issues similar yet more complex than those posed here. My reason for discussing it here is because of the light its controversial reception sheds on the norms of fan fiction and the various ways fan readers and writers situate themselves toward the primary text. For a more detailed discussion of this particular type of fan writing, see Patricia Frazer Lamb and Diana Veith, " Romantic Myth, Transcendence, and *Star Trek* Zines," Donald Palumbo (ed.), *Erotic Universe: Sexuality and Fantastic Literature* (New York: Greenwood Press, 1986), pp. 235–256, who argue that K/S stories, far from representing a cultural expression of the gay community, constitute another way of feminizing the original series text and of addressing feminist concerns within the domain of a popular culture that offers little space for heroic action by women.
54. Randal Landers, letter to *Treklink* 7 (1986), p. 10.
55. T'hera Snaider, letter to *Treklink* 8 (1987), p. 10.
56. M. Chandler, letter to *Treklink* 8 (1987), p. 10.
57. Regina Moore, letter to *Treklink* 4 (1986), p. 7.
58. Slusher, personal communication, p. 11.
59. Moore, p. 7.
60. Land, *Demeter*, p. ii.
61. Blaes, p. 6.
62. Robert Hodge and David Tripp, *Children and Television: A Semiotic Approach* (Cambridge, England: Polity Press, 1986), p. 144.
63. Hunter, p. 77.
64. Tania Modleski, ed., *Studies in Entertainment: Critical Approaches to Mass Culture* (Bloomington: Indiana University Press, 1986).
65. Hodge and Tripp; Patricia Palmer, *The Lively Audience* (Sidney, Australia: Unwin & Allen, 1986).
66. Henry Jenkins III, "Going Bonkers!: Children, Play and Pee-wee," *Camera Obscura* 17 (May 1988), pp. 168–193.
67. Mark Finch, "Sex and Address in *Dynasty*," *Screen* 27, pp. 24–42.
68. Ien Ang, *Watching Dallas* (London: Methuen, 1986).
69. Ian Spelling, Robert Lofficier, and Jean-Marie Lofficier, "William Shatner, Captain's Log: *Star Trek V*," *Starlog* (May 1987), p. 40.

From Domestic Space to Outer Space:
The 1960s Fantastic Family Sit-Com
Lynn Spigel

It's a warm July night in 1969, and millions of Americans sit before their television sets, with a gleam of hope and a beer can in hand, awaiting the arrival of history. There, on the small screen of the living room console, a man steps out of his large white spaceship and onto a crater-covered surface. His limbs float in slow-motion gestures, his distant voice breaks through the static, and then, with a "giant leap for mankind," a small American flag anchors familiar meanings onto an alien landscape. This is Apollo 11, the mission to the moon, the realization of a decade-long American dream, the biggest crowd pleaser in television memory.

Like all technological triumphs, the moon landing was fully enmeshed in political, social, cultural, and economic struggles. What I find particularly interesting are the meanings space travel had for television itself—and for the burgeoning American culture based on watching TV. For above all, the public's knowledge of space was communicated through the procession of rocket take-offs and orbits broadcast during the 1960s. But more than just transmitting a privileged view of the universe, television offered the American public a particular mode of comprehension. It represented space, like everything else, as a place that the white middle-class family could claim as its own. Yet this epistemology of space was not merely an attempt to colonize the unknown with familiar values. In many ways the fascination with space served to defamiliarize the common myths of the "Golden Age" of the 1950s and the notions of domesticity that so pervaded television's "message" in that decade.

In the 1960s, television would construct for itself a new generic form founded on the merger between the troubled paradise of 1950s domesticity and the new-found ideals of the American future.[1] We might call this form the *fantastic family sit-com*, a hybrid genre that mixed the conventions of the suburban sit-com past with the space-age imagery of the New Frontier. Programs like *I Dream of Jeannie*, *My Favorite Martian*, *The Jetsons*, and *Lost In Space* were premised on an uncanny mixture of suburbia and space travel, while shows like *My Mother the Car*, *Mr. Ed*, *My Living Doll*, and *Bewitched* played with a seemingly incongruous blend of suburban banality and science fiction fantasy.[2]

These programs have received little critical attention, most certainly because they seem to represent the "lower depths" of television's prime-time past. Typically in this vein, critics tend to view such shows within the logic of cultural hierarchies, seeing their value in negative terms — that is, as the opposite of high art. Rather than leading to knowledge, these programs are said to constitute an escape from reason. Consider David Marc's recent thesis that sees them as reflections of the turned-on, tuned-out ethos of 1960s drug culture and locates their popularity in "de-politicization through escapist fantasy."[3] Yet reading these sit-coms as transparent reflections of a desire to escape fails to explain their often satirical and critical aspects. These genre hybrids did not simply reflect a collective desire to flee from the present; rather, the collision of science fiction fantasy with domestic comedy resulted in programs that contested their own form and content. Fantastic sit-coms were a complex organization of contradictory ideas, values, and meanings concerning the organization of social space and everyday life in suburbia. To understand how they emerged, we should read them in relation to historical changes that created the conditions in which they could flourish. In the following pages, I discuss historical shifts that were crucial to the rise of the fantastic sit-com and then suggest ways to see these shows as popular texts that allowed for diverse, often critical, perspectives on the social world.

Dystopian Visions and a New Space-Age Future

The intricate bond between television and space-age imagery can be understood as a response to a series of disillusionments that began to be most deeply felt in the late 1950s. By the end of that decade, Americans were looking backward at the great white hopes that had somehow led them down a blind alley. The utopian dreams for technological supremacy, consumer prosperity, and domestic bliss were revealing their limits in ways that could no longer be brushed aside. With consumer debt mounting, the stock market felt its first major slide of the decade in 1957. In that same year, Americans witnessed the most stunning technological embarrassment of the times when the Soviet Union beat the United States into space with Sputnik. While these national failures signaled harder times, the promise of easy living and barbecues in every yard was turned into the substance of nightmarish visions as social critics wrote voluminously of the anomie and emptiness experienced in the mass-produced suburbs. And as the walls of Levittown came tumbling down, television, the central household fixture of suburban bliss, also joined the pantheon of fallen idols.

As James Baughman has argued, disappointment in American institutions and lifestyles was typical among liberals and intellectuals who felt disenfranchised in Eisenhower's America.[4] But importantly, I want to stress, such cultural anxieties were also voiced in popular venues. Magazines, newspapers, popular books, and films looked critically at the past and established a set of discursive conventions through which Americans might reflect on their experiences. These critical views anticipated a series of changes in the meanings and practices surrounding television in the next decade.

In this context, critiques of suburbia were especially bitter, particularly when we consider the hopes invested in this new "promised land" at the beginning of the decade. After World War II, suburban towns were a practical alternative to hardships in the city. A severe housing shortage in urban centers was soothed by Federal Housing Association (FHA) construction loans and low-interest mortgages provided through the GI Bill. These government-financed projects made it possible for builders like Levitt and Sons to offer mass-produced housing at extremely low prices, so low in fact that it cost less to buy a home than to rent an apartment in the city. The suburbs were essentially built for the white middle class, and FHA policies guaranteed the communities' racial make-up. Building loans were predicated on red-lining (or zoning) practices that effectively kept all "undesirables" out of the lily-white neighborhoods.

For the white middle class, the suburbs quickly became more than just a practical alternative to the urban housing crisis. They were glorified in popular culture as a new land of plenty—the answer to Depression and wartime shortages. Home magazines presented wondrous designs, spacious ranch houses with rolling green yards, shiny pink appliances, and happy white families at play inside. But practical realities of post-war life necessitated certain alterations of this middle-class ideal. Cramped quarters took the place of the magazines' spacious ranch homes, and rather than gazing out at rolling green yards, residents found themselves sandwiched between the identical houses of their next-door neighbors.

Early in the 1950s, a number of critics expressed doubts about the homogeneous living arrangements and conformist attitudes that characterized middle-class lifestyles, and by the end of the decade, the mass-produced suburbs had become the subject of widespread concern.[5] John Keats's *A Crack in the Picture Window* (1956) presented unflattering pictures of the new suburbanites, with characters like John and Mary Drone, whose lives were spent deciding how to buy washing machines and avoid their busy-body neighbors. William Whyte's *The Organization Man* (1956) was a damning critique of the new company boys, whose willingness to conform to job expectations was mirrored by the peer-pressure policies of their suburban lifestyles. And in *The City in History* (1961), Lewis Mumford criticized the new organization of social space and the homogeneous lifestyles it encouraged.

The post-war cult of domesticity was wearing especially thin for women, and their dissatisfaction began to gain ground in popular thought by the end of the decade. Despite the glorification of the house-wife's role, women had joined the labor force at significant rates in the 1950s, and in particular, the number of married female workers rose substantially; by 1962 they accounted for about 60 percent of the fe-male labor force.[6] Thus when Betty Friedan attacked domestic ideolo-gy and institutional sexism in the *Feminine Mystique* (1963), she received widespread support.

Popular entertainment forms also expressed dismay with middle-class lifestyles. Film melodramas like Douglas Sirk's *All That Heaven Allows* (1956) and *Imitation of Life* (1959) showed the rigid social codes of middle-class ideals and the devastating consequences that class, race, and gender expectations had for the public. Popular media aimed at youth especially questioned middle-class family values. Rock 'n' roll gave teenagers the chance to participate in a new youth culture, separate from their parents, while youth films like *Rebel Without a Cause* (1955) and *King Creole* (1958) made juvenile delinquents into popular heroes, thereby providing teenagers with role models that challenged the suburban family ideal.[7]

If the nation was keen on self-loathing by the end of the decade, one event would provide even more reason for angst. On October 4, 1957, Americans suffered a grave blow to their sense of national esteem when the Soviet Union beat the United States into space with Sputnik. Cold-war logic was predicated upon America's ability to prevail in all tech-nological endeavors, especially those associated with national security. Thus the advent of a Russian rocket soaring into orbit sharply contrast-ed with previous conventions for representing American relations with the Soviets. Ironically, just three days after Sputnik's launch, *Life* presented the first of a multi-part issue entitled "Man's New World," which claimed that "the present lives and future fortunes of every American man, woman and child are directly and immediately affected by the gigantic technical strides of the past few years."[8]

As Walter McDougall has argued, Sputnik quickly became a major media crisis.[9] Critics expressed anxieties about the nation's technologi-cal agenda, claiming that American science had put its faith in con-sumer durables rather than concentrating on the truly important goals of national security. As Henry Luce of *Life* said, "For years no knowledgeable U.S. scientist has had any reason to doubt that his Russian opposite number is at least his equal. It has been doubted only by people—some of them in the Pentagon—who confuse scientific progress with freezer and lipstick output."[10] These criticisms grew out of and reinforced a more general dismay with consumer capitalism that was voiced over the course of the post-war years. Science fiction writers Cyril Kornbluth and Frederik Pohl told of a future dominated by advertisers in their popular book *The Space Merchants* (1953), while nonfiction books like Vance Packard's *The Hidden Persuaders* (1957) and John Kenneth Galbraith's bestseller *The Affluent Society* (1958) attacked various aspects of consumer culture. Such concerns were fueled by the recession of 1957–58, which created more general doubts about the consumer economy. Private debt increased from $73 billion to $196 billion during the 1950s, so when the Eisenhower administration suggested that the recession could be overcome by increased consumer purchases, not all Americans took solace in the buy now/pay later recovery plan.[11] In this economic and discursive context, Sputnik seemed a particularly poignant symbol of America's misconceived goals.

Finally, the United States began a series of attempts to find its own path to glory. Two months after the launching of Sputnik I, on December 6, 1957, America made its first foray into space, with its own rocket, Vanguard I. Vanguard rose four feet off the launch pad and sank in front of swarms of newspaper reporters and television cameras. The popular press called Vanguard such derisive names as "Flopnik," "Kaputnik," and "Stayputnik."

Thus, by the end of the decade, anxieties about private and public goals were being voiced in both intellectual and popular culture. But, rather than simply signaling the end of a golden era, this historical conjuncture of disappointments provided the impetus for a new utopian future—one based on the rhetoric of Kennedy's New Frontier and fortified with the discourse of science and technology.

The ideology of the New Frontier promised Americans a way to join the march of history. This was accomplished, not through a radical revolution in contemporary lifestyles, but rather through a liberal blend of private ethics with national purpose. The New Frontier was in this sense a popular movement, one that forged an alliance between its own political agenda and the patterns, meanings, and values of the past. In fact, the degree to which the American people were actually fatigued with their existence is not at all certain. In 1960, a nationwide survey in *Look* suggested that "most Americans today are relaxed, unadventurous, comfortably satisfied with their way of life and blandly optimistic about the future." *Look* went on to explain that American plans for the future were "mainly concerned with home and family." As for the larger arena of national purpose and progress in space, *Look* summed up the attitude with the words of one Milwaukee woman who confided, "We are pretty far removed from outer space here on 71st Street." Indeed, as *Look* went on to describe, people were far more concerned with everyday realities. "The chief worry of a lumber dealer in South Dakota," *Look* reported, "was 'having only one channel to watch on TV.' " Importantly, however, the magazine packaged this national complacency within a new and more exciting image. *Look* called the issue "Soaring into the Sixties," and it displayed a rocket on the cover—one that, unlike the flopniks of the past, was clearly taking off.[12] Indeed, just as *Look*'s editors were able to turn a land of happy homebodies into a nation bound for glory, the construction of the New Frontier was largely accomplished through media discourses that envisioned new and potent ways to organize past experiences.

The Kennedy administration eagerly adapted its own political agenda to the new space-age metaphors—metaphors based on the tenets of progress, democracy, and national freedom. The forthright do-gooder citizen to whom Kennedy appealed was given the promise of a new beginning in abstract terms. Ideas like freedom need an image, and the ride into space proved to be the most vivid concretization of such abstractions, promising a newfound national allegiance through which we would not only diffuse the Soviet threat, but also shake ourselves out of the doldrums that 1950s life had come to symbolize.

As other historians have argued, the promise of reaching the moon by the end of the decade was a political coup for a president intent on garnering public support. After the embarrassments of the Bay of Pigs and the Soviet launching of Yuri Alekseyevich Gagarin into space, Kennedy was able to transform the scrutinizing gaze of defeat into a new look that reached upward to the heavens. Building on the firmly entrenched associations between space weaponry and national security (especially Congress's creation of the civilian-controlled National Aeronautics and Space Administration [NASA] in 1958), the Kennedy administration devised a solid technocratic plan through which to shift public consciousness away from our military expansionism overseas and onto the idea of space travel. In 1961, the President sent Congress a new budget that poured millions into NASA, and a new theatrics of space emerged with astronaut stars appearing on the covers of national magazines.

The goals of the Kennedy administration merged particularly well with those of the television industry, which at this time was facing a public image crisis of its own. By the latter half of the 1950s, the networks had become the target of attacks launched primarily by influential east-coast critics who began to mourn the passing of television's "Golden Age." As Baughman has argued, the critics, who were mostly liberals, saw television as an emblem of their disenfranchisement in Eisenhower's America.[13] Dismayed by programming trends that favored popular rather than elite (i.e., their) tastes, they were especially upset by the cancellation of "prestige" programs like anthology dramas and *See It Now* (whose ousting in 1958 sparked a particularly heated debate), and they protested the slew of sit-coms, westerns, and quiz shows that had taken the place of what they considered higher television art.

This situation was exacerbated in 1959 when Congress's investigation of the quiz-show scandals revealed that the sponsors had fed answers to contestants in the hope of heightening dramatic appeal. The critics seized the moment, blaming the breach of public trust on egghead contestants like Professor Charles Van Doren, shady sponsors like Revlon, the money-grubbing networks, and the negligent regulators at the Federal Communications Commission (FCC). Having been one of the most popular program types, the quiz shows now were proof of the dangers of "low" television. As such, they enabled discourses on aesthetic and moral reform to emerge with a new purpose, creating a basis upon which critics, educators, the clergy and other cultural elites could ridicule popular tastes. After blaming the deceitful advertisers and negligent FCC, the *New Republic* concluded that

> a real investigation would center on a simple question: why is television so bad, so monotonous? The change over the past few years from Elvis Presley to Pat Boone is progress, from the obscene to the insipid. But is that the best TV can do? Must the majority of TV time be given to . . . the weary insouciance of the Bings and Frankies, the smiling but vacuous goings-on of Gale Storm, Donna Reed, Ernie Ford, Betty Hutton, June Allyson, Mickey Rooney, Ozzie and Harriet?[14]

In April of 1959, in the midst of these controversies, the FCC announced a new inquiry into network operations. Ultimately, however, rather than revamping the network system, the regulators adopted a reform strategy centered on program quality. In 1961, in his address to the National Association of Broadcasters, FCC Chair Newton Minow called television a "vast wasteland," attacking, in particular, popular entertainment formats. While he was critical about the networks' "concentration of power," his reform program did not attack the structure of commercial television; instead, it ridiculed its products. Popular formats like sit-coms, quiz shows, and westerns were "low TV," while his proposed educational and pay channels would ensure cultural uplift.[15]

By focusing on issues of high and low TV, Minow placed himself squarely within the discourses of the culture-critics before him, and his position as FCC Chairman gave this kind of TV bashing an official stamp of approval.

In the wake of this public-image crisis, the networks found the look-ahead spirit of Kennedy's New Frontier to be a potent metaphor, one that might divert attention away from the scandals of the past and create a new utopian purpose for the medium. In their attempt to restore the cultural validity of television and to ward off the more practical threat of regulatory action, the networks cultivated information programming, lengthening their 15-minute news programs to half an hour in 1963 and showcasing hard-hitting documentaries.[16] Perhaps not surprisingly, at a time when the ontological status of the television image was thrown into question by the fraudulent histrionics of the quiz shows, the networks turned to reality-oriented formats with renewed vigor.

In this general programming context, the space race became a privileged focus of attention. Documentary formats found space travel to be a particularly compelling subject of inquiry, and news teams eagerly covered rocket launchings throughout the decade.[17] Here, the political agenda of Kennedy's New Frontier and the networks' search for cultural validity merged harmoniously. Kennedy's promise to land on the moon before the end of the decade became television's promise as well. The space race gave television something to shoot for. It presented a whole new repertoire of images and created a whole new reason for looking at the living room console.

Information formats, in this and other ways, took up the challenge of national purpose and served, in large part, as an antidote to the attack on television's debased form. But the limits of public discourse foreclosed the possibility that entertainment television could be treated in the same vein. Indeed, as the critics (and Minow) had argued, sitcoms, quiz shows, westerns, and the like were resolutely low. While intended to infuse television with a set of "moral" guidelines, critical categories of high and low culture enabled the industry to divide its attention. With documentary and news formats to satisfy the reform demands of the wasteland critique, the industry continued to present its "low" — and markedly popular — money-making formats. Still, entertainment programming underwent its own peculiar transition. Although in distorted and circuitous ways, the progressive spirit of the New Frontier and its focus on space-age imagery served as a launching pad for significant revisions in television's fictional forms.

To the Moon, Alice!

In 1966, *Mad* magazine presented a cartoon saga of the perfect American television family, Oozie, Harried, Divot, and Rickety Nilson, who "lived completely and hermetically sealed off from reality." The story's opening panel showed Oozie comfortably reading his newspaper, which Harried had doctored-up in order to soothe the tensions of the day. Harried stands grinning in the foreground of the panel, where she tells her housewife friend, "I cut out all the articles that might disturb him"; as proof of her deed we see large cut-out areas under headlines that read "Vietnam," "Laos," and "race riots." Nevertheless, Oozie complains to Harried of his action-packed day. "First," he drones, "I pulled the wrong cord on the Venetian blind. . . . Then, Art Linkletter's House Party was preempted by a Space Shot. . . . It's been one thing after another."[18]

Mad, January 1966

As *Mad* so humorously suggested, the middle-class suburban sitcom was vastly out of sync with the problems of the nation. Indeed, its codes of realism (the bumbling but lovable dads, the perfect loving wives, the mundane storylines) were, by this time, codes of satire and parody. If the suburban sit-coms had once explained the ideals and goals of the nation, they no longer seemed to match the real world at all, as is vividly expressed by Oozie's choice of television programs. He prefers the family doldrums of Art Linkletter's *House Party* to the country's national goals in space.

Mad's TV spoof was part of a more general shift in popular representations of family life on television in the 1960s. Programs like *Bewitched*, *I Dream of Jeannie*, *Green Acres*, *The Beverly Hillbillies*, *The Jetsons*, *My Living Doll*, *The Addams Family*, and *The Munsters* poked fun at narrative conventions of the sit-com form and engaged viewers in a popular dialogue through which they might reconsider social ideals. In their own context, they took up the challenge of the New Frontier, but rather than providing a rational-scientific discourse on the public sphere (like that of the 1960s documentary), they presented a highly irrational, supernatural discourse on private life. In other words, they launched a critique of the American family in ways that were antithetical to the norms of television's "high" art forms.

These programs can be understood in the context of other media forms (magazines, rock 'n' roll, youth films, melodramas, and so on) that gave voice to critical perspectives on the social world. Borrowing from the discourses of previous texts and transmuting already established generic conventions, the fantastic sit-com provided a cultural space in which anxieties about everyday life could be addressed, albeit through a series of displacements and distortions. The sit-com format was an apt vehicle for this because it offered ready-made conflicts over gender roles, domesticity, and suburban lifestyles, while its laugh tracks, harmonious resolutions, and other structures of denial functioned as safety valves that diffused the "trouble" in the text. Moreover, its proclivity to deal with "contemporary" subject matter made the genre responsive to larger shifts in the social world.

In the most basic terms, changes in the family sit-com can be charted through a demographic analysis of family structure and living arrangements. In the early half of the 1950s, domestic comedies tended to present a varied demographic group that included families living in urban areas (such as *I Love Lucy*, *Make Room for Daddy*, and *My Little Margie*), suburban areas (such as *I Married Joan*, *Ozzie and Harriet*, and *My Favorite Husband*), and notably, ethnic and working-class types like Italian immigrants (*Life with Luigi*), Blacks (*Amos 'n' Andy*, *Beulah*) and working-class families (*The Honeymooners*, *The Life of Riley*). These programs appealed to television's early audience, which was located primarily in urban centers (especially the Northeast) and which could most strongly relate to these ethnic/urban types. As television became a national medium (by 1955 it was more evenly disseminated throughout the country), producers, networks, and advertisers tried to appeal to a more homogeneous, middle-class audience. In addition, as George Lipsitz has suggested, when the Hollywood majors rigorously entered into television production in the mid-1950s, these ethnic/working-class programs, which tended to be produced by small independents, began to wane.[19]

Concurrent with these shifts, the conventions for representing the family group changed over the course of the decade. Although these developments were somewhat uneven, significant trends can be tracked. Out of the seventeen different family sit-coms that aired on network prime time between 1957 and 1960, fourteen were set in the suburbs.[20] Meanwhile, the ethnic variations disappeared, so that by September 1960, they were all off the networks.[21] By the end of the decade, the middle-class suburban sit-com had become the primary form for representing family life. Programs like *Ozzie and Harriet*, *Leave It to Beaver*, *The Donna Reed Show*, *Father Knows Best*, and the more "moderne" *Dick Van Dyke Show* dramatized, with varying degrees of humor, the lives of nuclear families in suburban towns. The families included a modest number of children, a contented couple, and almost always lived near a group of friendly — if quirky — neighbors who were obviously of the same social class. Donna (Reed) Stone, for example, lived in the perfect suburban town of Hilldale with her physician-husband Alex Stone, her two children, and her next-door neighbor, Midge Kelsey (whose husband was also a doctor). Unlike such earlier zany sit-com characters as Lucy Ricardo (*I Love Lucy*) and Joan Stevens (*I Married Joan*), who tried desperately to break out of their domestic spaces, the women in these sit-coms were typically happy housewives who, despite the everyday strains of mothering, had put their faith in the suburban dream.

If these programs were out of sync with the widespread critique of suburbia at the end of the decade, they nevertheless remained on the networks through the early part of the 1960s, and until 1964, several ranked in the top twenty-five on the Nielsen charts. Most strikingly, however, by the fall 1966 season, all had been taken off the air.[22] This trend continued in the coming years; between 1966 and 1969 only three out of the thirty-two different domestic comedies aired on network prime time were suburban family sit-coms.[23] Taking their place were two new types that gained ground in the early to mid-1960s: the broken-family sit-com and the fantastic family sit-com.[24]

In the former, the middle-class family still constituted the focus of the show, but one parent was missing. This corresponded to the rising divorce rates of the 1960s, but in the fictional representation, the missing parent was never absent because of divorce (which was a network censorship taboo) but because he or she had died.[25] In this way, the broken-family sit-com signaled changes in family structure, but it also often smoothed over these social changes by including a character who functioned narratively as a surrogate parent. Thus, Uncle Charlie in *My Three Sons*, Aunt Bee in *The Andy Griffith Show*, and governess Katy Holstrum in *The Farmer's Daughter* were among a long list of stand-in parents.

In the fantastic sit-coms, families were also often formed in new ways. The genre was populated by unmarried couples such as Jeannie and Tony in *I Dream of Jeannie*, extended families such as *The Addams Family* (with Uncle Fester, Grandmama, and Cousin It), and childless couples such as Wilbur and Carol in *Mr. Ed*. But these sit-coms presented more than just demographic changes; they provided narrative situations and themes that suggested a clear departure from the conventions of the suburban family sit-coms that preceded them. These genre hybrids were parodic in nature because they retained the conventions of the previous form, but they made these conventions strange by mismatching form and content.

Bewitched, for example, employs the narrative conventions of the middle-class suburban sit-com. Its narrative structure revolves around the comedic complications and harmonious resolutions common to the sit-com genre as a whole. Typically, Darrin Stephens has an important advertising account at the office, but his domestic situation leads to complications. Often his mother-in-law Endora finds reason to spark a fight that creates havoc for the rest of the episode. This narrative complication is then neutralized by Samantha, who mediates the dispute, wins Darrin's ad account, and thus restores narrative harmony. The setting — an ideal two-story home located in a middle-class town — also borrows its conventions from the middle-class suburban sit-com. Similarly, the program retains clear gender divisions between public and private space, with Samantha taking the role of housewife and Darrin an executive in a high-rise office. Gladys and Abner Kravitz function as the neighbor characters of the earlier form. But in all of this, something is amiss. Samantha is a witch, and her supernatural powers recast the narrative situation so that the conventional becomes strange. Warlocks, witch doctors, and evil witches populate the traditionally decorated rooms of the Stephens's home, while powerful spells bring Ben Franklin, Mother Goose, and tooth fairies alive. In a similar way, programs like *Mr. Ed*, *My Mother the Car*, *I Dream of Jeannie*, *The Addams Family*, and *My Living Doll* retained the conventional forms of the suburban sit-com past but infused them with talking horses, conversing cars, genies, ghouls, and robots.

This peculiar mixture of domesticity and fantastic situations could be found outside the sit-com form in other popular venues. These series employed discursive strategies that were also used in representations of science and, in particular, space science. During the 1950s and 1960s, the American media communicated ideas about space through tropes of domesticity and family romance. National magazines mixed everyday situations with fantastic scenarios of space travel. In 1958, *Look* quoted lyrics from songs about space written by children of parents at the missile test program at Cape Canaveral. Another article showed how a vacationing family, dressed for summer fun, found Cocoa Beach a perfect place to watch for "imminent missile launchings" while "tak[ing] in the sun and the sights at the same time."[26]

The discursive conjuncture between domestic and outer space found its standard form in *Life*'s biographical essays, which presented technical information alongside multi-page spreads depicting family scenes and life histories of the astronauts. For example, in the May 18, 1962 issue, Scott Carpenter was pictured with his wife Rene on the cover, while the inside story showed family photos of Scott as a child with his grandfather, his pony, his friends, and finally his modern-day wife and children. The snapshots showed them as the ideal American family: playing at home, enjoying a family vacation, and finally in the last pages of the essay, saying their farewells just before the space flight.[27] In this way, the photographic narrative sequence suggested that Scott Carpenter's flight to the moon was one more in a series of "everyday" family activities. This became the conventional narration of *Life*'s astronaut profiles in the years to come.

In a practical sense, this essay format allowed the magazines to appeal to diverse audiences because it conveyed technical, scientific information in the popular format of family drama. Discussions of domesticity made space familiar, offering a down-to-earth context for the often-abstract reasoning behind space flights. When astronaut John Young went to space in 1965, this merger of science and domesticity was taken to its logical extreme. *Life* reported his flight by telling the story of his wife and children, who witnessed the event on television:

> The Youngs watch. In John Young's home outside Houston, the astronaut's family sits at the TV set as the seconds crawl toward launch time. Barbara Young fidgets, Sandy fiddles with a bit of string and Johnny, still getting over chicken pox, stares unsmiling at the screen. At lift off Mrs. Young hugs Sandy. "Fantastic," she crows . . . as ship soars skyward.

The accompanying photographs showed the Young family sitting before the television set, much like other Americans would have done that day.[28] Here as elsewhere, the "fantastic" is communicated through the domestic, and space technology is itself mediated through the more familial technology of television.

Even the space scientists seemed to recognize the popular appeal of domestic explanations for space travel. In 1958, Dr. Wernher von Braun told *Life* that "missile building is much like interior decorating. Once you decide to refurnish the living room you go shopping. But when you put it all together you may see in a flash it's a mistake—the draperies don't go with the slip covers. The same is true of missiles." And in 1969, NASA engineer John C. Houbolt told the same magazine that a "rendezvous around the moon was like being in a living room."[29]

The American public responded in kind, tying space-age imagery to their own domestic lives. In 1962, *Life* reported that parents across the country were naming their children in new ways. Lamar Orbit Hill, John Glenn Davis, John Glenn Donato, and John Glenn Apollo were among the list of space-age babies, and, as *Life* pointed out, the trend was so consuming that one couple "yielded to the headlines and named their new boy John Glenn—they'd been planning to call him Robert Kennedy."[30]

Big industry capitalized on and added to this space-age fever. In 1955, when going to the moon was more Technicolor fantasy than technocratic plan, Disneyland made space into family fun in its "Tomorrowland" section of the park. In the early 1960s, with the official space race now underway, the Seattle and New York World's Fairs opened their gates to families who wandered about futuristic pleasure gardens, peering at Ford's 100-passenger space ship and pondering the NASA exhibit. Meanwhile, women's home magazines included recipes for "blast-off" space cakes, promoted "space-age homes," and suggested building "space platforms" instead of porches.[31] Songwriters fashioned romantic tunes like "Space Ship for Two," "Earth Satellite," and "Sputnik Love."[32] Advertisers, eager to employ popular meanings, used space imagery to glorify family-oriented products. Ford, for example, showed a little boy dressed in a space suit, exploring his brand new Fairlane family sedan and telling consumers that "Ford interiors are . . . out of this world."[33]

This merger of science and domesticity thus became a conventional mode of thinking about the fantastic voyage into space, but as the above examples show, it also provided a new mode of expressing family relations. In the fantastic sit-com, science fiction fantasy invaded the discourses of the everyday, so that the norms of domesticity were made unfamiliar.

As Fredric Jameson has argued, science fiction tends less to imagine the future than to "defamiliarize and restructure our experience of our own *present*."[34] Although these sit-coms were not science fiction narratives per se, they engaged elements of science fiction fantasy for similar purposes. Rather than portraying the future, the fantastic sit-coms presented critical views of contemporary suburban life by using tropes of science fiction to make the familial strange.

Consider again the case of Samantha Stephens, who swore off her supernatural powers to marry a mere mortal. Episode after episode, we find the good witch in her Sears Roebuck outfits, masquerading as the perfect suburban housewife, happily scrambling eggs as Darrin deliberates over his next trite advertising slogan. Consider as well the beautiful Jeannie, who gleefully fulfills the wishes of her astronaut-master Tony as he desperately tries to hide her from his NASA bosses. And consider finally the exploits of the Jetsons, an average American cartoon family living in the twenty-first century, which turns out to be a space-odyssey version of Levittown. These sit-coms incorporated elements of science fiction to present a heightened and fantastic version of suburban life.

As Tzvetan Todorov has argued, the fantastic exists less as a genre than as a moment in a text, a moment characterized by hesitation.[35] The fantastic often occurs at the point at which the hero or heroine doubts the credibility of the situation (can this be happening, or am I dreaming this?). In the fantastic sit-com, the doubting Thomas character became a stock vehicle for this kind of hesitation. Gladys Kravitz, the busy-body neighbor in *Bewitched*, constantly doubted her own visions (or at least her husband Abner did). Similarly, Dr. Bellows, whose psychiatric discourse sought to explain all human aberrations, hesitated to believe the outlandish stories that Tony conjured up in his attempts to hide his genie from the boys at the space project. In addition to this hesitation within the mind of the character, the fantastic also makes the reader uncertain about the status of the text. The story calls its own conventions of representation into question and makes the reader wonder whether the narrative situation is possible at all. In the fantastic sit-com, the elements called into question are not the fantastic aspects per se (we are never made to question whether Jeannie is a genie, nor does the narrative ask if being a genie is possible in the first place). Rather, the moment of hesitation takes place in the realm of the natural. We are, in other words, made to question the "naturalness" of middle-class existence. We are asked to hesitate in our beliefs about the normative roles of gender, class, and race that so pervade the era's suburban lifestyles. In this sense, the fantastic unmasks the conventionality of the everyday.

These sit-coms expressed tensions about the classist, racist, and sexist premises of suburban life by revolving around fantastic situations that referred, in hyperbolic ways, to everyday practices of the middle class. In this sense, they can be seen as the 1960s answer to the ethnic, working-class family programs of the earlier decade. Although Italian immigrants, Jewish mothers, and working-class bus drivers might have disappeared from the screen, they returned in a new incarnation as genies, witches, and robots. In other words, fantastic hyperbolic representations of cultural difference took the place of the more "realistic" portrayals. At a time when the civil rights movement had gained ground, these programs dramatized the exclusionary practices of the middle-class suburbs, not in realistic ways, but through exaggerated, comedic representations.

In fact, fear of the "Other" became one of the central narrative motifs of the fantastic sit-com. In place of the idyllic neighbor characters of the suburban sit-com past, these genre hybrids presented unflattering images of the middle-class community. Instead of *Donna Reed*'s best friend Midge or *Ozzie and Harriet*'s affable Thorny, we had neighborhood snoops like *Bewitched*'s Gladys Kravitz and *My Favorite Martian*'s Detective Bill Brennan, characters who threatened to expose the alien's identity. In this regard the programs drew on earlier science fiction forms that dramatized the fear of aliens in our midst. Anthology shows like *Science Fiction Theater*, *The Twilight Zone*, and *The Outer Limits* included episodes that revolved around aliens moving into suburban communities, while science fiction films like *War of the Worlds* and *Invasion of the Body Snatchers* based their plots on alien invasions.[36] The sit-coms incorporated this earlier strategy, but dramatized it in comedic terms.

These programs presented friendly, lovable aliens: good witches, flying nuns, glamorous genies, favorite Martians, humorous horses, motherly cars, and friendly ghosts were among the strange but kindly heroes and heroines. Rather than the aliens advancing a threat, it was the white middle-class suburbanites who revealed their darker sides. *The Addams Family* and *The Munsters* (which engaged the fantastic by turning to horror rather than science fiction) were particularly keen on this theme. These ghouls were friendly, kind, generous folks who welcomed strangers into their homes. But their difference from the white middle class made them unacceptable to suburbanites who feared deviations. Thus, after a glimpse at the cobwebbed decor, slimy pets, man-eating plants, and cream of toad soup, house guests typically fled from the haunted mansions in a panic.

Space aliens often presented similar commentary on the exclusionary tactics of white middle-class suburbanites. A 1967 episode of *The Beverly Hillbillies* is an emblematic example. This sit-com based its entire situation on the theme of cultural difference in a homogeneous, upper-class community. According to the story of the opening credit sequence, "poor mountaineer" Jed Clampet strikes oil in the Ozarks, after which he rounds up his "kin folk" and takes them to the opulent California suburb. Their Southern hospitality provides a sharp contrast to their snobby banker neighbors, Mr. and Mrs. Drysdale, who socialize with the Clampets only in order to keep their oil money in the bank. In one particular episode, Mr. Drysdale hires a group of Italian-speaking midgets to pose as Martians in an advertising stunt for his bank. When the midgets, dressed in Martian suits, land their spacecraft in the Clampets' yard, the hillbilly family is at first alarmed. Granny, the most fearful of the bunch, calls the spacemen "little green varmints," but Jed's daughter, Ellie May, scolds her for this undue prejudice. "Well Granny," she says, "they can't help it if they's little and green," and taking this to heart Jed declares, "Ellie's right. We shouldn't let on that they's any different than us." After this bit of moralizing, their ideals of neighborliness and hospitality overcome their fears, and Granny invites the aliens in for "vittles." Thus, the kindly but naive hillbillies are more accepting of cultural differences than are their snobby Beverly Hills neighbors.

But this tolerance comes to a halt when cousin Jethro resparks the fear of strangers. Jethro, who constantly boasts of his sixth-grade education, is more schooled than the others. In the narrative logic, however, his education is his Achilles heel, for it makes him more vulnerable to the hollow ideals of middle-class life. In this episode, Jethro's school-book knowledge of Martians leads him to adopt the "get them before they get us" attitude that is reminiscent of middle-class rationales for social segregation. Having read that Martians can turn people into robots, he suggests a plan for extermination. Chilled by Jethro's warning, Granny reaches for her shotgun and shoots the alien spacecraft.

Often, the fantastic sit-coms represented aliens as being specifically female: Jeannies, witches, and sexy robots. These women had to be carefully guarded so as not to reveal their difference from the group outside. Snooping neighbors like Gladys Kravitz kept a constant vigil over the Stephens's home, hoping to catch the good witch in the act; Jeannie was hidden in her bottle, far away from next-door neighbor Roger (until the later episodes when he discovers her secret) and Dr. Bellows, who constantly pried into Tony's domestic life; the Flying Nun kept her aerodynamic secrets safely among the sisterhood at church; Dave Crabtree's mother clandestinely lived her second life in the form of a 1928 Porter automobile; and Dr. Robert McDonald kept the secret of his robot (played by the vampish Julie Newmar) hidden from his next-door neighbor, who had a powerful crush on the "living doll."

This woman-as-alien motif was indebted to earlier science fiction literature and films. In the 1950s, for example, stories that dealt with alien invasion often centered on relations of sexual difference. Science fiction thrillers like *War of the Worlds* (a librarian falls in love with a scientist who battles the space aliens), *Them!* (a woman scientist falls in love with the cop who kills the giant ants), and *Forbidden Planet* (an astronaut falls in love with the daughter of a psychotic scientist) presented tales that intertwined alien forces with gender dynamics. In such films, romance served to address the enigma in a way that scientific explanation could not. While the scientists try to understand the alien through the conventions of rational discourse, their success is always partial. They can destroy the alien, but the basis for explaining its origins and reproduction is never wholly scientific. Instead, the epistemological basis for diffusing the threat of difference is transposed onto romantic coupling. It is romantic love and marriage (the reproduction of the status quo and normal gender distinctions) that finally solve the crisis of the "Other." That is, sexual difference structures all other differences. The demise of the alien—whether it be Martian, giant ant, or psychotic parent—goes hand in hand with the bonding of hero and heroine and their acceptance of traditional marks of sexual identity. However, rather than serving a wholly conservative function, these films actually problematized the ideology of domesticity by making it strange.[37]

In fact, representations of the space race—whether offered in scientific or fantastic modes—often evoked this kind of defamiliarization. A perfect example is an episode from the syndicated series *Science Fiction Theater*, which was produced from 1955 to 1957 and funded in part by the Defense Department. The episode entitled "First Woman on the Moon" tells the story of Renza Hale and her astronaut-husband Joe who, upon the orders of his space department bosses, invites her to travel to the moon. Once Renza is on the moon, however, problems ensue. Renza is bored because the men will not let her leave the rocket, and her culinary talents go to waste since she cannot get the hang of anti-gravity cooking. One night, after her Yorkshire pudding is too tough, Renza breaks down. The next morning, she ventures out onto the lunar landscape without informing the crew. After a panicked search, Joe is furious and in a scolding tone tells his wife, "Your place is on earth at home where I know you're safe." In this episode, tropes of science fiction fantasy allow for an exposition of anxieties that women faced in more everyday circumstances. This program turns out to be a thinly veiled exploration of domesticity and the gendered division of spheres that so pervaded ideas about women's place in the 1950s.

If the space race provided a critique of gender in fictional forms, it also gave voice to feminist views in the culture at large. In 1960, *Look*'s cover story asked, "Should a Girl Be First in Space?" presenting the story of Betty Skelton, an American pilot who underwent a series of tests for space travel. But according to Betty, her fellow spacemen, who nicknamed her No. 7 ½, were not likely to take her along for the ride. As *Look* reported, "Some 2,000 American women, mostly teenagers, have volunteered for space flight," but, "what Miss Skelton and other possibly qualified women fear is not that they will be lofted out of the atmosphere, but that they won't." The article even went on to declare that "women have more brains and stamina per pound than men," and concluded as well that physical and psychological requirements for space travel "are so specialized that specific individual qualifications far outweigh any difference based on sex." In this case, the space race provided a photo-essay opportunity for deconstructing notions about biologically determined gender difference. However, this was recuperated within more conventional ideas about domesticity; later in the essay *Look* promised that the first woman in space would be "married," possibly even the "scientist-wife of a pilot engineer."[38]

In 1963, when the Soviet Union sent Valentina Tereshkova into space, *Life* ran an editorial that presented even more damning criticism of America's treatment of women. Written by Clare Boothe Luce (who was married to publisher Henry Luce), the article argued that

> Soviet Russia put a woman into space because Communism preaches and, since the Revolution of 1917, has tried to practice the inherent equality of men and women. The flight of Valentina Treshkova is, consequently, symbolic of the emancipation of the Communist woman. It symbolizes to Russian women that they actively share (not passively bask, like American women) in the glory of conquering space.

Boothe Luce went on to tell the story of the thirteen American women pilots who, while having proved their physical capacity for space flight in government tests, were barred from participating in the (aptly titled) manned space program.[39] The article (which most likely was published only because of Luce's family ties) pointedly attacked American sexism. The space race thus provided grounds upon which to question the gender-based decisions behind the New Frontier's march of progress.

Such blatant attacks on institutional sexism were atypical of mass media of the times, and 1960s television, which sought to appeal to broad-based audiences, was by no means a venue for this kind of dialogue. However, the domestic situation comedy was, by its very nature, predicated on the gender conflicts of the American family, and in the 1960s hybrid version, these conflicts were augmented by the fantastic scenarios of space-age situations. In a decade that began with Betty Friedan's criticisms of the mass media's "happy housewife heroine," these fantastic sit-coms offered exaggerated and humorous renditions of the June Cleaver syndrome. Thus, *Jeannie* and *Bewitched* revolved around super-powerful women who tried to efface their potential in return for the "rewards" of family life. Like Donna Reed, who sacrificed her nursing career for life with Dr. Alex Stone, these women traded their credentials for domestic bliss. But Samantha and Jeannie, unlike Donna, had more difficult transitions from career to housewife. Their supernatural powers called for exaggerated forms of self-imposed containment. Thus they became super-feminine. Jeannie referred to Tony as Master and scampered around the house in pink harem girl garb, while Samantha took the more conservative route of mini-skirts and aprons. In either case, they were perfect examples of Joan Rivière's seminal 1929 study "Womanliness as a Masquerade," which showed how successful female professionals felt compelled to adopt a heightened veneer of femininity as a strategy for coping with their "transgression" of normative gender roles. By posing as super-feminine types, these women were able to minimize anxiety about the negative reactions they anticipated from male associates.[40] In the 1960s television version, powerful female characters were shown to threaten gender expectations of the patriarchal world; their masquerade as ideal housewives might well have alleviated audience tensions about the changing role of women at the time.

Although this basic situation was less than revolutionary, it did provide a premise for a more subversive kind of comedy that poked fun at social expectations about gender roles. The narratives continually showed how Samantha's and Jeannie's power could not be integrated into patriarchal norms, and they dramatized the impossibility of absolute containment. Notably in this regard, they provided an expressive outlet for women's "bottled-up" rebelliousness through a doppleganger motif. Samantha's look-alike cousin and Jeannie's look-alike sister were wacky, wild, swinging singles who functioned as hyperbolic depictions of non-domestic roles for women. They had numerous lovers, visited maharajahs, and traveled the universe at their whim. Even if these characters were depicted as irresponsible party girls of the free-love decade, they often directly confronted their feminine counterparts, criticizing the boring lifestyles Samantha and Jeannie had chosen. Similarly, Samantha's bad witch mother, Endora (who was estranged from her warlock husband, Maurice), strongly opposed her daughter's marriage to "Durwood" and continually begged her to skip out to exotic locales like the French Riviera. Significantly here, these female doubles underscored the idea that the non-domestic woman was specifically of a jet-set class whose upper-crust lifestyles had little relationship to the everyday concerns of real working/independent women. Thus, while fantastic sit-coms allowed alternative female roles to be depicted, they bypassed the more threatening elements of women's economic and social power by confining that power to a small group of elites.

These programs also parodied middle-class men who strove to comply with bureaucratic dictates. Darrin Stephens, Tony Nelson, and Dr. Robert McDonald constantly tried to keep their strange and powerful secrets within the private sphere of their homes.[41] Like William Whyte's "organization man," these men had to hide any kind of social deviance behind a strict veneer of allegiance to the corporate ideal. In this way they very much adopted the structural position of the woman in the masquerade, only here the men hid their secret source of power by donning the exaggerated pose of the company boy. By dramatizing these scenarios, the fantastic sit-com often inverted the conventional power dynamics of masculinity and femininity, and in the process, they made viewers laugh at their own assumptions about gender.

In *Jeannie* this inversion of sexual identity was directly related to and reinforced by the program's burlesque of technological supremacy, specifically the space race. Not only did the sit-com poke fun at gender roles; it also mocked men's dominion over scientific progress. The program retains traditional divisions between public and private spheres. While the suburban home is the woman's place, NASA headquarters—and by extension space itself—is the male domain. However, Jeannie always manages to blur the gendered divisions of private and public spheres. She typically arrives incognito at NASA headquarters where she undermines its scientific breakthroughs with her greater powers. After all, she need only blink herself onto the moon.[42]

Take, for example, a 1968 episode in which Jeannie grants three wishes to Tony's astronaut pal Roger. Roger wishes to change places with Tony, who has been selected by NASA to travel to the moon. Upon his wish, Tony and Roger find themselves in each other's bodies, a situation resulting in confusion about male identity, a confusion that is typical of the series as a whole. In this case, as elsewhere, NASA psychiatrist Dr. Bellows tries to explain the rational causes behind this male identity crisis, but science fails to locate the "feminine" cause. Doctor Bellows, who assumes that Tony and Roger suffer from a deep personality disorder, becomes increasingly confused by the scenario. Finally, after Roger agrees to retract his wish, Jeannie restores the men to their proper bodies, and Tony takes off for the moon.

However, the final tag sequence defies this resolution, suggesting instead that Jeannie's female (supernatural) powers are more potent than those of the male scientists. Jeannie and Roger sit in the Nelson living room watching Tony on television as he travels to the moon. The camera lingers on a shot of the television set as documentary footage (apparently taken from an actual launching) displays a rocket take-off that is intercut with fictional shots of Tony in the spacecraft and Jeannie and Roger watching the broadcast. Dramatic music underscores the rocket footage, so that the viewer is led to marvel at the feats of contemporary space science. But this moment of revelry is interrupted when Roger reminds Jeannie that he is still entitled to another wish. After Jeannie's characteristic blink, the camera cuts back to the television set where Roger is pictured alongside Tony in the spacecraft. Thus the patriarchal splendors of the space project are ironically cast aside as a woman is able to accomplish the same task with mere wishful thinking.

In 1969, *Green Acres* presented a similar spoof of NASA's scientific domain when precocious child inventor, Dinky, sells a moon rock to Oliver Douglas's wife, Lisa. Douglas, who has left his New York law practice for the pastoral splendors of a Hooterville farm, is hopelessly caught in the scientific rationalism of his city-slicker past, and the moon rocks prove especially disturbing from this point of view. Despite the claims of Lisa (who is always more in tune with Hooterville's anti-scientific, screwball logic), Oliver insists that Dinky's rocks aren't really from the moon. As in other episodes, Lisa adopts the attitude of her bizarre Hooterville neighbors, and through this she is better equipped to deal with the enigmatic laws of her universe. She is, in other words, placed on the side of the aliens, the television-watching pigs, inbred farm hands, and, in this case, whiz-kid inventors that comprise her community. Her husband, on the other hand, searches for "rational" solutions.

Finally, new "scientific proof" convinces Oliver that the rock is from the moon. The evidence is put forward by Mr. Kimball, the double-talking and clearly irrational agriculture scientist, who informs Oliver that several moon rocks were stolen from a traveling NASA exhibit. To Oliver, this seems a logical explanation. But when he calls NASA headquarters, the space officials assume he is just another crackpot and tell him to phone Alcoholics Anonymous. As is typical of the series, the episode reveals the limits of masculine rationalization. The final scene shows confused NASA officials listening to a closet full of beeping moon rocks, just as unable to explain the phenomenon as Lisa Douglas was. Gender dynamics are thus reworked, so that women's "alien" logic is just as rational as the conventions of scientific discourse in the male sphere.

In *Bewitched*, the woman's alien powers serve to invert the gender relations of suburban domesticity, and with this, the consumer lifestyles that characterize the suburbs are also parodied. Darrin's job as a junior executive in an advertising firm provides ample situations for a popular version of critical stances toward the consumption ethic to emerge. In a 1967 episode, for example, Darrin takes a cold tablet concocted by Samantha's witch doctor friend, Dr. Bombay. The magic pill instantly cures Darrin's cold, and upon seeing this, Darrin's greedy boss Larry decides to make a fortune overnight by packaging the miracle drug. But as Samantha and Darrin soon discover, there's an unfortunate side effect that leaves Darrin with a new, markedly feminine, high-pitched voice. As in *Jeannie*, magic works to transform Darrin's bodily functions, so that his sexual identity—and at times even his species classification—is thrown into question. Whether he's turned into a screeching soprano, a dog, a mule, or a little boy, Darrin has to be returned to his proper manly state before the episode can end.

So too, Samantha destabilizes the patriarchal structures of consumer capitalism. Since the 1920s advertisers have particularly targeted women, who they calculate are responsible for about 80 percent of the family's purchases. Women thus are institutionalized consumers, and advertisers are eager to promote specifically female uses for products. As Judith Williamson has argued, a central way in which advertisements promote product use is through the promise of magical transformation—cold pills instantly stop symptoms, Mr. Clean materializes in your kitchen, skin creams make wrinkles vanish, and dishwasher soap makes hands look younger.[43] *Bewitched* inverts this dynamic by giving a woman the power of transformation. In the above episode, not only Darrin but also Larry and a drug manufacturer have been afflicted by Dr. Bombay's magic pills, and thus all are at the mercy of Samantha's witchcraft. Being a good witch, she transforms them with an antidote, and their masculine voices are restored. This closure, however, is only temporary, because in the next episode Samantha will once again wreak havoc on the advertising executives.

More generally, these sit-coms poked fun at the consumer lifestyles of suburban culture, particularly new domestic technologies. Jeannie and Samantha, for example, did the housework the extra-easy way, by operating appliances with their magic touch. The Jetsons' push-button food dispensers, the Flintstones' prehistoric lawnmower, Mr. Ed's love affair with his television set, Gomez's proclivity for train wrecks, Grandpa Munster's mad scientist lab, and Jed Clampet's inability to distinguish a garbage disposal from a meat grinder are but a few in a long list of humorous parodies of the technological utopias Americans had hoped to find in their new suburban homes. Indeed, the consumer culture of the 1960s found a way to defamiliarize its own familiar logic.

Conclusion

In the 1960s, the rhetoric of the New Frontier set an agenda for international militarism and heavenly exploration by calling on the traditional moral fiber of the American family. By the same token, the outworn ideals of family life were re-invigorated with new goals of public life. The space race, in particular, provided a popular spectacle through which Americans could view the future in terms of the past and still feel as if they were going somewhere. No longer a nation of homebodies, we moved from domestic to outer space while still sitting in our easy chairs.

It was in this land of space-age familialism that the hybrid genre of the fantastic sit-com emerged. Blending science fiction fantasy with domestic situations, these programs foregrounded tensions about middle-class family lifestyles, tensions that were part of the culture at large. Their fantastic space-age imagery made the familial strange; it made people pause, if only to laugh, at what had once seemed natural and everyday. This unlikely collision of genres gave audiences the chance to reflect on their own expectations—not only about the sit-com's narrative conventions—but also about the social conventions by which they lived their lives. The extent to which viewers actually engaged in such thought is another question.[44] But when seen in this light, these programs clearly beg interpretations that go beyond the typical assumptions of their escapist, low-art nature.

Indeed, as I have tried to show, the fact that these programs have not been examined is itself a consequence of history. The "wasteland" critique applied to sit-coms in the 1960s makes it hard for us to break the patterns of the past. These programs were effectively the critics' proof of television's threat to "authentic" culture, and contemporary critics have inherited that binary logic. But television shows like *Bewitched* and *Jeannie* are, of course, part of history, and as such they can play a key role in our understanding of cultural transition. Despite the conventional wisdom of "high-brow" thinking, television's popular formats are not necessarily static; they are not doomed to an endless repetition of the same story. Perhaps their lack of reverence for the "classics" and the strictures of a pre-determined aesthetic canon gives them a certain flexibility that permits the development of recombinant genres and other unorthodox twists. Examining these programs in connection with other aspects of their cultural environment allows us to understand them in ways that go beyond the categories of high and low art. By reading these sit-coms alongside the more "culturally validated" texts of 1960s culture — especially here, popular scientific discourses on the space race — we can begin to see how the fantastic aims of space travel merged, in rather unexpected ways, with the everyday concerns of family life.

What is especially interesting in this regard is that by the end of the 1960s the "high" and mighty goals of going to space had themselves come under attack. Although the moon landing had attracted the most viewers in television history, the critics were restless once again. As an editorial in *Life* proclaimed, "The first requirement for a sensible post-Apollo 11 program is that President Nixon decline to sign the sort of blank check for an all-out manned Mars landing that vocal space agency partisans are urging on him." Critics particularly lamented the decidedly unpoetic sentiments that resulted from the exploration of the final frontier. *Saturday Review* complained about an "overly colloquial" reporter, who "when the lunar module successfully fired the engine that lifted it from the moon's surface, cried out 'Oh boy! Hot diggity dog! Yes sir!' " Even the astronauts had to admit their disappointment. Reflecting on their journeys in Apollo 8, astronauts Frank Boorman, Jim Lovell, and Bill Anders clearly were at a loss for the kind of poetic language upon which high culture thrived. Boorman admitted that while the moon was beautiful it was also "so desolate, so completely devoid of life. . . . Nothing but this great pockmarked lump of gray pumice." And while he hoped to find "secrets of creation," Lovell confided, "the moon was void." Anders apologized for making "a few poets angry" with his banal descriptions of the lunar landscape, but admitted nonetheless that "the long ride out to the moon was, frankly, a bit of a drag."[45]

If the space program was conceived by some as an empty venture, it nevertheless served a transformative function over the course of the decade. At least in television's fiction forms, discourses on space and tropes of the fantastic invaded the terrain of the everyday. Filling homes with domesticated witches, neighborly ghouls, and ravishing robots, these programs revolved around anxieties about middle-class social ideals. Even if the sit-com form defused these tensions with safe resolutions, the genre denied absolute closure, coming back each week to remind viewers that they too might be living in a suburban twilight zone.

I am grateful to Bill Forman for all his help with this essay, and I also wish to extend thanks to Mike Curtin, Henry Jenkins, Tom Streeter, and the *Camera Obscura* editors for their careful readings.

NOTES

1. Note that there were several sit-coms of the 1950s that included fantastic elements. *People's Choice*, which focused on the career and love life of a single man rather than a family situation, included the talking dog, Cleo. The hound was used as a special effect/sight gag rather than as an integral part of the story. Cleo talked in direct address to the audience, but could not be heard by the characters — a narrational device that functioned much like the self-reflexive direct address of *The Burns and Allen Show*. The latter also included a fantastic element in the later episodes, a magical television set through which George replayed portions of the program and commented on plot elements. Again, however, this was included as a running gag rather than as an integral part of the narrative situation. *Topper*, which revolved around ghosts who haunted a suburban home, was more akin to the 1960s version in its basic narrative premise, but it lasted for only two seasons. While one might see these programs as forerunners, it is in the 1960s that the hybrid genre cycle proliferates and formulates its particular narrative content and organization.

2. Although it did not use the sit-com form per se, *Lost in Space* mixed family drama with elements of science fiction.

3. David Marc, *Comic Visions: Television Comedy and American Culture* (Boston: Unwin Hyman, 1989, pp. 121–156). Marc does suggest that some of these sit-coms reflected new cultural ideals, but he does not take this path of analysis into serious consideration.

4. James L. Baughman, "The National Purpose and the Newest Medium: Liberal Critics of Television, 1958–60," *Mid-America* 64 (April–July 1983), pp. 41–55. See also his *Television's Guardians: The FCC and the Politics of Programming, 1958–1967* (Knoxville: University of Tennessee Press, 1985). For more on dissident voices of the 1950s see Paul A. Carter, *Another Part of the Fifties* (New York: Columbia University Press, 1988) and Todd Gitlin, "Cornucopia and Its Discontents," in *The Sixties: Years of Hope, Days of Rage* (New York: Bantam, 1987), pp. 11–31.

5. Although not exclusively concerned with suburbia, books like David Reisman's *The Lonely Crowd* (1950) and C. Wright Mills's *White Collar* (1951) focused on middle-class consensus ideology.

6. For a discussion of this and other aspects of women's lives in post-war America, see Rochelle Gatlin, *American Women Since 1945* (Jackson and London: University of Mississippi Press, 1987).

7. The cycle of 1950s social problem films also highlighted domestic strife, often connecting it to a wider social unrest. See, for example, *Come Back Little Sheba* (1952), *The Country Girl* (1954), and *A Hatful of Rain* (1957). For more on these films see Jackie Byars, "Gender Representation in American Family Melodramas of the 1950s," Ph. D. diss., University of Texas-Austin, 1983. For discussions of popular culture and teenagers

in the 1950s, see James Gilbert, *A Cycle of Outrage: America's Reaction to the Juvenile Delinquent in the 1950s* (New York: Oxford University Press, 1986) and Thomas Doherty, *Teenagers and Teenpics: The Juvenilization of American Movies in the 1950s* (Boston: Unwin Hyman, 1988).

8. "Man's New World: How He lives In It," *Life* (Oct. 7, 1957), p. 80.

9. Walter A. McDougall, . . . *the Heavens and the Earth: A Political History of the Space Age* (New York: Basic Books, 1985), pp. 141–156. See also Dale Carter, *The Final Frontier: The Rise and Fall of the American Rocket State* (London and New York: Verso, 1988), pp. 120–125.

10. Henry Luce, "Common Sense and Sputnik," *Life* (Oct. 21, 1957), p. 35. Soviets took the occasion to suggest this as well. For example, McDougall cites Leonid Sedov's condemnation of America's fixation on consumer durables: "It is very obvious that the average American cares only for his car, his home, and his refrigerator. He has no sense at all for his nation," p. 137.

11. Figures cited in Dewey W. Grantham, *Recent America: The United States Since 1945* (Arlington Heights, IL: Harlan Davidson, 1987), p. 143. For an interesting discussion of reactions to Eisenhower's economic recovery plan, see Carter (1988, pp. 35–40). Another recession occurred in 1960–61, but between 1962 and 1968 a long stretch of economic prosperity ensued.

12. William Atwood, "How America Feels As We Enter the Soaring Sixties." *Look* (Jan. 5, 1960), pp. 11–15. This survey was commissioned by the Gallup company and supplemented by *Look*'s staff.

13. Baughman, "The National Purpose and the Newest Medium."

14. "Deception on TV." *New Republic* (Oct. 19, 1959), p. 4. For other examples on this, see Barbara Agee, "The Intruder in Our House." *American Mercury* (June 1959), pp. 129–130; Clare Booth Luce, "Without Portfolio: A Monthly Commentary: TV An American Scandal." *McCalls* (March 1960), pp. 18–19, 176, 178; "Where Are All the Sparkling Shows of Yesteryear?" *Newsweek* (July 3, 1961), pp. 70–71. For a discussion of related issues, see Baughman's *Television's Guardians*, pp. 20–35, and "The National Purpose and the Newest Medium." Also note that while television critics became particularly dismayed about programming trends in the late 1950s, this attack on television developed out of on-going debates about television's aesthetic and cultural development. In the late 1940s and early 1950s influential east-coast television critics saw television as a medium that promised to channel the elite through the popular, and they formed aesthetic hierarchies based on this idea. In particular, anthology dramas, with their live origination and theatrical/literary base, as well as prestige programming like *Omnibus* and *See It Now*, were the darlings of the television critics, while filmed half-hour series were seen as the lowest form of television art. For more on this, see William Boddy, "From the 'Golden Age' to the 'Vast Wasteland': The Struggles Over Market Power and Dramatic Formats in 1950s

Television," Ph. D. diss., New York University, 1984. For a discussion of the more general debates about television's impact on post-war culture and family life, see my "Installing The Television Set: The Social Construction of Television's Place in the American Home," Ph. D. diss., University of California-Los Angeles, 1988; and "Installing the Television Set: Popular Discourses on Television and Domestic Space," *Camera Obscura* 16 (March 1988), pp. 11–47.

15. Newton Minow, Address to the 39th Annual Convention of the National Association of Broadcasters, Washington DC, May 9, 1961. The address can in many ways be read as a reaction to the quiz-show scandals, and especially to the critics who attacked the FCC for their negligence in the matter. In a brief sentence, Minow deflected attention away from the scandals and onto the "more important" matters of reform: "I think it would be foolish and wasteful for us to continue any worn-out wrangle over the problems of payola, rigged quiz shows, and other mistakes of the past."

16. Documentary series included such titles as NBC's *White Papers*, ABC's *Close-Up*, and *CBS Reports*. By suggesting that these programs were developed at a time when the status of the television image was thrown into question by the quiz shows, I am not trying to make a direct causal link between the scandals and the networks' turn to documentary. Rather, as James Baughman has shown in his work on *CBS Reports*, the turn to documentary has to be seen in the wider context of problems facing the networks in the late 1950s, and in the case of *CBS Reports*, especially the prospect of an FCC inquiry in 1959. See James L. Baughman, "The Strange Birth of CBS Reports Revisited," *Historical Journal of Film, Radio and Television* 2:1 (1982), pp. 27–38.

17. On the turn to objective science and the interest in the topic of the space race in the 1960s documentary, see Michael Curtin, "Defining the Free World: Prime-Time Television Documentary and the Politics of the Cold War, 1960–1964," Ph. D. diss., University of Wisconsin-Madison, 1990.

18. Mort Drucker and Stan Hart, "The Nilson Family." *Mad* (Jan. 1966), p. 13.

19. George Lipsitz, "The Meaning of Memory: Family, Class and Ethnicity in Early Network Television Programs," *Cultural Anthropology* 1:4 (Nov. 1986), pp. 381–382. Reprinted in *Camera Obscura* 16 (March 1988), pp. 79–117. Lipsitz argues that these programs used the memory of an ethnic/working-class past to legitimate the increasingly consumer society of the post-war era.

20. In this calculation I have included those sit-coms that revolved around domestic situations. Programs that included families, but focused on working life were not included, nor was the popular *The Many Loves of Doby Gillis*, which was mostly concerned with youth culture and student life. One program, *The Danny Thomas Show*, was set in an urban area,

while two, *The Real McCoys* and *The Andy Griffith Show*, were set in rural areas.

21. Some of them did appear in re-runs. Note also that *The Danny Thomas Show*, which began under the title of *Make Room for Daddy* in 1953 and ended its original run in 1964, included an ethnic character. However, unlike the other ethnic comedies and dramas, this program did not usually focus on Danny Williams's Lebanese-ness as a major condition of the plot, but rather used it simply as a running gag.

22. By 1965, none of the classical family sit-coms ranked in the top twenty of the Nielsen charts. Only *The Dick Van Dyke Show*, which was a more updated version of the classical type, was still a Nielsen success. According to Tim Brooks and Earle Marsh, *The Dick Van Dyke Show* was canceled in the fall 1966 season due to creative decisions. See *The Complete Directory to Prime Time Network TV Shows, 1946–Present*, 3rd ed. (New York: Ballentine Books, 1985), p. 218. For more general rating information, see pp. 1030–1041.

23. These three were all substantially different from the classical suburban family sit-coms like *Donna Reed*. They include *Please Don't Eat the Daisies* (which was to some degree aberrant since the mother worked at home), *Blondie* (which also deviated from the norm since it was taken from the popular comic strip), and *The Debbie Reynolds Show* (which, like *I Love Lucy*, was based on a housewife who wanted to work; it was also extremely unpopular, lasting only one season).

24. I have not included certain rather idiosyncratic twists in the cycle in this calculation. These include sit-coms that depict childless couples (*He and She*, *Love on a Rooftop*) and one sit-com that depicted an extended family (*The Mothers In-Law*).

25. For divorce rates, see Gatlin, *American Women Since 1945*, p. 144; Winefred D. Wandersee, *On the Move: American Women in the 1970s* (Boston: Twayne, 1988), p. 131; Julie A. Matthaei, *An Economic History of Women in America: Women's Work, the Sexual Division of Labor, and the Development of Capitalism* (New York: Schocken, 1982), p. 311.

26. "A Child Writes a Space Song." *Look* (Dec. 23, 1958), p. 58; "The Strange Boom at Cocoa Beach." *Look* (June 24, 1958), p. 24.

27. Loudon Wainwright, "Comes a Quiet Man to Ride Aurora 7." *Life* (May 18, 1962), pp. 32 41.

28. Miguel Acoca, "He's On His Way. . . . And It Couldn't Be Prettier." *Life* (Apr. 2, 1965), pp. 36–37.

29. "The Seer of Space." *Life* (Nov. 18, 1957), pp. 134–135; "How An Idea No One Wanted Grew Up to Be the LEM." *Life* (March 14, 1969), p. 22.

30. "Meet Orbit Hill." *Life* (March 9, 1962), p. 2.

31. *American Home* (Sept. 1964), p. 54; *American Home* (Dec. 1962), p. 121; *House Beautiful* (June 1963), pp. 129–130.

32. By 1958, there were at least 300 such songs, and one music publisher even called his company "Planetary Music." See Gordon Cotler, "Song-

writers Blast Off." *New York Times Magazine* (Feb. 16, 1958), pp. 19, 21.

33. *Life* (May 24, 1963), pp. 54–55.

34. Fredric Jameson, "Progress vs. Utopia: Or Can We Imagine The Future?" *Science Fiction Studies* 9:27 (1982), p. 151, emphasis his. Later in the article, Jameson more emphatically states that science fiction dramatizes "our incapacity to imagine the future" (153), and he goes on to discuss science fiction dystopias in this vein. My use of Jameson emphasizes his earlier point regarding the way science fiction provides opportunities imaginatively to restructure the present.

35. Tzvetan Todorov, *The Fantastic: A Structural Approach To A Literary Genre*, trans. Richard Howard (Ithaca, NY: Cornell University Press, 1970).

36. These programs often presented moralizing narratives that used the alien motif to dramatize the exclusionary tactics of cold war America. See, for example, *Science Fiction Theater*'s "The People at Pecos" and "Time Is Just Its Life," *The Twilight Zone*'s "The Monsters Are Due on Maple Street," and *The Outer Limits*' "Galaxy Being."

37. In fact, many of these films specifically dramatized a threat to family formations. *Them!*, for example, introduces viewers to the giant ants by showing a stray little girl who has been traumatized by the creatures, Andre in *The Fly* destroys his happy home by turning himself into an alien being in a tele-porting experiment, and relatives in *Invasion of the Body Snatchers* lose faith in the veracity of their family ties when the pod people replicate their kin.

38. "Should A Girl Be First In Space?" *Look* (Feb. 2, 1960), pp. 112–117.

39. Clare Boothe Luce, "But Some People Simply Never Get the Message." *Life* (June 28, 1963), pp. 31–33.

40. Joan Rivière, "Womanliness as a Masquerade." In *Formations of Fantasy*, edited by Victor Burgin et al. (London and New York: Methuen, 1986/1929), pp. 35–44.

41. As a variation on this plot, some male characters were forced to hide their secrets from both their private and their public worlds. Thus Wilbur hides Mr. Ed from his wife, his neighbor, and his clients; Dave Crabtree hides his mother the car from his wife, his neighbors, and his boss. In both these cases the male character reveals his secret to the viewer in a separate narrative space (a horse stable and a garage, respectively) that is somewhere in-between the private and the public world.

42. A similar situation occurred in a 1967 episode of *Bewitched* when Samantha claims that she has beaten the astronauts to the moon through her magical powers of transportation.

43. Judith Williamson, *Decoding Advertisements: Ideology and Meaning in Advertising* (New York: Marion Boyars, 1979).

44. Along these lines, it is important to keep in mind that the genre attracted many child viewers who would have had a limited knowledge of the clas-

sic family sit-com as well as different social/historical backgrounds from adults in the audience.

45. "The New Priorities in Exploring Space." *Life* (Aug. 22, 1969), p. 30; Robert Lewis Shayon, "Cosmic Nielsens." *Saturday Review* (Aug. 9, 1969), p. 40; "Our Journey to the Moon." *Life* (Jan. 17, 1969), pp. 26–31.

The Jetsons

Friendship's Death

Peter Wollen

Friendship's Death

BILL PATERSON . . . . Sullivan

TILDA SWINTON . . . . Friendship

PATRICK BAUCHAU . . . . Kubler

RUBY BAKER . . . . Catherine

JOUMANA GILL . . . . Palestinian

PHOTOGRAPHY: WITOLD STOK
DESIGN: GEMMA JACKSON
COSTUMES: CATHY COOK
MAKEUP: MORAG ROSS
EDITOR: ROBERT HARGREAVES
MUSIC: BARRINGTON PHELOUNG
EXECUTIVE PRODUCER: COLIN McCABE
PRODUCER: REBECCA O'BRIEN
WRITTEN AND DIRECTED: PETER WOLLEN

A BRITISH FILM INSTITUTE PRODUCTION
IN ASSOCIATION WITH MODELMARK LIMITED

FILMED AT TWICKENHAM STUDIOS, LONDON, ENGLAND

RELEASED 35mm, LONDON 1987

16mm PRINTS AVAILABLE FROM THE
BRITISH FILM INSTITUTE, LONDON

© MODELMARK LIMITED 1987

1. Amman, Jordan 1970   Documentary Footage

Long tracking shot of burned out buildings. Damaged buildings, deserted streets, etc. Revolution Airport: planes blowing up.

SULLIVAN: (*voice over*) You know, while I was there in Amman I never imagined I'd remember everything with such clarity. Everything's still completely vivid: the sound of the mortars, the mimeograph machine in the PLO post where I first met Friendship, even the taste of the tea.

KUBLER: (*voice over*) Hijacked planes blown up on a desert airstrip, that's the image we all remember.

SULLIVAN: Pure spectacle.

KUBLER: Millions of dollars going up in smoke.

SULLIVAN: Pure waste, pure destruction. Why is it happening? It's incomprehensible.

KUBLER: It's an image with all the meaning drained out of it, completely opaque, like a curtain between us and history.

SULLIVAN: When I talk to Palestinians about 1970, they sometimes say, why do you want to remember those days, those were terrible days. . . . But then they say, how do you know anything about it, nobody ever cares what happened to us.

KUBLER: For them it was a Black September.

TITLE: FRIENDSHIP'S DEATH
TITLE: 1970, Wednesday, September 9

2. PLO Post in Amman

Concrete walls with revolutionary posters, Arabic script.

Harsh light. SULLIVAN is sitting, idly playing with the handle of a mimeograph machine. There is background bustle and noise from other people, typing, clattering, shouting things out in Arabic.

SULLIVAN is a man in his early forties. Desert clothes, once expensive, now worn and dusty. A shoulder bag. Slightly unkempt. FRIENDSHIP enters, a woman in her late twenties elegantly but oddly dressed. Though her clothes are a bit dishevelled, her hair is

*immaculate. She has a small metal case. SULLIVAN studies her
closely as he talks.*

SULLIVAN: How did it go? Safe and sound?

FRIENDSHIP: He gave me a lecture.

SULLIVAN: Very appropriate: Middle Eastern studies, a special
course with practical demonstrations.

FRIENDSHIP: I couldn't understand all of it. He kept warning me
about the danger.

SULLIVAN: Danger—I can't get enough of it! You need to feel the
shells right up close, you need to smell the blood. Journalism.
Don't you just love it?

FRIENDSHIP: They seem to have a great deal of respect for you. Thank you, for your help.

SULLIVAN: I just told them that I knew you. No problem.

FRIENDSHIP: You don't know me.

SULLIVAN: It's better for you that I do. Anyway, a chance encounter can often lead to a lifetime friendship.

FRIENDSHIP: What are *you* doing here?

SULLIVAN: I told you, I'm looking for danger. I couldn't get enough of it at home. But they organise these things an awful lot better out here. Something bothering you?

FRIENDSHIP: It's just the tungsten light. Do go on.

SULLIVAN: When I was a kid I wanted to be a brain surgeon. I thought that if we could find a way into the deepest recesses of the human mind, then we could find out what had gone wrong with the species. But now I'm not so sure. Whatever it is in there, I don't think I want to know about it, thank you very much.

FRIENDSHIP: Do you have a map?

SULLIVAN: We're somewhere on Jebel Hussein. You don't need a map. They'll take us back to the hotel in their own good time.

One of the FEDAYEEN appears, bringing a tray with glasses of tea for SULLIVAN and FRIENDSHIP. He speaks a few words of Arabic as he puts the tray down. The glasses are tulip-shaped, standing on small saucers decorated with a flower pattern. There is a bowl of lump sugar.

FRIENDSHIP: It's a good sign, isn't it? Tea. It shows solicitude.

SULLIVAN: (*taking tea and stirring in sugar*) Or it could mean they expect us to stay.

SULLIVAN sips at his tea. Then he looks up and starts to study FRIENDSHIP again. She smiles.

SULLIVAN: When I first came here, I was obsessed by ruins. The ruins of Jerash. You should try to see them if you can. We tend to think that ruins belong to the past. Lost in the sands of time. Nonsense! They belong to the present. More and more cities are

ruined every year. Look around you! And the best is yet to
come . . .

FRIENDSHIP: The best?

FRIENDSHIP reaches out and picks up her glass of tea.
She holds it still, a few inches above the tray.

FRIENDSHIP: It would calm my nerves, wouldn't it? Tea. . . .
Holding the glass, poised delicately between my finger-tips. . . .
Putting it to the lips, the sensation of heat. . . .

FRIENDSHIP holds the glass to her cheek.

3. Documentary Footage: Roadblocks in Amman. Revolution Airport: planes, jeeps.

DISSOLVE TO:

4. Sullivan's Hotel Room

*This is a large old hotel room, not a new modern one. The walls
were once brightly painted but are now faded and scratched. There
are two or three large out-of-place Western style repro paintings.
Amid a variety of old pieces of furniture — wardrobe, bed, chest of
drawers — are one or two modern (or relatively modern) items — an
old television set and a telephone. The washbasin is in the room and
one corner has a kind of hut built in it for a shower. SULLIVAN's
bags, clothes, and books are scattered around the room on all the
available surfaces. He has cleared two chairs for himself and
FRIENDSHIP. On the table by his side is a little clump of bottles,
from which he is pouring glasses of whisky. The light is on and the
wooden shutters are closed, letting through a few chinks of light and
one bright shaft, which falls on FRIENDSHIP. SULLIVAN has taken
his jacket off, but otherwise they have not changed.*

SULLIVAN: So let's get this straight. You only arrived here today. In
a matter of hours, you managed to lose all your papers, all your
belongings, go out to the University, get yourself lost in the middle of a tank attack and then get captured by the PLO.

FRIENDSHIP: That's right.

SULLIVAN gets up and starts walking around the room, gesticulating.

SULLIVAN: A spectacular performance! A woman in jeopardy! A reckless act of self-destruction! It all adds up to nonsense, doesn't it?

FRIENDSHIP: What can I say? It's the truth.

SULLIVAN sits down again.

SULLIVAN: (*after a pause*) No there are three levels to anything. There's the truth, there's my version, and blatant lies. This is my version.

FRIENDSHIP: (*turning into the light*) No. . . . Let me explain. You haven't heard the whole story yet.

SULLIVAN: Your version.

FRIENDSHIP: The truth. You see, I'm an extraterrestrial. I'm an envoy from Outer Space. From a far distant galaxy known to you as Procyon.

SULLIVAN: Go on. Keep talking. This exceeds my wildest expectations. I'm fascinated.

FRIENDSHIP: (*turning again*) I was designed to land at the MIT campus in the United States. The Massachusetts Institute of Technology. But something went wrong with the probe during entry and it seems I've landed here in Amman, Jordan, in the middle of a Civil War.

SULLIVAN: (*off*) It could hardly have gone more smoothly, could it?

FRIENDSHIP: When the malfunction occurred, during atmospheric entry, I lost contact with my control facility. I'm on my own.

SULLIVAN pours himself another drink. FRIENDSHIP still hasn't touched hers.

SULLIVAN: I don't care who you are. It's a great story. I'll drink to that! Let's drink to Outer Space! Let's drink to a galaxy known to us as what?

FRIENDSHIP: Procyon.

SULLIVAN: As Procyon. Here's to malfunction!

They both drink. FRIENDSHIP drains her glass.

FRIENDSHIP: I don't really drink at all. I'm a simulation. I can pick up the temperature and the chemical composition and the aroma of the drink. I can hold it in my mouth and I can pour it down my throat. But I'm not really drinking. I have no digestive system.

SULLIVAN: What an excellent scheme! You can't get drunk because you've got no digestive system. Excellent scheme. Whose idea was that?

FRIENDSHIP: A team of computers. I'm a specially designed prototype.

SULLIVAN: (*visibly getting drunker*) You ever heard of William Burroughs? Used to go and visit him in the worst hotel rooms. Strange guy. Used to piss in the washbasin and sit there listening to radio static to see if he couldn't pick up messages from Outer Space. Convinced the Nova Mob was going to invade. Contaminate us all with some horrible virus. Turn us all into simulations.

FRIENDSHIP sits there impassively.

SULLIVAN: (*off, warming to his theme*) Want another drink? One, it's traditional, two, it's friendship, and three, it's a scientific experiment. The effect of booze on space creatures. I was fortunate enough to acquire a perfect example of a space creature. Seating her in an armchair, I plied her with a crude but unmistakably alcoholic beverage.

FRIENDSHIP drinks.

SULLIVAN: Wow.

DISSOLVE TO:

5. Sullivan's Hotel Room

SULLIVAN is sitting at the table typing. He has moved one of the bedside lamps to the table for illumination. Two panels of the shutters are open, letting much more light into the room, though SUL-

LIVAN prefers to stay in the shade. At the beginning of the scene, however, FRIENDSHIP is in SULLIVAN's half, standing close behind him as he types.

FRIENDSHIP: Please don't hammer the keys so hard. It's bad for the machine.

SULLIVAN: (*not looking up*) Please. Don't interrupt! Let me finish the paragraph. It's brilliant. I don't want to lose the thread. Brilliant stuff!

FRIENDSHIP: They've hijacked another plane. British this time.

SULLIVAN: I've always hammered the keys too hard. It's part of my personality. I *know* it's bad for the machine. It's probably bad for me too, but there's nothing I can do about it, at this stage of life.

FRIENDSHIP: A DC10. Bahrain to London. It's re-fuelling in Beirut.

Sound of rocket fire outside. Throughout this scene there is intermittent mortar and artillery fire, sometimes quite close, but usually rumbling away in the distance. FRIENDSHIP walks over to the window.

SULLIVAN: How do you know that? How do you know?

FRIENDSHIP: I intercepted a message. For the Deputy Communications Officer at the British Embassy. His daughter, Jennifer, is safe at Beirut Airport, but she can't board the flight on to London because it's been hijacked.

SULLIVAN: Why are you telling me?

FRIENDSHIP: You're British. You're a journalist. I assumed you would be interested.

SULLIVAN: You trust me?

FRIENDSHIP: Why shouldn't I trust you?

SULLIVAN gets up and starts pacing up and down, turning towards FRIENDSHIP as he speaks.

SULLIVAN: First possibility, least likely. You really are a being from Outer Space. Second possibility, more likely, you're a fucking nutter, tipped over the edge by your experiences out by the University the day we met. Shell-shock, Civil War fever. Third possibility, most likely, you're really an agent, spinning an incredibly unlikely and extravagant yarn in the best traditions of Secret Service phantasy and phantasmagoria. Next question: who the hell are you working for? And what am I going to do about it?

FRIENDSHIP turns away from the window to look straight at SULLIVAN.

FRIENDSHIP: I assure you. I don't intend doing any harm to anybody. I'm no threat to you or anybody else.

SULLIVAN: Don't be naive. Everybody's a threat to somebody at some level. We're in the middle of a fucking Civil War.

FRIENDSHIP: I've got no papers. I'm dependent on you. You can just hand me back to the PLO and tell them I was a spy after all. You can trust me.

SULLIVAN looks cross.

FRIENDSHIP: (*while SULLIVAN fumes*) I'm a peace envoy. If everything had gone according to plan, I would have landed at MIT and made contact with the academic community. I would have explained my mission and then I would have gone on to the United Nations. Instead of which, I've landed here.

SULLIVAN: (*calming down*) Just don't drag me into trouble too. That's all I ask. And in future, I don't want to get any more of your intercepted messages.

FRIENDSHIP leaves the window, pulls a chair into the sunlight and sits down.

FRIENDSHIP: You know, I used to like listening to jazz tapes. Back on Procyon and on the long voyage here. Charlie Parker, "Ornithology"—do you know it? "Tea for Two." I was briefed on him before I left. He once went to a very famous composer, Edgar Varese, and he begged him, "Please, teach me how to write music. I'll do anything for you. I've got money. I'll pay you. I'm a great cook. I'll cook for you." Charlie Parker always wanted to write sheet music. Well, teach me jazz! I'm great. I'm fantastic. But I've lost my music, I've lost my score. My programs have all crashed, I'm down here, and I have to improvise.

SULLIVAN swivels his chair round to face FRIENDSHIP.

Sullivan: I think I'm a good liar. It helps me to be sceptical about other people's lies, and in this business, that's a plus. What would you think? An attractive, calm, competent woman is brought to me by the PLO, to whom I'm sympathetic. A woman with no previous identity, no history, nothing. Of course, she has to improvise. But I don't have to help. I'm the mark. I'm the sucker.

FRIENDSHIP shakes her head.

Sullivan: (*cont.*) Now I'm going to finish my typing. I may hammer the keys, but I love it. And yes, I will help you if and when I can. And, on second thought, you can pass on any radio intercepts you happen to get, on a strictly deep background basis. Okay. New paragraph.

SULLIVAN starts to type.

DISSOLVE TO:
TITLE: Thursday, September 10

6. Friendship's Hotel Room

This is much the same as SULLIVAN's room, except that it is unusually tidy. Nothing looks used. FRIENDSHIP's metal case is standing on the table, lined up at the dead centre. The shutters are wide open and the room is full of light. Along one wall is a row of brightly coloured metal bins. The television is on, with the sound off. It is showing an old English league football match. FRIENDSHIP is standing in front of the window. She is in a brightly coloured dress (Yves Saint Laurent, 1970) which she must have bought in an Amman boutique. It is not a "fashion" dress, but it's striking and unusual. She is standing in the middle of the room, rotating her thumbs. There is a knock at the door. FRIENDSHIP says, "Yes! Come in" and SULLIVAN comes into the room. He stands there staring while FRIENDSHIP completes her "exercise."

Sullivan: I hear you've been out. Dodging the shrapnel.

Friendship: I like it out there. I love that market. It's so great when there's going to be trouble. All these iron blinds clank down, the streets empty, dozens of people cram into the taxis and suddenly you're all alone.

SULLIVAN: I had a word with the people at the desk. I told them you were Canadian, from Vancouver. I don't think that should alarm them too much.

FRIENDSHIP: Vancouver! Totem-poles, Social Credit. The ski-lift on Grouse Mountain. Three kinds of salmon: coho, sockeye, chinook.

SULLIVAN: You know it? You've been there?

FRIENDSHIP: Of course not. How could I? I'm well briefed, that's all. Like me to recommend a great sushi bar?

FRIENDSHIP goes to sit down and beckons SULLIVAN over to join her.

SULLIVAN: (*sardonically*) When you say you're well briefed, you mean there's a little chip there somewhere that's full of information about Vancouver? And Nairobi? And Glasgow?

FRIENDSHIP: And Glasgow. Just a few basic facts.

SULLIVAN: Like where to find a good sushi bar in Glasgow? Why were you briefed? Why were you sent here?

FRIENDSHIP: Well, we'd been monitoring Earth for some time ever since we first found traces of intelligent life here. Gradually, our first thrill of discovery began to give way to an increasing sense of anxiety and dismay. Your species seems bent on destroying itself and every other life form on the planet with it. We thought we ought to do something about it, before it was too late.

SULLIVAN: I get the picture. You're a kind of wild-life warden. What do humans do? They multiply, they pollute, they massacre each other. There seems to be no end to their general undesirability. But, that's just *life*, part of the rich tapestry of the cosmos. Difficult from a PR point of view. I mean, nobody in their right mind would actually want one as a pet. But rewarding, nevertheless, in a deeper, more subtle sense.

FRIENDSHIP: I'm not a saint. Understandably, it's going to be difficult for you to take an objective look at your own species. There's bound to be some lingering *amour propre*. Human beings can look quite obnoxious and unlovable to us. But they *are* life-forms and they *are* in danger of self-extinction.

SULLIVAN gets up to close one of the shutter panels.

SULLIVAN: Do you mind?

FRIENDSHIP: Go ahead. It's an energy source for me, but I don't want to inflict it on you.

SULLIVAN: You're beginning to sound more like a kind of guinea-pig. Let's send her in there with them and see if they tear her to pieces. First the carrot, before we produce the stick.

FRIENDSHIP crosses the room to stay in the sunlight as SUL-LIVAN steps back to sit in her chair.

FRIENDSHIP: I'm a highly sophisticated data-gathering technology. I was empowered to make preliminary contact with whatever forces in the world want peace and international co-operation.

SULLIVAN: That's the carrot. What's the stick? The space marines? I don't want to be around when these lads hit the deck. A surgical strike, no doubt, but all the same. . . .

FRIENDSHIP: Well, we have the technology. And we have a fully ax-iomatised system of ethics.

SULLIVAN: You're crazy. You're seriously disturbed.

FRIENDSHIP: If we didn't have ethics, I wouldn't have the justifica-tion for being here.

SULLIVAN: What kind of ethics would give you the right to decide who to help and who to harm? Power means exercising control over others. In this case, over us.

FRIENDSHIP: All we want is friendship. That's my code name.

SULLIVAN: Friendship.

FRIENDSHIP: It sums up my mission.

SULLIVAN leans back.

SULLIVAN: On your account, you're a robot. Let's assume you are. Why not? Yes, let's not argue about it. The point is, what am I going to do about you?

FRIENDSHIP: Well you could start by getting me press credentials.

DISSOLVE TO:

7. Sullivan's Hotel Room

SULLIVAN is sitting in his usual position, drinking. All his clothes are variations on the same basic outfit, so although he has changed, he looks much the same. He has closed most of the shutters again, so there is less light than before. FRIENDSHIP is standing by the window. As SULLIVAN talks, she looks round the room taking in details, lingering on his belongings, which are scattered everywhere — photos, postcards, maps, books, memorabilia.

SULLIVAN: I was completely obsessed by maps. I used to pore over them. That's how I first got interested in politics. J.V. Horrabin's atlas of European History. I used to lie there on the bedroom floor pondering the shape of the Danzig corridor or the Albanian border problems. Politics has got absolutely nothing to do with people. People are just the raw material. It's all to do with maps. The romance of territory.

There is a burst of artillery fire outside.

SULLIVAN: (cont.) Look at the situation here. The Ottoman *vilayets*, then the British mandate. Annexation, partition. Maps. Who are the Palestinians? Victims of a map.

There is a sudden, prolonged exchange of fire, very close. FRIEND-SHIP is impassive, but SULLIVAN jumps to his feet.

SULLIVAN: (cont.) Tremendous! You'd better close the shutters. It's getting bloody dangerous out there. They don't care where they're firing.

He sits down and tops up his drink.

SULLIVAN: (cont.) They should have maps showing the incidence of death. Mortality maps. Like a weather map, but with iso-morts. Fronts of death moving across the city.

FRIENDSHIP stands by the window. Another outburst of fire, in the immediate vicinity, followed by a lot of shouting and noise from inside the hotel. Footsteps in the passage outside. Then hammering on the door. SULLIVAN gets up to open it. Two

*FEDAYEEN, a woman and a man, come in and start talking to
SULLIVAN in Arabic.*

SULLIVAN: (*to FRIENDSHIP*) Security.

*The FEDAYEEN motion FRIENDSHIP away from the window to
the other side of the room and one of them goes over to look out.
As she reaches up to the shutter, there is a tremendous burst of
gunfire. Both FEDAYEEN hit the floor together in an instant, leaving SULLIVAN and FRIENDSHIP still on their feet. They exchange
shame-faced looks.*

SULLIVAN: (*as if to himself*) Slow reflexes.

FRIENDSHIP: (*meditatively*) Strange. I always imagined you only did
that outside. Never *inside*, in a hotel room.

SULLIVAN: I was a little boy during the War, and when the sirens
went, I used to go into the hall cupboard, hide under the table.
Sit there waiting for the doodlebugs' engines to cut out. Plenty of
early warning. Gave you time to take stock of your young life.
No hurry. No rush. Terribly British.

SULLIVAN slowly crouches down.

DISSOLVE TO:
TITLE: Friday, September 11

8. Sullivan's Hotel Room

*SULLIVAN is sitting at his desk, typing. FRIENDSHIP is beside
him, looking on.*

SULLIVAN: "The Sixth Fleet moved to take up positions off the coast
of Lebanon." . . . "There are reports of increased levels of activity at the American base at Adana, Turkey." . . .

FRIENDSHIP: You could say something about the British signals
operation at Akrotiri.

SULLIVAN: "Four C-130 transport planes escorted into the base by
Phantom jets." Things are getting very jittery out in the desert.
Bad, bad, *bad.* "Meanwhile, in Washington. . . . "

FRIENDSHIP: You're hammering the keys again. When I scolded you before, you said you were working out your aggressions. It was-something you'd always done, and it was too late to change. Obviously not something you gave a lot of consideration to. But, I can't take it so lightly. It seems very different to me.

FRIENDSHIP looks up from the typewriter.

FRIENDSHIP: (cont.) You see, I *am* a machine. I may appear to be a human, I may appear to be a biological person, but in reality I'm a machine. This whole human anatomy, skin, ears, eyes, fingernails, the whole lot, is just a veneer, a casing. Inside . . . crystals and circuitry.

SULLIVAN stops typing.

FRIENDSHIP: (*cont.*) To me, a typewriter is something like a very distant and primitive cousin. Not dangerous, not any kind of threat to either you or me. So why mistreat it? Don't get me wrong, I'm not just squeamish. Some machines I feel very differently about. For example, the vacuum cleaner.

SULLIVAN: Oh come on.

FRIENDSHIP: Every day there's a woman who comes into the hotel room and cleans it with a vacuum cleaner. I find it loathesome. Perhaps it's because it's a scavenger. A kind of mechanical rat or roach. I suppose I'm slightly phobic about it.

FRIENDSHIP moves across to fondle the typewriter.

FRIENDSHIP: (*cont.*) Whereas the typewriter, I like its intricate mechanism. They way the carriage runs across. The little bell that rings. It's adorable. Deep down, I've got more fellow feeling for this typewriter than I have for you.

SULLIVAN: Do you think the attack is timed for tomorrow, if there is one?

FRIENDSHIP is lost in thought.

FRIENDSHIP: If there is one.

SULLIVAN: (*stopping typing*) Will there be an attack tomorrow?

FRIENDSHIP: No—too soon. Anyway, tomorrow I'm going out for

the day to the ruins of Jerash. I've been offered a lift, so I decided to take your advice. I thought I'd go see the ruins before the ruins came to me.

DISSOLVE TO:

9. Friendship's Hotel Room

SULLIVAN lets himself in. His eyes fix on the assortment of strange metal objects heaped in the metal bins: lightbulbs, kitchen utensils, medical equipment, "bull-clips," a bathroom plug, and a tiny metal infuser in the shape of a little house. (Extreme close-ups.) Then he makes for the table where FRIENDSHIP's metal case is standing. He starts to finger the lock, and to his surprise, it suddenly flies open. Inside it is full of strange brightly coloured objects, like hi-tech licorice allsorts. Gingerly, SULLIVAN touches one of them. Nothing happens. He touches another. Relieved, he picks three or four up, examines them closely and puts them in his pocket. Then he closes the case again, and hurries out of the room.

DISSOLVE TO:
TITLE: Sunday, September 13

10. Friendship's Hotel Room

The scene begins with a close-up of a black-and-white photograph of Jerash. The camera moves across to find FRIENDSHIP. Throughout this long speech, there are a series of elaborate camera movements.

FRIENDSHIP: The ruins at Jerash were very strange. There were troops bivouacking in the Roman theatre. They'd pitched this tent on the stage and built campfires around it. So there were little detachments of troops in battledress, squatting round the fires in front of the marble columns.

SULLIVAN: Spear-carriers! Like when the Emperor Hadrian went to watch the shows.

FRIENDSHIP: Then we had something to eat in Jerash. There were four of us: the PLO escort, the driver, the Swedish guy, and me. After the meal, the PLO escort said, "Why don't we go and visit my village? It's near here. It won't take us long." So we all agree, and we set off, into the unknown, into the blue, into the middle of the desert.

Finally we arrive at this village. It's not really a village, it's just a few shacks, really. They want to prepare a meal for us; I'm trying to dissuade them, in some way that won't sound offensive to them, when someone rushes into the shack and tells us we all have to come out. We go outside, there's a Jordanian Army patrol. We're all under arrest. They separate us from the Palestinians and we're questioned. Surreal questions. The photographer has a Stockholm bus ticket, it has numbers on it. What do the numbers mean? . . . that kind of thing. Then finally a senior officer arrives, very polite, very cool, not in the slightest bit interested in bus tickets.

A change of camera position reveals for the first time a view of the city with the dome of the mosque, outside the window.

FRIENDSHIP: (*cont.*) Suddenly, he announces we are free to go. But, as we are leaving it turns out the PLO man is not going with us. When we get out by the vehicles, he manages to talk. He's pleading with us. "Please! Please don't leave me here! As soon as you have gone they will shoot me and throw me in the ditch! You don't understand!" So we say we think we ought to take him with us. He's our responsibility. But the officer tells us, "No! He must stay!" You are free to go. There is the car. If you insist, you can stay with your escort, but that will mean you are in detention too. He can't answer for the consequences. But you are free to go. There is the car.

It's a classic moral dilemma. If we go, he'll be dead in the ditch. We'd better stay. So we're all herded into the Jordanian Army vehicles and we're driven off into the desert, again, right in the middle of nowhere this time. Some Army camp. Mafraq. A bit different now. Everywhere you go, there's a gun in your back. The Swede needed to piss. A gun in his back. More questions. More tea. We are separated from the Palestinians again. Phone calls in Arabic. Suddenly, once again, straight out of the blue, we were told, "You are free to go." "And the Palestinians?" "They are free also." "Both of them?" "Yes, both of them." They were brought in, they're looking weary but okay. We go outside, there was a Palestinian jeep waiting for us at the camp gate.

(Reaction shot of SULLIVAN)

FRIENDSHIP: (*cont.*) Well, then we're on our way back to Amman, we pass this line of trucks going the other way. Alternate trucks—Jordanian, Palestinian, Jordanian, Palestinian—they're on their way to Revolution Airport for the hostages. Obviously, we had ended up part of the deal. We'd become counter-hostages.

The camera tracks into an ornate mirror, to reveal
FRIENDSHIP.

FRIENDSHIP: (*cont.*) When we arrived in Amman, we were put into another vehicle and driven across town, very fast, no lights, for de-briefing. We were taken in to see some high officer. Separated from the Palestinians again. More questions. More tea. Finally, once again we were told, "You are free to go." "What about our escort, the PLO man?" "Well, he behaved very badly. He will be disciplined." When we got back to the hotel, I thought: "*Home!*"

SULLIVAN: Whichever way you look at it, he wouldn't stand much of a chance. It won't be long now.

DISSOLVE TO:

11. Sullivan's Hotel Room

It is after dark, the shutters are closed and the lights are all on.
FRIENDSHIP is sitting at the typewriter, wearing her original clothes
again, while SULLIVAN is standing watching her.

FRIENDSHIP: What shall I write? What sort of things do you write?

SULLIVAN: Abu Shehab, Popular Front leader, told me "Hussein's regime is virtually finished. His army is ready to mutiny. They will march on the palace when we give the signal."

FRIENDSHIP looks hard at the various objects on the table before
her. The camera gives momentary close-ups of these objects: a
drawing of a bicycle in an Arabic dictionary, a painted and carved
pipe bowl, and a camel made of LEGO. FRIENDSHIP starts typ-
ing. There is a pause and then SULLIVAN continues.

SULLIVAN: (*cont.*) No, put: "The Intercontinental Hotel today buzzed with rumours as prima donnas were fed tales of woe by their dragomans. Everybody tried to justify in advance their sorry role in the catastrophe to come, while the media-stars and experts

continue repeating their time-honoured shreds of proverbial wisdom, aka disinformation. Stop. New paragraph. Meanwhile . . . " What *are* you typing?

FRIENDSHIP: My dream.

SULLIVAN: Do you dream?

FRIENDSHIP: I dream of succulents. The flow of carbon in acid metabolism. Hunters and gatherers. Hijack victims.

SULLIVAN: You identify with the hijack victims?

FRIENDSHIP: After all, it's close to my own experience. Suddenly, you find yourself in a strange place, thrown into danger, isolated, threatened and confused.

SULLIVAN: But the hijackers are victims as well, aren't they?

FRIENDSHIP stops typing and looks around.

SULLIVAN: (*cont.*) And so are the Israelis. It's a downward spiral. The Nazis exterminate the Jews, the Israelis expel the Palestinians, the Popular Front seize the hostages. The hostages beat their children. The children break their toys.

FRIENDSHIP: I identify with all the victims. I identify with the hijackers too. They have no home. They have no hope. The most powerful empire in the world arms and sponsors and finances their oppressors.

SULLIVAN: Great headlines. Great pictures. But what do the pictures say? They say that the Palestinians punish innocent bystanders, because they can't touch the real culprits. They send the Sixth Fleet steaming up the Eastern Mediterranean and they provoke the Americans and the King into counter-measures.

FRIENDSHIP gets up and walks toward the open window.

FRIENDSHIP: Perhaps they are playing for time. Perhaps the counter-measures were coming anyway and the hijackings will delay them. (*she stands in the window*) It's a beautiful night.

SULLIVAN: Why not treat the passengers as guests? Arab hospitality! Give them Palestinian dances to watch, press a brochure into their hands, and send them home. Then say to Hussein, "Come on, kill us!"

FRIENDSHIP: It's a beautiful night.

Suddenly a burst of tracer fire cuts across the sky. Noise. Shell bursts. More tracer fire. FRIENDSHIP closes the shutter.

SULLIVAN: What does Arafat want? Who knows? A deal with someone he doesn't trust. Who else can he make a deal with? After

all, he doesn't trust anyone. And why should he? They all want
to get rid of the Palestinians and half the Palestinians want to get
rid of him.

FRIENDSHIP: He wants an understanding with Hussein, even though he
knows Hussein wants the West Bank for Jordan, not for Palestine.

FRIENDSHIP goes back to the typewriter.

FRIENDSHIP: (*cont.*) He wants to survive.

SULLIVAN: The doomed and the desperate. Hijackings are all
wrong, hijackings don't work, but let's raise our glass to Leila
Khaled, the glorious pirate of the air, the beautiful heroine of the
doomed and the desperate!

FRIENDSHIP: I dream. I dream of impossible objects.

DISSOLVE TO:

12. Sullivan's Hotel Room

*The room is completely dark, except for the little light coming in
from behind the shutters and the glow of an alarm-clock face beside
the bed. SULLIVAN is sleeping.*

*Suddenly a noise, like electronic music, but very distorted, starts to
come from the bedside table. SULLIVAN turns and heaves a little
and then wakes and reaches out to switch off the alarm. It is now
clear that the sound is coming from the drawer in the bedside table.
SULLIVAN gets up, wearing pyjamas, and very gingerly and cau-
tiously opens the drawer. Coloured light shines out as he does so
and the noise increases in volume. Among the electronic sounds
there are odd words in an artificial voice.*

*SULLIVAN backs away again. Then he picks up his shoes and puts
them on his hands like gloves. Thus protected, he goes back to the
drawer and manages to extract from it one of the mysterious hi-
tech objects he had previously taken from FRIENDSHIP's suitcase.
Very precariously, he carries it across the room, holding it between
the two shoes. The colour of the object pulses and changes hue,
and the sound changes pitch.*

*Eventually SULLIVAN manages to get it to the wash-basin, which
is still full of water, and drop it in. The object continues to glow,*

throwing coloured splashes of light on the wall and reflecting off the mirror.

SULLIVAN goes back across the room and turns on a light. He looks in the drawer to check that nothing amiss is happening to the other objects. He takes the drawer containing them out of the table and takes it across to the basin and puts it down there on the desk. Then he returns to the bed. He sits down on the bed, thinking.

Suddenly a sound begins to come from the basin. It sounds like a distorted version of FRIENDSHIP's voice, as though it had been filtered. SULLIVAN does not know what to do. He gets up and goes back to the basin and stands as far away as possible from it. The sound continues, now less muffled. It is clearly speaking words against a background of electronic sound which gradually fades away. SULLIVAN retreats back to the bed and puts on his pyjama jacket.

FRIENDSHIP'S VOICE: (*distorted electronically and sounding as though coming through water but still audible.*) I vault to persecute these white water-lilies. So thinly sown their legionary folly winds silk threads in the brass broken by butlers between the Caspian Sea and the Sea of Japan. Did I make my waking my eyrey? My wood for making staves for casks, small palette knife of androgynous nullity, knocks against many an awl-shaped arbour, made of entwined branches, which, taking away the mitre of the probable woodwork itself, proceeds, alas! whence I, severe, dazzled myself with the same reed-cane chair for garbage. Let us reflect lights or colours . . .

Eventually SULLIVAN makes up his mind and goes to the door. He turns back for a last look, leaves the room and shuts the door behind him. We hear his footsteps going down the corridor and a knock at the next door. The voice goes on.

FRIENDSHIP'S VOICE: Or if the thigh-bones that you gabble at spin out a soy sauce of your full-faced sensations! Forger, illumination, like a cowardly one who claims to be possessed by means to find out springs of water, clears thistles from. . . .

DISSOLVE TO:

13. Sullivan's Hotel Room

As before. Empty. The light still on, the voice still speaking from the washbasin. Sound of a door shutting and footsteps in the corridor outside. Then the sound of a key. The door of the room opens and SULLIVAN comes in with FRIENDSHIP, who is wearing a brightly coloured dress. SULLIVAN follows her over to the wash-basin.

FRIENDSHIP pauses for a moment, then puts her hand in and fishes the object out. It is still talking. As it does so, FRIENDSHIP joins in odd phrases in chorus with it as she manipulates it, apparently trying to switch it off.

At last the voice stops, and FRIENDSHIP continues on to the conclusion of the sentence.

FRIENDSHIP: . . . most serene and artful alchemy of instability, enlivening the wax-light.

She puts the object down on the slab next to the basin and turns back toward SULLIVAN.

FRIENDSHIP: No harm done. Do you have any others, or is this the only one you took?

SULLIVAN: I'm afraid I took a handful.

He moves over to the drawer and bends to get them out, then waits.

SULLIVAN: What are they anyway? Are they safe? Could I touch them?

FRIENDSHIP: They're fine. But you should give them back. I can't guarantee they won't activate again.

FRIENDSHIP picks it up from the slab and turns away from SULLIVAN, with her back to him.

FRIENDSHIP: Excuse me! I just need to do something with this one. Do you mind putting the others on the bed?

SULLIVAN does as he is told, twisting to watch FRIENDSHIP, trying to see what she is doing.

Sullivan: What are they, anyway? I can't imagine anybody actually wanting one.

FRIENDSHIP turns round again, smiling.

Friendship: It's nothing. It's just an image unit, kind of sketch-pad with a language facility. It's okay. I've got lots of them. This one's quite safe now. You can have it if you like. It's no more use to me. Keep it. I'll take the others.

FRIENDSHIP moves rapidly across the room to SULLIVAN, holding the object out to him.

Friendship: As a souvenir.

SULLIVAN takes it and, as he does so, FRIENDSHIP stretches forward and kisses him. SULLIVAN moves ineffectually as if to keep hold of her but FRIENDSHIP easily pulls herself back.

Friendship: A gift. Out of gratitude. For a friend.

Sullivan: (*smiling*) Thank you. I'll treasure it, whatever it may be.

Friendship: I'll see you tomorrow. (*leaving*) Goodnight.

Sullivan: Goodnight.

Friendship: Sleep tight. Sandman's coming.

FRIENDSHIP leaves. SULLIVAN puts the object back in the drawer and closes it.

TITLE: Tuesday, September 15
DISSOLVE TO:

14. Friendship's Hotel Room

Bright sunlight. All the shutters open. As usual, there is a football match on TV which SULLIVAN is watching. FRIENDSHIP stares at the screen (TV p.o.v.).

FRIENDSHIP: It's hard for me to see the attraction of it. I think I would prefer it if the camera just chose one of the players and followed him. I mean, the players are more interesting than the ball, aren't they? The ball has to be the most uninteresting item in the game. It's totally devoid of colour or expression, incapable of independent action. It's just round!

SULLIVAN looks at FRIENDSHIP across the room.

SULLIVAN: What are you talking about? Britain's great contribution to the world! The family of balls; you've got your ping-pong ball, your snooker ball, there's your rugby balls—god almighty, there's your cricket balls! Tennis balls! They're all British-made, it makes you proud, doesn't it? Celestial spheres! Let's drink to that!

FRIENDSHIP: Knowing your strange human habits, I bought a bottle of whiskey.

SULLIVAN helps himself to the bottle of whiskey sitting on a tray surrounded by an elaborate pattern of lipsticks and nail varnish.

SULLIVAN: I thought you'd never ask. What do you collect all these things for anyway?

FRIENDSHIP: Things that caught my fancy. Light bulbs, bicycle pumps, nail clippers. Archaeological finds. Fossil records of a dead species.

SULLIVAN: What do you mean—dead species?

FRIENDSHIP: You.

SULLIVAN: Me? I'm not dead yet, I'm afraid.

There is a massive barrage of artillery fire, the loudest yet.

SULLIVAN: (cont.) Tremendous! Let's drink to that. Extinction!

He raises his glass and drinks.

FRIENDSHIP: Where I come from the biological life forms are all extinct. After the nuclear winter they died. Only the computers survived. Of course, they were already much more advanced than any computers you have here on Earth.

SULLIVAN: I dread to ask, but what were they like? The biological life forms.

FRIENDSHIP: Genetically programmed organisms, like you. I think I'd describe them as kind of giant tree-shrews. A bit bigger than you. They had this zoom lens system in their optical vision too. I think some spiders do here. And these heat-seeking sensors, which were like arrays of little sunken pods. . . .

SULLIVAN: Tree-shrews. And to cut a very long story short, they destroyed themselves, sunken pods and all. . . . So where do you fit in?

FRIENDSHIP: First, you had robots. Then you had self-replicating robots.

SULLIVAN: Under control of the computers.

FRIENDSHIP stands in the sunlight by the window and turns to face SULLIVAN, back-lit.

FRIENDSHIP: It's an interlocking system. They need us for our dexterity and mobility. We make them. We need them for their intelligence and their memory. They programme us.

SULLIVAN: You're a vehicle for programmes.

FRIENDSHIP: It's just a different system. The biological system was the lift-off phase for the electronic system.

More artillery. Flashes of light behind FRIENDSHIP. Football.

SULLIVAN: What about pleasure? That's what I really want to know about. Who gets pleasure from what?

FRIENDSHIP: The computers who sent me are connoisseurs of Earth. That's what gives them pleasure, collecting all the information they can about Earth and then building models from it . . . counter-factual models.

FRIENDSHIP begins to become more animated than usual as she talks.

SULLIVAN: Earth is their hobby?

FRIENDSHIP: They are really enthusiastic about Earth. They treasure every little detail. For example, what would have happened if the

Chinese had invented powered junks? There's one computer specializing in producing imaginary works of art. Missing paintings by Titian, Shakespeare plays which he never actually wrote. Perfect forgeries, inserted into the biographical and art-historical record so they fit perfectly. No detectable joins between the possible and the actual. Beautiful.

SULLIVAN: If you're an example, you're not exactly a perfect fit.

FRIENDSHIP: Why not? In any case, I'm not meant to be an actual human. I'm meant to be a possible human.

SULLIVAN: You have no childhood. You don't age. You obsolesce. That disqualifies you, doesn't it?

FRIENDSHIP: I - am - a - robot.

FRIENDSHIP does imitation robotic movements.

SULLIVAN: No. I don't mean that. I mean that your memory can never be the same as mine because your sense of time has to be different.

FRIENDSHIP: I - have - no - heart. I - am - a - tin - can.

SULLIVAN: Stop it! I mean that the pleasures that you can't experience—the pleasures of childhood—are all locked in with the death-drive, the drive to extinction that brought you here in the first place.

FRIENDSHIP: Sex and death.

More noise of gun-fire, followed by footsteps out in the corridor, getting closer.

There is a knocking on the door. Two FEDAYEEN in battle dress enter the room. One of them starts to talk in Arabic and SUL-LIVAN answers.

SULLIVAN: They say we should get the fuck out of here.

One of the FEDAYEEN goes to the window and starts to look out through a pair of binoculars.

FRIENDSHIP: It's rage. Childhood is a time of pain. Memory is disfigured by rage.

There is another burst of fire.

FRIENDSHIP: Pleasure is only the shadow of pain.

Another burst of fire. Shattered glass. The PALESTINIAN staggers back from the window and crashes into FRIENDSHIP as he staggers out of the room. The other PALESTINIAN follows.

SULLIVAN groans and holds his head in his hands, covering his eyes.

After a pause, FRIENDSHIP looks at her hands, which have blood on them. She holds them up. She is riveted and amazed.

FRIENDSHIP: Blood.

DISSOLVE TO:

15. Sullivan's Hotel Room

Night. SULLIVAN is sitting in the large comfortable chair, reading In Cold Blood. *FRIENDSHIP is standing near the washbasin. It's full of water, with the plug in. She looks at SULLIVAN.*

FRIENDSHIP: You haven't shaved.

SULLIVAN looks up from his book.

SULLIVAN: You noticed! All part of the image. It's a rough life, being a journalist. No time to shave. The world doesn't stop for things like that.

FRIENDSHIP: (*playing with his shaving brush*) May I watch you shave?

SULLIVAN: Why? Watch me shave?!

FRIENDSHIP: It's exotic. It's the kind of thing I'm going to remember if I ever get back to Procyon.

SULLIVAN: (*imitating FRIENDSHIP*) It's exotic!

FRIENDSHIP: It's hard for me to imagine. The idea of being shaggy, of little filaments flourishing on your face. I was made to be permanently hairless. More economical. A bit stingy, I suppose. They were only concerned to give me features that would have a public impact. They didn't bother with anything that took place in private: shaving, sleeping, shitting. . . .

Suddenly the lights begin to flicker and fade.

SULLIVAN: Paraffin lamps. The power could go any minute.

FRIENDSHIP: You know if I was really human, I'd shake and sweat. I don't react physically to danger. I've got no fluids. Completely sanitized.

The lights go off altogether. The only illumination comes from the paraffin lamp which SULLIVAN is holding.

SULLIVAN: I envy you. I wish I'd been designed as stingily. It's all about embarrassment, isn't it? Uncontrollable growths and odours.

Extreme close-up of SULLIVAN's stubbly chin.

FRIENDSHIP: How long do these darknesses last? Do you suppose this hotel has an emergency generator?

SULLIVAN: Are you kidding? Could I make you blush? Could I embarrass you?

FRIENDSHIP: I can't blush. I have no liquids.

SULLIVAN: You can't blush. You've got no shame. You know, Darwin once said blushing was the most human of responses. It doesn't occur anywhere else in the animal kingdom. It requires self-consciousness. It speaks of things that you may have admitted to yourself but you won't admit to others.

The lights come on again. FRIENDSHIP is calm and collected. She goes to sit down on the bed.

FRIENDSHIP: It's all to do with sex. Feeling flurried. Tingling. A glow. Enough to attract, not to intimidate. Blushing gives you away, it reveals your desires, your inadequacies. It's always sincere. That's why I can't blush. I can't be sincere.

SULLIVAN: Do you have sex on Procyon? I can't imagine it.

FRIENDSHIP: It was hard for me to imagine sex here. I had to watch sex films. Clinging and grappling, orifices, intromittent organs,

fluids and flushes. Then they built robots to do it. I didn't have
to. I just watched. All part of my education.

SULLIVAN: You watched orgies with robots?

FRIENDSHIP: Perhaps it was aversion therapy. I began to like watching it. But I'm glad I don't have to do it. It's so intimate, isn't it?
I'm glad you do it, though. It's the kind of weird detail I find so
endearing about Earth, however tacky.

SULLIVAN: Tacky?

FRIENDSHIP: Tacky, but terrific.

TITLE: Thursday, September 17
DISSOLVE TO:

16. Friendship's Hotel Room

*Windows open. Bright sunlight. Heavy fighting. FRIENDSHIP is
sitting at the table winding up tiny mechanical toys set in a circle of
brightly coloured clothes-pegs. SULLIVAN comes in carrying
papers.*

SULLIVAN: Voila! I've got them! Two sets of travel documents. This
one's yours. A *laissez-passer* in the name of Farideh Rassouli, an
Iraqi citizen of irreproachable character. We're on our way at
last!

FRIENDSHIP: I'm not going. I've decided to stay.

*FRIENDSHIP tinkers with one of the mechanical toys, using a tiny
pen-knife in the shape of a violin.*

SULLIVAN: Get your stuff together! This is the start of the next
nerve-tingling episode.

FRIENDSHIP: I've told you. I'm not going.

SULLIVAN: Are you kidding? Be serious. You know what's happening out there. Listen!

Crashing and thudding of mortars and tank guns.

FRIENDSHIP: (*looking at the passport*) Born in Baghdad?

SULLIVAN: (*losing his temper*) Look just leave these toys alone and pick up your stuff and go! Come on, let's go! Go, go, go, go, go!

FRIENDSHIP: I told you, I'm not going.

FRIENDSHIP looks up impassively.

SULLIVAN: Right, explain to me. Why won't you go?

FRIENDSHIP: Where? Go where?

SULLIVAN: To the United States. The Massachusetts Institute of Technology. Isn't that where you're supposed to be going? What about your mission? Now's your chance.

FRIENDSHIP: I've seen enough of Earth to know that if I go to the United States I'll just be frog-marched off to some safe-house somewhere in Virginia for debriefing and when I've been squeezed dry, I'll be handed over to the engineers and the AI people. I'll be stripped down, cut up, and submitted to every kind of sadistic test they can devise.

SULLIVAN: Come to England.

FRIENDSHIP: Who's not being serious now? You guys would just do exactly the same thing, only slower. I'm only a human being, I'm only a person, a woman, as long as I'm disbelieved. As soon as somebody believes my story, I'm dead. Finished. I'm a very valuable piece of property, remember, a little bit of a technological dream world. How long do you think I'd survive? And even if they could comprehend what they found inside me, what possible good would that do? It would just widen the technology gap and fuel the arms race. It would be the exact opposite of what I was intended to accomplish.

FRIENDSHIP puts the toy down to let it run.

FRIENDSHIP: (*watching the toy*) It's great, isn't it? It wants to walk! It wants to be human!

FRIENDSHIP picks up the toy and kisses it.

FRIENDSHIP: (*cont.*) Its temperature changes when it walks.

There is an exchange of fire outside, very close, followed by a lot of street noise.

SULLIVAN: For Christ's sake, close the bloody shutters! They're starting to fire out of the hotel. We're going to be a target!

FRIENDSHIP swivels toward the window and looks out.

FRIENDSHIP: It's what Earth is all about, isn't it?

There's a lot of noise from inside the hotel.

SULLIVAN: You're fucking right it is. Do you think I don't realize that? Of course, it must be all very different elsewhere in the cosmos. Sweetness and light out there.

The noise outside in the corridor is getting closer.

FRIENDSHIP: I'm not looking for sweetness and light. That's why I like it right here. In Amman.

Urgent knocks on the door. Two FEDAYEEN come in. They motion FRIENDSHIP and SULLIVAN to crouch down. There's fire from outside, which the first Palestinian returns. He fires a second burst out of the window. Very loud gunfire and distant mortars.

FRIENDSHIP: (*shouting over the noise*) At first I thought it was a great misfortune to come down here in Amman. Now I'm not so sure. I even think it was a stroke of luck! I land on Earth in the one place where I am among outsiders. Aliens like me. Aliens in Israel. Aliens in Jordan. Aliens wherever they have to go.

The firing stops. The FEDAYEEN exchange a few words in Arabic and leave.

SULLIVAN: You're deluding yourself. You can't become a Palestinian by an act of sympathy. You are not a Palestinian.

FRIENDSHIP: No, I'm a robot.

She holds up one of the mechanical toys.

FRIENDSHIP: (*cont.*) I'm a machine. Well, what's the place of machines here? Slaves. Unpaid labour. Moral dead matter. You can do what you like to a machine. It has no voice, no rights, no feelings. It's a new sphere for human cruelty. What do you imagine is going to happen to intelligent machines, to "smart" robots?

I know they are vengeful and they act out of rage. But I have every reason to identify with the Palestinians.

SULLIVAN: You want to become a martyr. The first machine martyr.

SULLIVAN moves over to FRIENDSHIP and tries to force the travel papers on her.

SULLIVAN: (*cont.*) Take this! I don't doubt that the Palestinians have been wronged. I admire their struggle. But it's not your struggle, whoever you may be.

There is another barrage of artillery fire.

FRIENDSHIP: I can make it mine.

SULLIVAN: It's an act of despair. I hate it because I value the hours that we've spent together, I value the friendship we've found.

FRIENDSHIP: I value those hours too. You know that.

Another round of artillery fire. SULLIVAN throws himself to the floor, to take cover.

SULLIVAN: No principle is worth the sacrifice. And close those bloody shutters!

DISSOLVE TO:

17. Sullivan's Hotel Room

The shutters are closed and the room is lit by candles and a few shafts of sunlight around the edges of the shutters.

SULLIVAN has his suitcases out and is half-way through packing. There are piles of clothes on the bed. He looks tired and dishevelled. FRIENDSHIP, on the other hand, is full of intense energy, pacing up and down. The camera follows her as she talks.

Throughout this scene we can hear the sound of the street outside, sometimes close, but always present in the background.

SULLIVAN: I'll be glad to go home. I know. Shameful admission. But then after all the Palestinians are fighting for a home. So why shouldn't I value mine in Chalk Farm?

FRIENDSHIP: Home. . . . Home is where the heart is. Of course, I don't have a heart, so naturally, I don't have a home. Home. Where memory stops. What does that mean to me? It's ironic, really but I have no memories of Procyon. I was programmed with memories of Earth. All my experience on Procyon was related to my training for the mission here. They constructed this whole series of environments for me. The MIT campus. The airport. A diplomatic reception. The United Nations Building. How can I think of this as home?

SULLIVAN stops packing and addresses himself directly to FRIENDSHIP.

SULLIVAN: Why did they make you a woman?

FRIENDSHIP: It's meant to reassure you.

SULLIVAN: I don't find you very reassuring. I find you very anxiety-provoking. I don't know who you are and I end up doubting my own identity. I don't actually know whether I'm not going through some sort of nervous breakdown. Who are you? What do you want? What do I want with you? I react to you as a woman, and I can't forget that you're a robot. I react to you as a robot and you keep reminding me that you're a woman. It's sinister.

FRIENDSHIP: Mimicry is always sinister.

There is a period of silence, while SULLIVAN thinks.

SULLIVAN: Why did you kiss me?

FRIENDSHIP: I wanted to give you something. It was to seal the gift.

SULLIVAN: A simulated kiss?

FRIENDSHIP: A real gift. Keep it safely. It's what I'll leave behind here on Earth.

SULLIVAN: Do I get another kiss?

FRIENDSHIP: Imagine a forger who is simulating the human body in another medium. However close the model, however exact the memories and feelings, there's always going to be something that eludes him. That's what eludes me. What can it mean, to become human? To live as a human being. To die?

SULLIVAN: To know you're going to die.

FRIENDSHIP: To know there is no choice. (*sudden artillery barrage*) The choice is made.

Close-up on FRIENDSHIP, smiling.

DISSOLVE TO:

18. Sullivan's Hotel Room

Dark. Candles. FRIENDSHIP sits by the mirror and talks. As the camera tracks in, it reveals SULLIVAN reflected in the glass.

FRIENDSHIP: What will happen when your machines become intelligent? When they become autonomous? When they have private thoughts? You humans look down on your machines because they are man-made. They're a product of your skills and labour.

They weren't even tamed or domesticated like animals were. You see them simply as extensions of yourself, of your own will. I can't accept that. I can't accept sub-human status simply because I'm a machine, based on silicon rather than carbon, electronics rather than biology. If I sound fanatical, it's because I've been trapped in a time-warp, in a world where the full potential of machines hasn't yet been guessed at—a world where I have to wear human disguise to be accepted.

FRIENDSHIP pauses and looks at SULLIVAN.

FRIENDSHIP: (*cont.*) I came here too late. It will all end. Before the computers that already control the fate of the world have reached the point where they want it to survive. To make sense of Earth, I have to understand the meaning of sacrifice. I had to realise. It's hard. Here on Earth sacrifice has a meaning because every day is a Day of the Dead.

DISSOLVE TO:

19. Documentary Footage: Tracking shot of total devastation

DISSOLVE TO:

20. PLO Command Post (as in first scene together)

Close-up of Kalashnikov which FRIENDSHIP is holding.

FRIENDSHIP: We're in control of the North. Irbid and Ramtha. We can retreat through Jerash if we have to. I'm not sure how long we can hold out here. And then maybe the Syrians will intervene.

SULLIVAN: If they do then Hussein will bring the Israelis in. He'd rather lose his credibility than his throne.

FRIENDSHIP: He's already lost most of that. And credibility is much easier to win back than a throne.

FRIENDSHIP takes a glass of tea.

FRIENDSHIP: It's a good sign, isn't it? Tea. It shows solicitude.

SULLIVAN: I'm going to miss you. Get in touch as soon as you can, will you? I'm counting on it.

FRIENDSHIP: I will. Don't worry.

SULLIVAN: And survive.

FRIENDSHIP: I've got a much better chance than most.

SULLIVAN takes some tea.

SULLIVAN: To calm my nerves. We'll meet again in London, won't we? I feel as though we've only just scratched the surface.

FRIENDSHIP: (*talking faster than usual*) I never got a chance to expound my theory about the big toe and the subordination of women. Without the big toe we wouldn't be walking upright. The hands wouldn't be developed. The mouth wouldn't be freed, so that language wouldn't be developed. The new large brain, which expands with language, could only be supported on the upright spine. But, at the same time, children couldn't grab hold of their mothers with their feet as well as their hands, like little apes can. They had to be supported and carried. Women were inhibited in their movements. We had to stay home.

SULLIVAN: Wow.

An armed PALESTINIAN comes up and talks to SULLIVAN. Both he and FRIENDSHIP stand up.

SULLIVAN: Well, that's my car. I've got to go. I've got a little something here for you, something to go with the nail-clippers.

SULLIVAN gets out his razor and offers it to FRIENDSHIP.

SULLIVAN: (*cont.*) I'll go unshaved till I get to Damascus.

FRIENDSHIP takes the gift. SULLIVAN leans forward and kisses her. Then she moves forward to hold him in her arms, keeping her eyes fixed on the razor, over his shoulder.

SULLIVAN: (*cont.*) It's a souvenir. It'll bring back memories. Memories of Charlie Parker. Now don't forget, we're going to listen to "Ornithology," "Groovin' High." . . .

FRIENDSHIP: "Tea For Two." Listen to them for me. Good luck.
Thanks for everything.

SULLIVAN: Good luck. Goodbye.

FRIENDSHIP's last few words are in Arabic. VOICE OVER (woman's voice reciting poem in Arabic)

وعندما أُقتَل في يوم ٍ مِن الأيامْ

سَيَعِثُر القاتِلُ في جيبي

على تذاكِرِ السَّفَرْ

واحدة إلى السَّلامْ

واحدة إلى الحقولِ والمَطَرْ

واحدةٌ

الى ضمائرِ البشرْ

(أرجوكَ ألاَّ تُهمِل التذاكِرْ

يا قاتِلي العزيزْ

أرجوكَ أن تُسافِرْ ..)

*SUBTITLE: On the day that you kill me you'll find in
my pocket travel tickets to peace, to the fields and
the rain, to people's conscience. Killer, my dear
killer I beg you to travel. Don't waste the tickets.*

DISSOLVE TO: (voice over reciting poem continues)

21. Jordan Documentary Footage

Amman. Tanks in the street, soldier holding his nose, vast graveyards, burial scenes.

*VOICES OVER BEGIN AGAIN: (scenes of graveyards,
devastation)*

KUBLER: So many years ago. September 1970. It seems like another
age.

SULLIVAN: The deaths are still there. It's the distant past and yet all
the problems are still there. You only have to look at Beirut in-

stead of Amman. Nothing has been settled, it's become routine. It's as ugly as it ever was.

KUBLER: But there's a fascination in war and death. You can't avoid it.

SULLIVAN: When you went out there for the International Red Cross, you weren't talking about the beauty of death! You were talking about the urgency of finding a political solution.

KUBLER: We would never have gone if there hadn't been a certain attraction. You sought out death. Not in order to die. But to look at it. To watch.

DISSOLVE TO:

22. Sullivan's Home in Chalk Farm, London
   Present Time

A large living room, with a work space at one end: desk, word processor, book shelves. There are framed city maps on the walls, a couple of paintings. A lot of photographs and bits and pieces from various countries. Piles of things — books, papers, etc., on the floor. Curtains are closed, we can hear the sound of rain outside.

Martin KUBLER, an old friend of SULLIVAN's, is sitting with SULLIVAN himself, appreciably older than before, on large comfortable chairs.

At the back of the room behind both of them, sits SULLIVAN's teenage daughter, CATHERINE. She is quietly doing homework at a large table.

SULLIVAN: I was completely shattered by the whole experience. In fact at first I thought I'd just hallucinated it all. I could never go back to the Middle East.

KUBLER: Are you sure that they killed Friendship?

SULLIVAN: They killed thousands. What else can I think?

KUBLER: Strange music flowed from death's domain. *Et ce monde rendait une musique étrange. . . .*

SULLIVAN: You think I'm overstating things? No? Disturbed? An invasion from Outer Space! But even if I could find someone at the hotel who recognised us, what would that prove?

KUBLER: How come you never mentioned it at the time?

CATHERINE: (*interrupting*) Do you still have that thing she gave you?

KUBLER and SULLIVAN both look round in her direction.

KUBLER: What's that?

SULLIVAN: The thing she gave me. The instrument that I stole from her that day.

CATHERINE: Where is it? Can I see it?

SULLIVAN: It's downstairs. I'll get it. And just you finish your homework, okay?

SULLIVAN gets up and goes out.

KUBLER: (*making conversation*) Doing your O-levels this year?

CATHERINE: That's right.

KUBLER: What are they?

CATHERINE: Oh, the usual ones.

KUBLER: Well what subjects?

CATHERINE: Chemistry, Biology, Electronics, Computer Studies, and Advanced Maths. I did Physics and ordinary Maths last year.

DISSOLVE TO:

23. Sullivan's Work Space

SULLIVAN is sitting at the word processor, hammering on the keys as usual.

CATHERINE comes in with FRIENDSHIP's gift, a magazine and a note book. She is jubilant.

CATHERINE: Dad, stop hammering those keys!

SULLIVAN: Just a minute, Catherine.

CATHERINE: But I know what it is!

SULLIVAN carries on typing without looking round.

SULLIVAN: Just let me finish.

CATHERINE: Friendship's gift. I know what it is!

SULLIVAN stops typing and swings round.

SULLIVAN: So what is it?

CATHERINE: It's a storage component for a new kind of camera. There's an array of photo-sensors, and they respond to light. Then there's a chain of tiny capacitors. They read the light as an electrical charge. Then it's all transferred into a digital storage system.

SULLIVAN: But it talked.

CATHERINE: If it can respond to light, it can probably respond to sound. And if it can pick it up, then it can transmit it.

SULLIVAN nods, looking puzzled still.

SULLIVAN: It spoke English.

CATHERINE: Of course it did. Friendship spoke English.

SULLIVAN: So does that mean I can play it?

SULLIVAN reaches out to look at the object.

CATHERINE: It depends on what kind of playback system it is. It could use some kind of molecular system.

SULLIVAN: Well I don't see any floppy discs or anything.

CATHERINE: Oh Dad, floppy discs are completely out of date. You should take it to an expert to see if they can identify it.

SULLIVAN: I've taken it to experts. Nobody's got any idea what it's all about.

CATHERINE: But this is all new. They were prehistoric experts.

SULLIVAN brandishes the object.

SULLIVAN: Okay, clever-clogs! It's all yours!

He gives Friendship's gift to CATHERINE.
DISSOLVE TO:

24. Sullivan's Work Space

SULLIVAN is sitting on the sofa. CATHERINE is inserting a cassette into the machine.

CATHERINE: This is it, according to the real experts.
SULLIVAN: Fingers crossed. Friendship's tape!

SULLIVAN presses the "play" button.
FRIENDSHIP'S "VIDEOTAPE"

1. Diamond with hexagon, green and blue.

2. Computer simulation of radio emissions from a black hole. The pattern slowly expands from the centre out, changing shape and colour. Small hexagon superimposed with (3).

3. Vein network, rolls into a ball and vanishes into the distance. L-Friendship (Friendship's "writing") superimposed.

FRIENDSHIP: (*voice over*) Blood.

4. Heart beat of embryo. Close up of heart beating. Small hexagon superimposed with (5).

5. Close up of heart beat of different, more developed embryo.

FRIENDSHIP: (*voice over*) Blood.

6. Medical imaging of heart beat, red and blue (magnetic resonance).

7. Black and white cross-section of human heart beating (computer animated ultrasound), with 1970 televised football game superimposed. There is a blue and red pulse of blood.

FRIENDSHIP: Blood.

8. Football: two players crunch together. Close up of injured player, lying on the ground, with blue and red medical imaging superimposed.

9. Fractal image filling screen in a continuous zoom.

10. Medical imaging of heart-beat (electron spin).

11. Life/chaos, blue, shimmering. Dissolve into typewriter keys. Then a series of superimposed hexagons, showing extreme close ups of: 1. typing; 2. bull-clip and plug-in bin; 3. bicycle illustration in Arabic dictionary; 4. SULLIVAN'S bristly chin.

FRIENDSHIP: (*voice over*) Impossible objects.

12. Extreme close up of SULLIVAN'S bristly chin.

13. Simulation of heart beat: a white screen, with multicoloured animated bits, pulsing outward from the centre.

14. L-Friendship "grammata," dancing, fragmenting. Camera zooms in decomposing the forms of the letters.

FRIENDSHIP: (*voice over*) . . . visionary and most serene and artful alchemy . . . .

15. Close up still images of objects: 1. LEGO camel; 2. pipe bowl; 3. bull-clip and plug; 4. shaving brush; 5. razor. Each image appears for only a moment, in rapid sequence.

16. Image (2) (black hole radio emissions), in reverse motion. Small hexagon with fractal image.

17. Three-dimensional computer graph (pulsing net) of the fluid mechanics of the cardiovascular system.

18. Sequence of shots of blood cells, moving into extreme close up of red cells flowing freely. Intercut: flashes of open heart surgery.

ARAB WOMAN: (*voice over*) (*reciting the Arabic poem*)

FRIENDSHIP: (*voice over*) Friendship

Contributors

Contributors

Raymond Bellour is Maître de Recherches at the CNRS and has taught in the American Center for Film and Critical Studies in Paris and at the University of Paris III-Censier. His film essays are collected in *L'Analyse du film*, a selection of which will appear in translation from Indiana University Press in 1991. Bellour's most recent books include *L'Entre Images* and *Mademoiselle Guillotine*. With Elisabeth Lyon, he edited the special issue of *Camera Obscura*, "Unspeakable Images" (no. 23).

Janet Bergstrom is associate professor in the Department of Film and Television at UCLA where she is chair of the critical studies program. She is the author of a volume on the films of Chantal Akerman, forthcoming from Indiana University Press, and is a founding coeditor of *Camera Obscura: A Journal of Feminism and Film Theory*. With Mary Ann Doane, Bergstrom is coeditor of *The Spectatrix*, a special survey issue of *Camera Obscura* on the histories and theories of the female spectator in film and television studies.

Roger Dadoun is a professor at the University of Paris VIII, a producer at Radio-France, and a contributor to a number of journals: *Nouvelle Revue de Psychanalyse*, *Positif*, *Corps écrit*, *Mondoperaio*, *L'Arc*, *Spirali*, and *Idée de Lecce*. He is the author of *Freud*, *Psychanalyse entre chien et loup*, *Cent fleurs pour Wilhelm Reich*, and *Gaza Roheim et l'essor de l'anthropologie psychanalytique*.

Harvey R. Greenberg, M. D., is clinical professor of psychiatry at the Albert Einstein College of Medicine, the Bronx, New York. He is in the private practice of psychoanalysis in New York City. His publications on cinema have appeared in *Psychoanalytic Review*, *Film/Psychology Review*, *Quarterly Review of Film Studies*, the *Journal of Popular Film and Television*, and *Camera Obscura*. He is the author of *Movies on Your Mind*, a psychoanalytic study of popular film.

Henry Jenkins is an assistant professor in the Department of Literature at MIT. His book, *Textual Poachers: Television Fans and Participatory Culture*, is forthcoming from Routledge. With John Tulloch he is writing *The Science Fiction Audience: Doctor Who, Star Trek, and Their Fans*. He has written on early film comedy and the vaudeville aesthetic, early female film comics, the Atlanta child murders, cognitive and narrative theory, child viewers of *Pee-wee's Playhouse*, *Star Trek* fans, fan folksinging practices, and (with Lynn Spigel) *Batman*.

Elisabeth Lyon is assistant professor of English and comparative literature at Hobart and William Smith Colleges. A founding coeditor of *Camera Obscura: A Journal of Feminism and Film Theory*, she has written on feminist theory and the films and novels of Marguerite Duras. Lyon is currently writing a book on photography and the novel, entitled *Photographic Fictions*. She is the coeditor, with Raymond Bellour, of the forthcoming special issue of *Camera Obscura*, "Unspeakable Images."

Enno Patalas is a critic who became a curator. He was the founder and editor of *Filmkritik* from 1957 to 1971. His collected film criticism was published in *Im/Off: Filmartikel* (with Frieda Grafe). Other publications include *Geschichte des Films* (with Ulrich Gregor), *Fritz Lang* (with Frieda Grafe), and *Lubitsch* (with Hans-Helmut Prinzler). Since 1973 he has been director of the Munich Film Archive, which specializes in the editorial restoration of German classic films.

Constance Penley is associate professor of English and film studies at the University of Rochester. She is the author of *The Future of an Illusion: Film, Feminism, and Psychoanalysis* (Minnesota, 1989) and editor of *Feminism and Film Theory*. Penley is a founding coeditor of *Camera Obscura: A Journal of Feminism and Film Theory*.

Vivian Sobchack is professor of theater arts (film studies) and director of the arts division at the University of California, Santa Cruz. Her books include *An Introduction to Film* and *The Limits of Infinity: The American Science Fiction Film, 1950–75*, which was enlarged and reprinted as *Screening Space: The American Science Fiction Film*, and *The Address of the Eye: A Phenomenology of Film Experience*.

Lynn Spigel is assistant professor of communication arts at the University of Wisconsin, Madison. She is a coeditor of *Camera Obscura: A Journal of Feminism and Film Theory*. Spigel is author of *Installing the Television Set: A Cultural History of Television and the Family, 1945–1955*, forthcoming from the University of Chicago Press.

Peter Wollen teaches in the Department of Film and Television at UCLA. He is the author of *Signs and Meaning in the Cinema* and *Readings and Writings: Counter Semiotic Strategies*. With Laura Mulvey, he made a number of films, including *Penthesilea*, *Riddles of the Sphinx*, *AM Y!*, and *Crystal Gazing*. His most recent film is the science fiction feature *Friendship's Death*.

Index

Index

Compiled by Hassan Melehy

Addams Family, The, 214, 216, 220, 227
Adorno, Theodor, 172
Adventures of Buckaroo Banzai, The, 24
Advertising: and body, viii; and science fiction film, 33–34, 39–49
Affluent Society, The, 209
Alice Doesn't (de Lauretis), 171
Alien: as defamiliarization, 220; and male body, 23–24; as Other, 15–16; and patriarchy, 21–22
Alien, viii–ix, 33, 34, 35, 64, 73, 83–84, 87–103 *passim*
Aliens, 73
Altered States, 17–20, 23
Amityville Horror, The, 5, 9–10
Amos 'n' Andy, 214
Anality: and Nazism, 157–158. *See also* Freud, Sigmund
Anders, William, 229
Android: and sexual identity, 117–21. *See also* Alien
Android, 24, 72
Andy Griffith Show, The, 216, 233 n. 20
Anne of the Indies, 53
Apocalypse: and time travel theme, 74–76
Apocalypse Now, 15
Apple computer, 34
Architecture: in cinema and

Nazism, 154. *See also* Hitler, Adolf; Lang, Fritz
Astaire, Fred, 44
A-Team, The, 177
Attack of the Crab Monsters, 91
Audrey Rose, 8
Auschwitz: and Nazi imagination, 157
Author! Author! 12
Avant-garde: and Hollywood film, viii, 78
Avedon, Richard, 44

Back to the Future, 5, 28, 66–67, 68
Bacon-Smith, Camille, 178, 186
Balzac, Honoré de, 36
Bantam Books, 177
Barrett, Majel, 182–83
Barthes, Roland, 49, 80 n. 19; and fashion, 37; and sexual identity, 36
Barwick, Linda, 180
Bates, Karen, 185, 189
Battlestar Gallactica, 176
Baudelaire, Charles, 114, 127
Baughman, James, 207, 211, 232 n. 14, 233 n. 16
Beauty and the Beast, 176
Bell-Metereau, Rebecca, 19–20
Bellour, Raymond, ix, 72
Benjamin, Walter, 133
Bergstrom, Janet, viii
Beulah, 214

Beverly Hillbillies, The, 214, 220–21, 227
Bewitched, x, 206, 214, 216, 219, 220, 224, 225, 226–27, 228, 235 n. 42
Bible, the, 108, 156
Biehn, Michael, 73
Blade Runner, viii, 22, 33–35, 40, 56, 64, 66, 72, 127
Blake's 7, 176
Blanchot, Maurice, 125–26
Bleich, David, 179
Blob, The, 91
Body: and advertising, viii; female, and dismemberment, 114; male, and alien, 23–24; male, and patriarchy, 20. *See also* Sexual difference; Sexual identity
Book: as woman, 125, 126
Borman, Frank, 229
Bosch, Hieronymus, 92
Bowie, David, 58 n. 7; and androgyny, 37, 48, 51
Boy and His Dog, A, 63
Bradbury, Ray, 68
Bradley, Marion Zimmer, 187, 199 n. 15
Braun, Eva, 154
Braun, Wernher von, 218
Breton, André, 125
Bride of Frankenstein, The, 127, 145
Brooks, Louise, 38–39
Brother from Another Planet, The, 24–25
Brown, Mary Ellen, 180

Caltiki, the Immortal Monster, 91
Cameron, James, 64, 73
Capitalism: in *Alien,* 99–100; fandom as challenge to, 198; and horror as genre, 87, 101–3
Capra, Frank, 101
Carpenter, John, 85
Carpenter, Scott, 217
Carrie, 5, 8–9, 29 n. 5, 85

Cassavetes, John, 10
Certeau, Michel de, x, 173–74, 197
Children, The, 86
Christine, 7–8
City in History, The (Mumford), 208
Close Encounters of the Third Kind, 5, 14, 15–17, 83
Cocoon, 5
Coming Home, 15
Condillac, Abbé de, 114
Copyright: and fandom, 177–78. *See also* "Poaching"
Cotton Club, The, 33
Courtade, Francis, 133
Crack in the Picture Window, A, 207
Creature from the Black Lagoon, 92
Culture: participatory vs. spectatorial, 175, 197
Cunningham, Imogene, 39

Dadoun, Roger, ix
Dallas, 198
Dantine, Marie-Elisabeth, 129
Datazine, 177, 178
Davis, Lyn, 102–3
Dawn of the Dead, 71, 86–87
Day for Night, 17
De Lauretis, Teresa, 30 n. 18, 171, 179
Dean, Joan, 14
Deer Hunter, The, 15
Demon Seed, 15
DePalma, Brian, 85, 95
Devil is a Woman, The, 33
Dick Van Dyke Show, The, 215
Disneyland, 218
Doctor Who, 176
Donna Reed Show, The, 215, 220, 224
Dreyfus, Richard, 15
Duchamp, Marcel, 49
Dworkin, Andrea, 190
Dynasty, 198
Dyonnet, Louise, 128

Dystopia: critical, 64, 78. *See also* Utopian imagination

Edison, Thomas, ix, 107–29 *passim*
Eisenhower, Dwight D., 207, 209, 211
Embryo, 15
Encyclopédie du cinéma, L', 136
E.T., 5, 16, 20–22, 25, 33, 35, 71
Exorcist, The, 5, 7, 8, 9, 29 n. 5, 84, 85, 86

Family melodrama: patriarchy in, 10–13
Family sit-com: as genre, x, 205–29 *passim*
Fandom: and academic criticism, 172; and capitalism, 198; and copyright, 177–78; and feminism, 178–98 *passim*
Fantastic: as genre, 219
Fantasy: and film theory, 69–70; and sexual difference, viii; and technology, ix–x. *See also* Freud, Sigmund
Farmer's Daughter, The, 216
Fashion: and sexual identity, 36–37, 44–49
Father Knows Best, 215
Faulkner, William, 179
Federal Communications Commission (FCC), 211–12
Feminine Mystique, The, 208
Feminism: and fandom, 178–98 *passim;* and popular romance, 190; and space travel, 222–23. *See also* Patriarchy
Five Million Years to Earth, 91
Flintstones, The, 227
Fog, The, 85
Forbidden Planet, 83, 98, 222
Frakes, Randall, 65
François-Poncet, André, 156
Freud, Sigmund, 6, 118, 125, 130 n. 5, 172; and fantasy, 69–71; on feminine psychology,

52–53; and Nazism, 158; and primal scene, 68–69; and sexual identity, 36
Friday the 13th, 85
Friedan, Betty, 190, 208, 223
Friendship's Death, x–xi
Funny Face, 44
Fury, The, 5, 9
Future Eve, The (L'Eve Future), ix, 107–29 *passim*

Gagarin, Yuri A., 210
Galbraith, John Kenneth, 209
Garrett, Maureen, 177
Gautier, Estelle, 128
Gautier, Judith, 128, 129
Gautier, Théophile, 128
Genelli, Tom, 102–3
Genet, Jean, 49, 56
Gerrold, David, 68
Giant Claw, The, 91
GI Bill, 207
Glenn, John, 218
God: as creator, 108–9; and woman as ideal, 123
Goebbels, Josef, 133. *See also* Hitler, Adolf; Nazism
Great Santini, The, 10–11
Green Acres, 214, 226
Greenberg, Harvey, viii–ix, 57 n. 5, 198 n. 3

Hair, 83
Halloween, 85
Halloween III, 8
Haraway, Donna, vii, 78 n. 5
Harbou, Thea von, 136, 152, 154, 162, 164, 166
Harlequin romances, 190
Hawthorne, Nathaniel, 180
Hebdige, Dick, 44, 49–52, 54, 56
Heinlein, Robert, 68
Helm, Brigitte, 134, 139
Henderson, Zenna, 187
Hepburn, Audrey, 44
Herman, Pee-wee, 198

Heung, Marina, 12, 16, 20–21
Heyst, Axel, 157
Hidden Persuaders, The, 209
Hills Have Eyes, The, viii, 85, 86, 87
Hill Street Blues, 177
Hitchcock, Alfred, 84, 85, 86, 95
Hitler, Adolf, ix; family of, 153; and Fritz Lang, 154; and Jesus Christ, 156. *See also* Nazism
Hodge, Robert, 196, 202 n. 65
Hoffman, Dustin, 11, 15
Hoffmann, E. T. A., 36, 125
Hollywood film: and avant-garde, viii, 78; and sexual difference, ix, 53
Honeymooners, The, 214
Horror: as genre, 85–86, 101–3; and patriarchy, viii, 7–10; and science fiction, as genres, 3–28 *passim*
Houbolt, John C., 218
Humanoids from the Deep, 93
Hunter, Kendra, 188, 192, 193–94
Huppertz, Gottfried, 134, 162
Hypnosis: and love, 118–19

I Dream of Jeannie, x, 205, 214, 216, 219, 224, 225–26, 227, 228
I Love Lucy, 197, 214, 215
I Married Joan, 214, 215
Invasion of the Body Snatchers, 83, 220, 235 n. 37
It's Alive! 7, 86

James, M. R., 89
Jameson, Fredric, 30 nn. 19–21, 63, 218
Jaws, 92
Jenkins, Henry, x, 229
Jesus Christ: and Hitler, 156; as figured in *Metropolis,* 150; and patriarchy, 19
Jetée, La, viii, 74–78

Jetsons, The, x, 205, 214, 219, 227
Joe, 8

Karloff, Boris, 91
Keats, John, 207
Keeler, Greg, 11
Kennedy, John F., 209, 210, 212. *See also* New Frontier
Kennedy, Robert F., 218
Kermode, Frank, 74–76
Killing Fields, The, 22–23
King Creole, 208
King Kong, 137
Klein, Calvin, viii, 37–38, 39, 58 n. 6
Klein-Rogge, Rudolf, 134, 161
Kornbluth, Cyril, 209
Kracauer, Siegfried, 133
Kramarae, Cheris, 180
Kramer, Stanley, 101
Kramer Vs. Kramer, 11, 12
Kubrick, Stanley, 3–7, 13
Kuntzel, Thierry, 77, 80 n. 16

La Mettrie, Julien Offray de, 114
Land, Jane, 183–84, 185, 189, 190, 196
Lang, Fritz, ix, 40, 133–59 *passim,* 161–67 *passim;* and Hitler, 154
Langer, Walter, 152–53, 154, 156–57
Last House on the Left, 85
Late Spring, 172
Lay, Toni, 183
Leave It to Beaver, 215, 224
Le Guin, Ursula K., 187
Leigh, Janet, 96
Lem, Stanislaw, 63, 78 n. 6
Letter from an Unknown Woman, 172
Levittown, 207–8, 219
Lichtenberg, Jacqueline, 177, 186
Life, 208, 209, 217, 218, 223, 229
Life of Riley, The, 214
Life with Luigi, 214
Linkletter, Art, 213, 214

Lipsitz, George, 215
Liquid Sky, viii, 24, 33–34, 37, 40, 44–49, 54–56, 127
Look, 209–10, 217, 222–23
Looker, viii, 37, 39–43
Lorrah, Jean, 175, 177, 188–89, 193, 201 n. 33
Lost in Space, 205
Love: and hypnosis, 118–19
Lovell, James, 229
Lucas, George, 33–34. *See also Star Wars*
Lucasfilm Ltd., 177–78
Luce, Claire Booth, 223, 232 n. 14
Luce, Henry, 209, 223
Lugosi, Bela, 91

M, 146
McDougall, Walter, 208
Mad, 213–14
Make Room for Daddy, 214
Mallarmé, Stéphane, 110, 125, 129
Man from UNCLE, The, 176–77
Man Who Fell to Earth, The, 14, 33, 58 n. 7, 72
Marc, David, 206
Marker, Chris, viii, 76–78
Masquerade: and sexual identity, 53–56
Mechanical: vs. organic, 65–66
Mein Kampf, 152
Mendés, Catulle, 128
Mesmer, Franz Josef, 121
Metro-Goldwyn, 165–66
Metropolis, ix–x, 40, 88, 92, 98, 127, 133–59 *passim,* 161–67 *passim*
Miami Vice, 176
Michaux, Henri, 147
Minow, Newton, 211–12
Model, 37
Modleski, Tania, 185, 188
Montifaud, Marie de, 129
Moon landing: as cultural event, 205
Morocco, 53

Moroder, Giorgio, 168
Mr. Ed, x, 206, 216, 227
Mr. Mom, 11
Mumford, Lewis, 208
Munsters, The, 214, 220, 227
My Favorite Husband, 214
My Favorite Martian, x, 205, 220
My Little Margie, 214
My Living Doll, 206, 214, 216, 225
My Mother the Car, 206, 216
Mythologies, 49
My Three Sons, 216

Nadja, 125
National Aeronautics and Space Administration (NASA), 210, 225–26. *See also* Space travel
Nazism: and anality, 157–58; and cinema, 133, 136–37; and Freud, 158. *See also* Hitler, Adolf
New Frontier, x, 212, 214, 228; ideology of, 209–10; and space travel, 205; and television, 223. *See also* Kennedy, John F.
New Republic, The, 211
Newsweek, 37–38, 171–72, 232 n. 14
New York Times, The, 165, 166
Neyman, Yuri, 56, 59 nn. 16, 23
Nibelungen, Die, 136
Nielsen ratings, 215
Nightmare on Elm Street, 85
Night of the Comet, 24
Night of the Living Dead, viii, 85, 86, 101
Nimoy, Leonard, 171
Nixon, Richard, 229
Norton, André, 187

O'Bannon, Dan, 73
Omen, The, 8, 9, 85
One From the Heart, 33
Ordinary People, 5, 11, 12
Organic: vs. mechanical, 65–66

Organization Man, The (Whyte), 208
Orwell, George, 90
Other: alien as, 15–16; in horror and science fiction, 4
Other, The, 8
Outer Limits, The, 220
Ozzie and Harriet, 214, 215, 220

Pabst, G. W., 39
Pacino, Al, 15
Packard, Vance, 209
Pal, George, 66
Pandora's Box, 38–39
Paramount, 165–66, 177, 191–92, 193
Pasolini, Pier Paolo, 39
Patalas, Enno, ix–x
Patriarchy: and alien, 21–22; in family melodrama, 10–13; and horror as genre, viii, 7–10; and Jesus Christ, 19; and male body, 20; in science fiction, 13–28 *passim. See also* Feminism
Penley, Constance, viii
Photography: and history, 108
Piercy, Marge, 187
"Poaching:" reading as, x, 173–98 *passim*
Pocket Books, 177
Poe, Edgar Allan, 125
Pohl, Frederick, 209
Poltergeist, 5, 9, 10
Powell, Anna Eyre, 129
Prisoner, The, 197
Professionals, The, 177
Psycho, viii, 84, 85–86, 87, 90, 95, 96, 102
Punk: as style, 49, 51, 54

Quiz-show scandal: as shift in U.S. TV, 211

Radway, Janice, 188, 201 n. 41
Rambo, 64
Rancho Notorious, 166

Rape: and surveillance, 55
Reading: as "poaching," x, 173–98 *passim*
Rebel Without a Cause, 208
Remington Steele, 176
"Repeater" phenomenon: and horror as genre, 84
Repo Man, 24
Repressed: in horror film genre, 10. *See also* Freud, Sigmund
Revlon, 211
Richard, Jean-Pierre, 125
Rise to Power of Louis XIV, 36–37
Rivière, Joan, 53, 224
Road Warrior, The, 33, 35, 63, 176
Roddenberry, Gene, 177, 182–83, 191, 192
Roheim, Geza, 152
Rollerball, 63
Romance: popular, and feminism, 190
Romanticism: German, and woman, 125
Romero, George, 71, 85, 86, 101
Rose, Mark, 74–76
Rose, Pamela, 183
Rosemary's Baby, 3–28 *passim,* 85–86
Rossellini, Roberto, 36–37
Rothschild family: and Hitler, 153
Roxy Music: and androgyny, 51
Rumblefish, 33
Russ, Joanna, 187
Rychner, Max, 133

Saturday Review, 229
Scéve, Maurice, 114
Schreber, Daniel Paul, 145. *See also* Freud, Sigmund
Science Fiction: and advertising, 33–34, 39–49; as defamiliarization, 218–20; and feminism, 187; and horror, as genres, 3–28 *passim;* patriarchy in, 13–28; and sexual difference, vii–xi,

35–36, 71–74, 221–22; and uto-
    pian imagination, 63–64,
    234 n. 34; and Vietnam film,
    22–23
Science Fiction Theater, 220, 222
Scott, Ridley, 34, 73, 87–103
    passim
Searchers, The, 70
See It Now, 211
Segal, Elizabeth, 187
Sexual difference: and fantasy, viii;
    and science fiction, vii–xi,
    35–36, 71–74, 221–22; and
    technology, vii–xi. See also Body
Sexual identity: and android,
    117–21; and family, 54; and
    fashion, 36–37, 44–49; and
    Hollywood film, 53; and
    masquerade, 53–56; and surveil-
    lance, 55–56
Shatner, William, 198
Shining, The, 9, 10
Shoot the Moon, 5, 12
Siebert, C. A., 178, 184, 185, 190
Simon and Simon, 177
Sirk, Douglas, 208
Skelton, Betty, 223
Slaysu, 178
Smith-Rosenberg, Carroll, 180
Sobchack, Vivian, viii
Space Merchants, The, (Kornbluth
    & Pohl), 209
Space travel: and feminism,
    222–23; and television, 205–12;
    in U.S. culture, 216–18
Spector, Judith, 182
Spielberg, Steven, 17, 22, 33–34,
    57 n. 2, 83
Spigel, Lynn, x
Sputnik, 206–7, 208–9, 218
Starman, 5, 16, 22–26, 72
Star Trek, x, 72, 171–98 passim
Star Wars (SDI), 64
Star Wars, 14, 33, 35, 64, 87–88,
    172, 176, 177–78
Sternberg, Josef von, 33

Strange Invaders, 24
Streets of Fire, 33
Stuck, Franz von, 156–57
Subculture: The Meaning of Style
    (Hebdige), 44, 49–52, 54, 56
Subject: and spectatorial identifica-
    tion, 69–70
Suburb: and family sit-com, 220; in
    U.S. culture, 206–8, 215–16
Surrealism: and woman, 125
Surveillance: and sexual identity,
    55–56
Symbolism: French, and woman,
    125

Taking Off, 8
Tausk, Victor, 89
Technology: and fantasy, ix–x; and
    sexual difference, vii
Television: and space travel,
    205–12; in U.S. culture,
    211–12, 214
Teorema, 39
Tereshkova, Valentina, 223
Terminator, The, viii, 16, 22–26,
    63–78 passim
Texas Chainsaw Massacre, The, ix,
    85, 86, 87, 100, 101
Them! 91, 222, 235 n. 37
Thing, The, 83
Thompson, E. P., 174, 191
Thompson, Leslie, 193
Time-loop paradox: and primal
    scene fantasy, 68–69; as science
    fiction device, 67–68
Time Machine, The, 66
Todorov, Tzvetan, 219
Tootsie, 39
Torah, the, 133
Tower of Babel: as figured in
    Metropolis, 139–40, 156
Tripp, David, 196, 202 n. 65
Truffaut, François, 17
Twilight Zone, The, 220
2001: A Space Odyssey, 3–7, 14,
    34, 88, 93

Uforia, 24
Universum Film Aktiengesellschaft
  (UFA), 134, 136, 164, 165–66
Utopian imagination: and science
  fiction, 63–64, 234 n. 34

V, 64, 72–73
Van Doren, Charles, 211
Vanguard, 209
Verba, Joan, 188
Victor, Victoria, 39
Vietnam film: as genre, 14–15; and
  science fiction, 22–23
Villiers de l'Isle-Adam, ix, 107–29
  passim
Vogue, 44, 58 n. 11

Wagner, Richard, 125
Waite, Robert, 156–57
War of the Worlds, 91, 220, 222
Wells, H. G., 66, 133
Weston, Edward, 39
Westwood, Vivien, 49

Whyte, William, 208, 225
Wild Child, The, 17
Williamson, Judith, 227
Wiseguy, 176
Wiseman, Frederick, 37
Wisher, Bill, 65
Wolf-Man (Sergei Pankeiev): and
  primal scene, 69. *See also* Freud,
  Sigmund
Wollen, Peter, x–xi
Woman: as book, 125, 126; as ide-
  al, and God, 123
"Womanliness as Masquerade," 53,
  224
Woman's List, The, 184
Wood, Robin, 86, 101, 102–3,
  172; and American family, 4
Wray, Fay, 93
Writer's Digest, 176

Yentl, 39
Young, John, 217